Saddarsanam
&
An Inquiry into the Revelation of Truth and Oneself

SOCIETY OF ABIDANCE IN TRUTH

Saddarsanam

by Sri Ramana Maharshi

translated by Nome

&

An Inquiry into the Revelation of Truth and Oneself

by Nome

Revealing the Truth,
Removing all obstacles,
Bestowing Knowledge,
As the Lord of all the retinues,
He abides.

Wielding undivided Knowledge,
Destroying a mountain of illusion,
Liberating all from delusion's dream,
As that which is excellent for the
Realization of Brahman,
He shines.

Existing without another,
Granting to all the nectar of
immortality,
Silencing all doubts forever,
As That which alone exists, Siva,
He is.

Society of Abidance in Truth

Printed in India.

ISBN: 9780981940908

For all inquiries contact the publisher:
Society of Abidance in Truth
SAT
1834 Ocean Street
Santa Cruz, California 95060 USA
(831) 425-7287 / sat@cruzio.com
www.SATRamana.org

Contents

Preface

Our beloved Bhagavan Ramana has told us:

> *"The One Self, the Sole Reality, alone exists eternally. When even the Ancient Teacher, Dakshinamurti, revealed It through speechless eloquence, who else could convey it by speech?"*
>
> - EKATMA PANCHAKAM, FIVE VERSES ON THE ONE SELF, *Collected Works of Sri Ramana Maharshi*

Sri Bhagavan blazes forth with the quintessential wisdom of Advaita Vedanta in His *Saddarsanam*. His great silence perpetually and eternally "speaks" to us so plainly. Though He tells us that the Reality cannot be conveyed by speech, still, we thrive on His lucid words of unparalleled wisdom, for they help us understand the depth of His silence.

Many times throughout the year, SAT conducts retreats, so that avid Ramana brothers and sisters may gather together to revel in Sri Bhagavan's silent speech. His illustrious teaching of Self-Inquiry and Self-Knowledge fills us with joy, and, through His teaching, we are able to directly experience His silence.

This *Saddarsanam* is reflected upon in one such retreat each year. At this retreat, we read *Saddarsanam*, and we experience Saddarsanam. As we read, we absorb ourselves in each phrase or verse of Ramana's exquisite wisdom, word for word, again and again, to extract the Knowledge essence and thus joyfully experience Its depth in our hearts. During the exposition of this exquisite scripture, illustrations are given and doubts are answered. Contained within this book are just such illustrations and dialogues. They are the reflected light of Saddarsanam and they are compiled into a commentary called *An Inquiry into the Revelation of Truth and Oneself.*

It is with immense gratitude for Sri Ramana's Grace and unending devotion and love for Him that SAT and Nome make this an offering to our Bhagavan Sri Ramana Maharshi. We sincerely hope that Sri Bhagavan's words of immense wisdom illumine your heart and you remain in the Bliss of Sri Ramana—the Bliss of which our beloved Guru silently speaks so plainly.

> *"The power of the word is inconceivable. As from the word, a person deep asleep wakes up, so too, by the power of the word, verily, the direct, immediate Knowledge is gained. By discrimination of the Self and the not-Self, blemishless Knowledge comes to be. A disciple instructed by a Guru transcends the words and attains the meaning—Brahman."*
>
> - ADI SANKARA, SADACARA, V. 18 & 19

Sasvati

Introduction

SADDARSANAM

Om Namo Bhagavate Sri Ramanaya

The Truth is silent. He is silent. He is the Silence. A name was given to him: Bhagavan Sri Ramana Maharshi, and the eternal Silence, itself, poured forth in luminous verses, expressing the sublime, supreme Truth. This is *Saddarsanam, The Revelation of Truth.* In Tamil, it is known as *Ulladu Narpadu, The Forty on What Is.*

Saddarsanam consists of verses selected from among over eighty verses. This larger body of verses consists of both verses composed by the Maharshi and verses derived from other texts that were translated into Tamil from their Sanskrit originals. The verses selected for the text of *Ulladu Narpadu (Saddarsanam)* were composed by the Maharshi. Those verses not selected for *Ulladu Narpadu (The Forty on What Is)* were compiled into the *Anubandham,* or *Supplement.* Though the *Supplement,* too, contains verses of great profundity, this present book concerns itself only with the *Saddarsanam* verses, which consist of the two invocatory verses, the forty verses, and the two concluding verses by Ganapati Muni that serve the function of a colophon.

The original verses were composed in Tamil by Bhagavan Sri Ramana Maharshi, arranged by Sri Muruganar, and entitled *Ulladu Narpadu (The Forty on What Is).* The Tamil verses were translated into Sanskrit by Kavyakantha Ganapati Muni (Vasishta Ganapati Muni), who had also selected which verses were to appear as the invocation, and entitled *Saddarsanam.* The Muni's Sanskrit version is used in this present volume. It is translated in a very literal manner, to the extent that even the order of the Sanskrit words is followed fairly closely in the English wherever possible, even if the English then reads a bit awkwardly. Whenever practical, the point where each English line breaks follows the pattern displayed in the Sanskrit text. In numerous instances, alternative translations of words, phrases, and lines are presented. The aim is to provide the literal meaning free of interpretation and, also, to present the numerous nuances of meaning that can be derived from the text without deviating from a literal translation. With this supplied, the meditating reader can easily, inwardly understand the significance of each verse and, if he chooses, mentally render the verse into a more smoothly flowing set of English words, for a consequence of this style of translation is the loss of the poetic quality of the original text. Reference to the portion of this book entitled "An Inquiry into the Revelation of Truth and Oneself" may be found to be helpful to the understanding of the applicability of this translation for Self-inquiry and Self-Realization and for an explanation of the meaning of those phrases of the translation that may elude complete comprehension at first glance. Words and phrases placed in parenthesis indicate alternative translations of the term or phrase immediately preceding them. Words placed in brackets are those inserted to make the English translation intelligible and are not actually in the Sanskrit text, though they may be implied. The intended result of presenting the translation in this manner is to provide the meditating reader with the full scope of meanings consonant with an experiential understanding of this nondual Knowledge.

Among the English translations of the text are the two by A. R. Natarajan, as found within his books *Sat-Darshana* and *Teachings of Ramana Maharshi,* the two that are found in earlier and later editions of *The Collected Works of Ramana Maharshi,* one of which is the translation by Professor K. Swaminathan, the one entitled *Truth Revealed (Sad-Vidya),* which is translated from the Tamil original, the one by "K," which is contained in his *Sat-Darshana Bhashya,* the one of Dr. T. M. P. Mahadevan from the Tamil text found in *Ramana Maharshi and His Philosophy of Existence,* the translation by K. Lakshmana Sarma ("Who") that accompanies his own Sanskrit rendition from the Tamil, as contained in his *Sri Ramanahrdayam, Revelation,* the one by Swami Tejomayananda as contained in *Saddarsanam of Bhagavan Sri Ramana Maharshi,* the translation by S. S. Cohen, which is said to be an edition derived from six other translations, and the translation by S. Ram Mohan, which is being serially published in the "Mountain Path." Several of these are published by Sri Ramanasramam, some by the Ramana Maharshi Centre for Learning, and some are by other publishers and by other spiritual institutions dedicated to Vedanta. The translation contained herein is intended to augment and not to substitute for these existing translations.

Presented in this volume are the Sanskrit in Devanagari for Sanskrit-knowing readers and for ease of recitation, with the transliteration as further assistance for recitation, the English translation for the understanding of the English-knowing reader, and the combination of all of these accompanied by "An Inquiry into the Revelation of Truth and Oneself."

There is deep gratitude to Sri Ramanasramam, the sacred abode of the Maharshi at Arunachala, and to its President, Sri V. S. Ramanan for preserving and disseminating, with devotion, the holy, liberating teachings of Sri Bhagavan, and for his kind encouragement to the SAT temple. There is heartfelt thankfulness to Sri V. S. Mani of Sri Ramanasramam for his kindness and sweet encouragement and for his devoted care with the preservation of the precious teachings of Sri Bhagavan. There is also heartfelt thankfulness to the late A. R. Natarajan of the Ramana Maharshi Centre for Learning, at Bangalore, as an exceedingly dear friend of SAT, for all his loving generosity toward devotees of Sri Ramana and for his life of selfless dedication to making Sri Ramana and His gracious teachings known. The help, without which this translation would not have been published, of Ganesh Sadasivan, Raman Muthukrishnan, and Sangeeta Raman for proofreading and of Sasvati for book design, proofreading, and seeing to the printing, is appreciatively acknowledged. There is gratitude toward Omkarananda Ashram for freely making available the Sanskrit font used in this book. There is thankfulness also to Raman Muthukrishnan for financially supporting this publication and to all those at the Society of Abidance in Truth who support its activities, including the publication of spiritual literature such as the present volume.

An Inquiry into the Revelation of Truth and Oneself

Om Namo Bhagavate Sri Ramanaya

The spiritual teachings contained in Bhagavan Sri Ramana Maharshi's *Saddarasanam* are the apex of Advaita Vedanta. They are undoubtedly the purest, clearest expression of Self-Knowledge.

The teachings of Bhagavan, replete with the perfection of the most sublime, profound, spiritual wisdom, require no explanation or commentary. They shine as self-evident for those who abide in the Knowledge that they reveal. It is possible, though, for disciples and devotees to revel together in this blissful Knowledge, giving expression to it, as well as to their devotion to the Sadguru. Praise thus becomes an expression of the spiritual instruction, and exegesis upon the teaching, along with reiteration and explanation, becomes praise. In this manner, several commentaries have been composed by them on the teachings, and verbal expositions on the same abound.

These essential teachings of Self-Knowledge form the foundation and peak of what is taught, adhered to, and practiced at the SAT temple. This particular text is frequently referred to at this temple consecrated to nondualistic Self-Knowledge, and in-depth immersion in its spiritual instructions is the entire focus of retreats regularly held there. These retreats are primarily filled with silence, yet some instruction is given in the form of reading *Saddarsanam* and discussion while meditating upon its meaning. Recitation of holy texts, such as *Ribhu Gita* and texts of Adi Sankara, in Sanskrit, Tamil, and English, also occurs, as well as puja performed as worship of the Maharshi.

In 2006 and 2007, the discussion portions of the retreats were recorded. Later, these recordings were transformed into transcripts by those who perceived the spiritual value and depth of such a revelation of the Truth. Other than the recited verses of *Saddarsanam,* the other texts recited, the chanting of Om and Om Shanti with which each day's spiritual instruction began and ended, and, of course, the silence were not included in these transcripts. It must be understood that each retreat was five days in length, so that the two transcripts that form the content of this present volume represent teachings, questions, and answers during a ten day period of time. The present text is composed of the combination of both transcripts. With the exception of just a few passages, generally, the verse is stated first, followed by the comments concerning its meaning and application from the earlier retreat, which is then followed by the comments of the later retreat. Thereafter, the dialogues of the earlier retreat are given, followed by those of the later retreat. In some instances, it was impractical to strictly adhere to this order in the editing of the text.

Care has been exercised to avoid excessive redundancy. In some cases, reiteration of an instruction or explanation was necessary to set the context of what followed or to indicate emphasis. In the event the reader or meditator does suppose that an explanation is merely a repetition of what has already been stated, a little meditation upon and experience of that which is being indicated will enable one to find the clarity and precision of the discrimination expressed and the revelation of Truth within.

A consequence of a compilation of transcripts that contain spiritual instruction that spans so many days is repetition, at points, which though helpful to the listener, may seem needless to the reader, at first glance. Therefore, the reader may find easier access to the intended experience by reading a small portion, perhaps one or a few verses with the comments pertaining to them, at a time. The singularity of Self-Realization shines clearly and magnificently through all the verses by the Maharshi, and the same is the consistent expression of the comments.

Most of the myriad questions raised during the dialogues directly pertain to the teachings presented in the text of *Saddarsanam,* their application in sadhana (spiritual practice), and experiential absorption in the spiritual Truth revealed. A minority of the questions is not directly related, but they have been included because the answers to them incorporate the teachings from a relevant portion of the text, and those questions comprise doubts that may be common to other spiritual aspirants. In many instances, the answers were given tersely in response to a series of questions in the course of a dialogue, and these have been edited by the transcriber so that the number of questions is less, or even only one, and the several answers that were given incrementally in the dialogue are conjoined to form a single answer of greater length. Most, if not all, of the spiritual instruction found in this present work is spiritually identical with what is stated in *Talks with Sri Ramana Maharshi* and *Day By Day with Bhagavan,* and, in all cases, is completely in accord with what is taught therein. Should any ambiguity appear to the reader or if any uncertainty regarding the meaning of a passage arises, the passage in question should be interpreted in light of the teachings given by the Maharshi as found in these two works. The teachings contained in the verses of this work and the comments pertaining to them are also identical to those expressed in *Self-Knowledge* and *Essence of Enquiry.*

This volume was not composed with any intention of creating a formal commentary. There are already several excellent commentaries upon *Saddarsanam,* by illustrious disciples and devotees of Sri Bhagavan. According to the Maharshi, a devotee is one who worships, and a disciple is one who adheres to the practice. It is certainly possible to be both. Among these wonderful commentaries are the two authored by A. R. Natarajan, as found with his translations in *Sat-Darshana* and *Teachings of Ramana Maharshi,* the one composed by "K," which is contained with his translation in his *Sat-Darshana Bhashya,* the commentary of Dr. T. M. P. Mahadevan with his translation from the Tamil text found in *Ramana Maharshi and His Philosophy of Existence,* the commentary by K. Lakshmana Sarma ("Who") that accompanies his own Sanskrit rendition from the Tamil along with his English translation, as contained in his *Sri Ramanahrdayam, Revelation,* the commentary by Swami Tejomayananda with his translation as contained in *Saddarsanam of Bhagavan Sri Ramana Maharshi,* the commentary by S. S. Cohen, and the commentary by S. Ram Mohan, which is being serially published in the "Mountain Path" and which is based upon Lakshmana Sarma's commentary. There may be others, too, and absence of their mention here is due only to lack of familiarity with them at this time. The reader is encouraged to also read all of those commentaries. The present text represents simply the comments and dialogues that occurred during these sacred events, edited slightly for the sake of brevity while retaining their informal tone, and it is hoped that the reader may find something of use in these passages. Whatever is of worth here is by the Grace of the Maharshi.

In this book, "N" signifies Nome, and "Q" and "Another Q" represent any of the questioners and the initial query by another questioner respectively. "Q" designates a speaker even if the speaker made a statement and did not ask a question. The use of the generic "Q" is to maintain the expression of the impersonal, non-ego nature of these teachings, and the use of "N" is solely to make the distinguishing of the comments and answers from the verses and questions readily comprehensible. Where "laughter" appears in parenthesis, it means that everyone present was laughing. "Silence" placed in parenthesis indicates that the silence was the instruction, though this is expressly indicated in this book for only some of the occasions of such absolute, formless teaching. It could be said that the entirety of what is recorded here is within Bhagavan's Silence.

Appreciation should be expressed here for those who saw to the publication of this book, inclusive of this portion. Especially to be acknowledged for their efforts are Eric Ruetz for recording and his ongoing insistence on the publication of these teachings, Raman Muthukrishnan for recording and his selfless service with the distribution of SAT publications, Chris Mair for his efforts in the loving labor of creating the transcripts from the original recordings, Ganesh Sadasivan for proofreading the Sanskrit and Nome's English translation and for suggestions pertaining thereto, and Sasvati for proofreading, layout, design, and seeing to the printing of the book.

Saddarsanam

॥ सद्दर्शनम् ॥
|| saddarśanam ||

॥ प्रार्थना ॥
|| prārthanā ||

सत्प्रत्ययाः किं नु विहाय सन्तं
हृद्येष चिन्तारहितो हृदाख्यः ।
कथं स्मरामस्तममेयमेकं
तस्य स्मृतिस्तत्र दृढैव निष्ठा ॥ १ ॥

sat-pratyayāḥ kiṁ nu vihāya santaṁ
hṛdyeṣa cintā-rahito hṛd-ākhyaḥ |
kathaṁ smarāmas-tam-ameyam-ekaṁ
tasya smṛtis-tatra dṛḍhaiva niṣṭhā || 1 ||

मृत्युञ्जयं मृत्युभियाश्रिताना -
महंमतिर्मृत्युमुपैति पूर्वम् ।
अथ स्वभावादमृतेषु तेषु
कथं पुनर्मृत्युधियोऽवकाशः ॥ २ ॥

mṛtyuñjayaṁ mṛtyu-bhiyāśritānām
aham-matir-mṛtyum-upaiti pūrvam |
atha svabhāvād-amṛteṣu teṣu
kathaṁ punar-mṛtyu-dhiyo'vakāśaḥ || 2 ||

सर्वैर्निदानं जगतोऽहमश्च
वाच्यः प्रभुः कश्चिदपारशक्तिः ।

चित्रेऽत्र लोक्यं च विलोकिता च
पटः प्रकाशोऽप्यभवत्स एकः ॥ १ ॥

sarvair-nidānaṁ jagato'hamaś-ca
vācyaḥ prabhuḥ kaścid-apāraśaktiḥ ।
citre'tra lokyaṁ ca vilokitā ca
paṭaḥ prakāśo'pyabhavat-sa ekaḥ ।। 1 ।।

आरभ्यते जीवजगत्परात्म -
तत्त्वाभिधानेन मतं समस्तम् ।
इदं त्रयं यावदहंमति स्यात्
सर्वोत्तमाऽहंमतिशून्यनिष्ठा ॥ २ ॥

ārabhyate jīva-jagat-parātma-
tattvābhidhānena mataṁ samastam ।
idaṁ trayaṁ yāvad-aham-mati syāt
sarvottamā'ham-mati-śūnya-niṣṭhā ।। 2 ।।

सत्यं मृषा वा चिदिदं जडं वा
दुःखं सुखं वेति मुधा विवादः ।
अदृष्टलोका निरहंप्रतीति -
र्निष्ठाऽविकल्पा परमाऽखिलेष्टा ॥ ३ ॥

satyaṁ mṛṣā vā cid-idaṁ jaḍaṁ vā
duḥkhaṁ sukhaṁ veti mudhā vivādaḥ ।
adṛṣṭa-lokā niraham-pratītir-
niṣṭhā'vikalpā paramā'khileṣṭā ।। 3 ।।

सरूपबुद्धिर्जगतीश्वरे च
सरूपधीरात्मनि यावदस्ति ।
अरूप आत्मा यदि कः प्रपश्येत्
सा दृष्टिरेकाऽनवधिर्हि पूर्णा ॥ ४ ॥

sarūpa-buddhir-jagatīśvare ca
sarūpa-dhīr-ātmani yāvad-asti |
arūpa ātmā yadi kaḥ prapaśyet
sā dṛṣṭir-ekā'navadhir-hi pūrṇā || 4 ||

यत्पञ्चकोशात्मकमस्ति देहं
तदन्तरा किं भुवनं चकास्ति ।
देहं विना पञ्चविधं तदेतत्
पश्यन्ति के वा भुवनं भणन्तु ॥ ५ ॥

yat-pañcakośātmakam-asti dehaṁ
tad-antarā kiṁ bhuvanaṁ cakāsti |
dehaṁ vinā pañca-vidhaṁ tadetat
paśyanti ke vā bhuvanaṁ bhaṇantu || 5 ||

शब्दादिरूपं भुवनं समस्तं
शब्दादिसत्तेन्द्रियवृत्तिभास्या ।
सत्तेन्द्रियाणां मनसो वशे स्यात्
मनोमयं तद्भुवनं वदामः ॥ ६ ॥

śabdādi-rūpaṁ bhuvanaṁ samastaṁ
śabdādi-sattendriya-vṛtti-bhāsyā |
sattendriyāṇāṁ manaso vaśe syāt
manomayaṁ tad-bhuvanaṁ vadāmaḥ || 6 ||

धिया सहोदेति धियास्तमेति
लोकस्ततो धीप्रविभास्य एषः ।
धीलोकजन्मक्षयधाम पूर्णं
सद्वस्तु जन्मक्षयशून्यमेकम् ॥ ७ ॥

dhiyā sahodeti dhiyāstam-eti
lokas-tato dhī-pravibhāsya eṣaḥ |
dhī-loka-janma-kṣaya-dhāma pūrṇaṁ
sad-vastu janma-kṣaya-śūnyam-ekam || 7 ||

भवन्तु सद्दर्शनसाधनानि
परस्य नामाकृतिभिः सपर्याः ।
सद्वस्तुनि प्राप्ततदात्मभावा
निष्ठैव सद्दर्शनमित्यवेहि ॥ ८ ॥

bhavantu saddarśana-sādhanāni
parasya nāmākṛtibhiḥ saparyāḥ |
sad-vastuni prāpta-tad-ātma-bhāvā
niṣṭhaiva sad-darśanam-ityavehi || 8 ||

द्वन्द्वानि सर्वाण्यखिलास्त्रिपुट्यः
किञ्चित्समाश्रित्य विभान्ति वस्तु ।
तन्मार्गणे स्याद्गलितं समस्तं
न पश्यतां सच्चलनं कदापि ॥ ९ ॥

dvandvāni sarvāṇyakhilās-tripuṭyaḥ
kiñcit-samāśritya vibhānti vastu |
tan-mārgaṇe syād-galitaṁ samastaṁ
na paśyatāṁ sac-calanaṁ kadāpi || 9 ||

विद्या कथं भाति न चेदविद्या
विद्यां विना किं प्रविभात्यविद्या ।
द्वयं च कस्येति विचार्य मूल -
स्वरूपनिष्ठा परमार्थविद्या ॥ १० ॥

vidyā katham bhāti na ced-avidyā
vidyām vinā kim pravibhātyavidyā ।
dvayam ca kasyeti vicārya mūla-
svarūpa-niṣṭhā paramārtha-vidyā ।। 10 ।।

बोद्धारमात्मानमजानतो यो
बोधः स किं स्यात्परमार्थबोधः ।
बोधस्य बोध्यस्य च संश्रयं स्वं
विजानतस्तद्द्वितयं विनश्येत् ॥ ११ ॥

boddhāram-ātmānam-ajānato yo
bodhaḥ sa kim syāt-paramārtha-bodhaḥ ।
bodhasya bodhyasya ca samśrayam svam
vijānatas-tad-dvitayam vinaśyet ।। 11 ।।

निद्रा न विद्या ग्रहणं न विद्या
गृह्णाति किञ्चिन्न यथार्थबोधे ।
निद्रापदार्थग्रहणेतरा स्यात्
चिदेव विद्या विलसन्त्यशून्या ॥ १२ ॥

nidrā na vidyā grahaṇam na vidyā
gṛhṇāti kiñcin-na yathārtha-bodhe ।
nidrā-padārtha-grahaṇetarā syāt
cid-eva vidyā vilasantyaśūnyā ।। 12 ।।

सत्यश्चिदात्मा विविधाकृतिश्चित्
सिध्येत्पृथक्सत्यचितो न भिन्ना ।
भूषाविकाराः किमु सन्ति सत्यं
विना सुवर्णं पृथगत्र लोके ॥ १३ ॥

satyaś-cid-ātmā vividhākṛtiś-cit
sidhyet-pṛthak-satya-cito na bhinnā ।
bhūṣā-vikārāḥ kim-u santi satyaṁ
vinā suvarṇaṁ pṛthag-atra loke ।। 13 ।।

तद्युष्मदोरस्मदि संप्रतिष्ठा
तस्मिन् विनष्टेऽस्मदि मूलबोधात् ।
तद्युष्मदस्मन्मतिवर्जितैका
स्थितिर्ज्वलन्ती सहजात्मनः स्यात् ॥ १४ ॥

tad-yuṣmador-asmadi sampratiṣṭhā
tasmin vinaṣṭe'smadi mūla-bodhāt ।
tad-yuṣmad-asman-mati-varjitaikā
sthitir-jvalantī sahajātmanaḥ syāt ।। 14 ।।

भूतं भविष्यच्च भवत्स्वकाले
तद्वर्तमानस्य विहाय तत्त्वम् ।
हास्या न किं स्याद्गतभाविचर्चा
विनैकसंख्यां गणनेव लोके ॥ १५ ॥

bhūtaṁ bhaviṣyac-ca bhavat-svakāle
tad-vartamānasya vihāya tattvam ।
hāsyā na kiṁ syād-gata-bhāvi-carcā
vinaika-saṅkhyāṁ gaṇaneva loke ।। 15 ।।

क्व भाति दिक्कालकथा विनाऽस्मान्
दिक्काललीलेह वपुर्वयं चेत् ।
न क्वापि भामो न कदापि भामो
वयं तु सर्वत्र सदा च भामः ॥ १६ ॥

kva bhāti dik-kāla-kathā vinā'smān
dik-kāla-līleha vapur-vayaṁ cet ।
na kvāpi bhāmo na kadāpi bhāmo
vayaṁ tu sarvatra sadā ca bhāmaḥ ।। 16 ।।

देहात्मभावे ज्ञजडौ समाना -
वेकस्य देहे हृदि दीप्त आत्मा ।
आक्रम्य देहं च जगच्च पूर्णः
परस्य मेयं तनुमात्रमात्मा ॥ १७ ॥

dehātma-bhāve jña-jaḍau samānā-
v-ekasya dehe hṛdi dīpta ātmā ।
ākramya dehaṁ ca jagac-ca pūrṇaḥ
parasya meyaṁ tanu-mātram-ātmā ।। 17 ।।

अज्ञस्य विज्ञस्य च विश्वमस्ति
पूर्वस्य दृश्यं जगदेव सत्यम् ।
परस्य दृश्याश्रयभूतमेकं
सत्यं प्रपूर्णं प्रविभात्यरूपम् ॥ १८ ॥

ajñasya vijñasya ca viśvam-asti
pūrvasya dṛśyaṁ jagad-eva satyam ।
parasya dṛśyāśraya-bhūtam-ekaṁ
satyaṁ prapūrṇaṁ pravibhātyarūpam ।। 18 ।।

विधेः प्रयत्नस्य च कोऽपि वाद -
स्तयोर्द्वयोर्मूलमजानतां स्यात् ।
विधेः प्रयत्नस्य च मूलवस्तु
सञ्जानतां नैव विधिर्न यत्नः ॥ १९ ॥

vidheḥ prayatnasya ca ko'pi vāda-
s-tayor-dvayor-mūlam-ajānatāṁ syāt |
vidheḥ prayatnasya ca mūla-vastu
sañjānatāṁ naiva vidhir-na yatnaḥ || 19 ||

यदीशितुर्वीक्षणमीक्षितार -
मवीक्ष्य तन्मानसिकेक्षणं स्यात् ।
न द्रष्टुरन्यः परमो हि तस्य
वीक्षा स्वमूले प्रविलीय निष्ठा ॥ २० ॥

yad-īśitur-vīkṣaṇam-īkṣitāra-
m-avīkṣya tan-mānasikekṣaṇaṁ syāt |
na draṣṭur-anyaḥ paramo hi tasya
vīkṣā svamūle pravilīya niṣṭhā || 20 ||

आत्मानमीक्षेत परं प्रपश्ये -
दित्यागमोक्तेः सुलभो न भावः ।
नात्मैव दृश्यो यदि का कथेशे
स्वयं तदन्नीभवनं तदीक्षा ॥ २१ ॥

ātmānam-īkṣeta paraṁ prapaśye-
d-ityāgamokteḥ sulabho na bhāvaḥ |
nātmaiva dṛśyo yadi kā katheśe
svayaṁ tad-annī-bhavanaṁ tad-īkṣā || 21 ||

धिये प्रकाशं परमो वितीर्य
स्वयं धियोऽन्तः प्रविभाति गुप्तः ।
धियं परावर्त्य धियोन्तरेऽत्र
संयोजनान्नेश्वरदृष्टिरन्या ॥ २२ ॥

dhiye prakāśaṁ paramo vitīrya
svayaṁ dhiyo'ntaḥ pravibhāti guptaḥ ।
dhiyaṁ parāvartya dhiyontare'tra
saṁyojanān-neśvara-dṛṣṭir-anyā ।। 22 ।।

न वक्ति देहोऽहमिति प्रसुप्तौ
न कोपि नाभूवमिति प्रवक्ति ।
यत्रोदिते सर्वमुदेति तस्य
धियाऽहमः शोधय जन्मदेशम् ॥ २३ ॥

na vakti deho'ham-iti prasuptau
na kopi nābhūvam-iti pravakti ।
yatrodite sarvam-udeti tasya
dhiyā'hamaḥ śodhaya janma-deśam ।। 23 ।।

देहो न जानाति सतो न जन्म
देहप्रमाणोऽन्य उदेति मध्ये ।
अहङ्कृतिग्रन्थिविबन्धसूक्ष्म -
शरीरचेतोभवजीवनामा ॥ २४ ॥

deho na jānāti sato na janma
deha-pramāṇo'nya udeti madhye ।
ahaṅkṛti-granthi-vibandha-sūkṣma-
śarīra-ceto-bhava-jīva-nāmā ।। 24 ।।

रूपोद्भवो रूपततिप्रतिष्ठो
रूपाशनो धूतगृहीतरूपः ।
स्वयं विरूपः स्वविचारकाले
धावत्यहङ्कारपिशाच एषः ॥ २५ ॥

rūpodbhavo rūpa-tati-pratiṣṭho
rūpāśano dhūta-gṛhīta-rūpaḥ |
svayaṁ virūpaḥ svavicāra-kāle
dhāvatyahaṅkāra-piśāca eṣaḥ || 25 ||

भावेऽहमः सर्वमिदं विभाति
लयेऽहमो नैव विभाति किञ्चित् ।
तस्मादहंरूपमिदं समस्तं
तन्मार्गणं सर्वजयाय मार्गः ॥ २६ ॥

bhāve'hamaḥ sarvam-idaṁ vibhāti
laye'hamo naiva vibhāti kiñcit |
tasmād-ahaṁ-rūpam-idaṁ samastaṁ
tan-mārgaṇaṁ sarva-jayāya mārgaḥ || 26 ||

सत्या स्थितिर्नाहमुदेति यत्र
तच्चोदयस्थानगवेषणेन ।
विना न नश्येद्यदि तन्न नश्येत्
स्वात्मैक्यरूपा कथमस्तु निष्ठा ॥ २७ ॥

satyā sthitir-nāham-udeti yatra
tac-codaya-sthāna-gaveṣaṇena |
vinā na naśyed-yadi tan-na naśyet
svātmaikya-rūpā katham-astu niṣṭhā || 27 ||

कूपे यथा गाढजले तथान्तः
निमज्ज्य बुद्ध्या शितया नितान्तम् ।
प्राणं च वाचं च नियम्य चिन्वन्
विन्देन्निजाहङ्कृतिमूलरूपम् ॥ २८ ॥

kūpe yathā gāḍha-jale tathāntaḥ
nimajjya buddhyā śitayā nitāntam ।
prāṇaṁ ca vācaṁ ca niyamya cinvan
vinden-nijāhaṅkṛti-mūla-rūpam ।। 28 ।।

मौनेन मज्जन्मनसा स्वमूल -
चर्चैव सत्यात्मविचारणं स्यात् ।
एषोऽहमेतन्न मम स्वरूप -
मिति प्रमा सत्यविचारणाङ्गम् ॥ २९ ॥

maunena majjan-manasā svamūla-
carcaiva satyātma-vicāraṇaṁ syāt ।
eṣo'ham-etan-na mama svarūpa-
m-iti pramā satya-vicāraṇāṅgam ।। 29 ।।

गवेषणात्प्राप्य हृदन्तरं तत्
पतेदहन्ता परिभुग्नशीर्षा ।
अथाहमन्यत्स्फुरति प्रकृष्टं
नाहङ्कृतिस्तत्परमेव पूर्णम् ॥ ३० ॥

gaveṣaṇāt-prāpya hṛdantaraṁ tat
pated-ahantā paribhugna-śīrṣā ।
athāham-anyat-sphurati prakṛṣṭaṁ
nāhaṅkṛtis-tat-parameva pūrṇam ।। 30 ।।

अहङ्कृतिं यो लसति ग्रसित्वा
किं तस्य कार्यं परिशिष्टमस्ति ।
किञ्चिद्विजानाति स नात्मनोऽन्यत्
तस्य स्थितिं भावयितुं क्षमः कः ॥ ३१ ॥

ahaṅkṛtiṁ yo lasati grasitvā
kiṁ tasya kāryaṁ pariśiṣṭam-asti |
kiñcid-vijānāti sa nātmano'nyat
tasya sthitiṁ bhāvayituṁ kṣamaḥ kaḥ || 31 ||

आह स्फुटं तत्त्वमसीति वेद -
स्तथाप्यसंप्राप्य परात्मनिष्ठाम् ।
भूयो विचारो मतिदुर्बलत्वं
तत्सर्वदा स्वात्मतया हि भाति ॥ ३२ ॥

āha sphuṭaṁ tat-tvam-asīti veda-
s-tathāpyasamprāpya parātma-niṣṭhām |
bhūyo vicāro mati-durbalatvaṁ
tat-sarvadā svātmatayā hi bhāti || 32 ||

न वेद्म्यहं मामुत वेद्म्यहं मा -
मिति प्रवादो मनुजस्य हास्यः ।
दृग्दृश्यभेदात्किमयं द्विधात्मा
स्वात्मैकतायां हि धियां न भेदाः ॥ ३३ ॥

na vedmyahaṁ mām-uta vedmyahaṁ mā-
m-iti pravādo manujasya hāsyaḥ |
dṛg-dṛśya-bhedāt-kim-ayaṁ dvidhātmā
svātmaikatāyāṁ hi dhiyāṁ na bhedāḥ || 33 ||

हृत्प्राप्यसद्धाम निजस्वरूपे
स्वभावसिद्धेऽनुपलभ्य निष्ठाम्।
मायाविलासः सदसत्सरूप -
विरूपनानैकमुखप्रवादाः ॥ ३४ ॥

hṛt-prāpya-sad-dhāma nija-svarūpe
svabhāva-siddhe'nupalabhya niṣṭhām |
māyā-vilāsaḥ sad-asat-sarūpa-
virūpa-nānaika-mukha-pravādāḥ || 34 ||

सिद्धस्य वित्तिः सत एव सिद्धिः
स्वप्नोपमानाः खलु सिद्धयोऽन्याः।
स्वप्नः प्रबुद्धस्य कथं नु सत्यः
सति स्थितः किं पुनरेति मायाम्॥ ३५ ॥

siddhasya vittiḥ sata eva siddhiḥ
svapnopamānāḥ khalu siddhayo'nyāḥ |
svapnaḥ prabuddhasya kathaṁ nu satyaḥ
sati sthitaḥ kiṁ punar-eti māyām || 35 ||

सोऽहंविचारो वपुरात्मभावे
साहाय्यकारी परमार्गणस्य।
स्वात्मैक्यसिद्धौ स पुनर्निरर्थो
यथा नरत्वप्रमितिर्नरस्य॥ ३६ ॥

so'haṁ-vicāro vapur-ātma-bhāve
sāhāyyakārī para-mārgaṇasya |
svātmaikya-siddhau sa punar-nirartho
yathā naratva-pramitir-narasya || 36 ||

द्वैतं विचारे परमार्थबोधे
त्वद्वैतमित्येष न साधुवादः ।
गवेषणात्प्राग्दशमे विनष्टे
पश्चाच्च लब्धे दशमत्वमेकम् ॥ ३७ ॥

dvaitaṁ vicāre paramārtha-bodhe
tvadvaitam-ityeṣa na sādhu-vādaḥ ।
gaveṣaṇāt-prāg-daśame vinaṣṭe
paścāc-ca labdhe daśamatvam-ekam ।। 37 ।।

करोमि कर्मेति नरो विजानन्
बाध्यो भवेत्कर्मफलं च भोक्तुम् ।
विचारधूता हृदि कर्तृता चेत्
कर्मत्रयं नश्यति सैव मुक्तिः ॥ ३८ ॥

karomi karmeti naro vijānan
bādhyo bhavet-karma-phalaṁ ca bhoktum ।
vicāra-dhūtā hṛdi kartṛtā cet
karma-trayaṁ naśyati saiva muktiḥ ।। 38 ।।

बद्धत्वभावे सति मोक्षचिन्ता
बन्धस्तु कस्येति विचारणेन ।
सिद्धे स्वयं स्वात्मनि नित्यमुक्ते
क्व बन्धचिन्ता क्व च मोक्षचिन्ता ॥ ३९ ॥

baddhatva-bhāve sati mokṣa-cintā
bandhas-tu kasyeti vicāraṇena ।
siddhe svayaṁ svātmani nitya-mukte
kva bandha-cintā kva ca mokṣa-cintā ।। 39 ।।

रूपिण्यरूपिण्युभयात्मिका च
मुक्तिस्त्रिरूपेति विदो वदन्ति ।
इदं त्रयं या विविनक्त्यहन्धी -
स्तस्याः प्रणाशः परमार्थमुक्तिः ॥ ४० ॥

rūpiṇyarūpiṇyubhayātmikā ca
muktis-trirūpeti vido vadanti |
idaṁ trayaṁ yā vivinaktyahan-dhī-
s-tasyāḥ praṇāśaḥ paramārtha-muktiḥ || 40 ||

सद्दर्शनं द्राविडवाङ्निबद्धं
महर्षिणा श्रीरमणेन शुद्धम् ।
प्रबन्धमुत्कृष्टममर्त्यवाण्या -
मनूद्य वासिष्ठमुनिर्व्यतानीत् ॥ ४१ ॥

sad-darśanaṁ drāviḍa-vāṅ-nibaddhaṁ
maharṣiṇā śrī-ramaṇena śuddham |
prabandham-utkṛṣṭam-amartya-vāṇyā-
m-anūdya vāsiṣṭha-munir-vyatānīt || 41 ||

सत्तत्त्वसारं सरलं दधाना
मुमुक्षुलोकाय मुदं ददाना ।
अमानुषश्रीरमणीयवाणी -
मयूखभित्तिर्मुनिवाग्विभाति ॥ ४२ ॥

sat-tattva-sāraṁ saralaṁ dadhānā
mumukṣu-lokāya mudaṁ dadānā |
amānuṣa-śrī-ramaṇīya-vāṇī-
mayūkha-bhittir-muni-vāg-vibhāti || 42 ||

Saddarsanam
The Revelation of Truth

Prayer

1

Can there, indeed, be the belief (faith, firm conviction, idea) of existence without that which exists?
In the Heart, free from (devoid of) thoughts, this is called the Heart.
How to think of (remember) (lit., How can we remember) that immeasurable one?
Remembrance of that, therefore, is, indeed, firm abidance (alone).
(Or: Remembrance of that is firm abidance therein alone.)

2

For those who have taken refuge, out of fear of death, in the Conqueror of death,
The "I" thought (notion) is the first to attain death.
Thereafter, in them [who] are naturally (by their own nature) immortal,
How again can there be space for the thought of death?

Text

1

By all, an original (first) cause (original essence) of
 the universe (world) and of the "I"
Is to be said, the Lord (who is the powerful Master),
 someone with boundless power.
Variegated here (in this) (In this picture here), the
 seeing one (the seer) and the seen, and
The screen, and the Light, only (also) He, the One,
 became.

2

With naming the individual, the world, and the
 Supreme Self
Principles (verities), all suppositions (doctrines)
 begin.
(Or: Naming the individual, the world, and the
 Supreme Self is inherent in suppositions.)
This triad is so long as the "I"-notion will exist (be).
The best of all is abidance void of the "I"-notion
 ("I"-assumption).

3

True or false, this is consciousness or inert,
Suffering or happiness, thus to no purpose (vain) is
 the dispute (quarrel).
The world is not seen, no "I"-belief (no going toward
 the "I")(clear ascertainment of no "I"),
Abidance without differentiation (without doubt), the
 Absolute (the Supreme), is agreeable for (dear to)
 all.

4

With-form idea (belief) the world and the Lord [are]
So long as the with-form idea the Self is (the with-form idea in the Self is)(in oneself is).
If the Self is formless, who is to see?
That vision (eye, wisdom, beholding) is one (single), limitless, [and] certainly perfectly full.

5

The body is of the nature of the five-fold sheaths (lit.: Which five-fold sheaths forming the nature is the body.)
Without that does the world shine?
Without the five-fold body, that, this here (now),
Who at all see the world? Let them speak.

6

[Of] the form of sound and others is the entire world.
The existence of sound and others is a mode of the senses made to appear (brought to light).
The existence of the senses in the mind's power (control) is.
Full of the mind (Composed of the mind) is that world, we say. (or: Full of the mind, therefore, the world is, we say.)

7

With the idea (thought, intelligence, mind) rises, with the thought (mind) sets
The world. Therefore, of the mind's (thought's) light is this.
The abode (glory, splendor, light) [in which] the mind and world are born and decay (are destroyed, perish) is the perfect fullness,
The real thing (the true Reality), devoid of birth and decay (destruction, perishing), the One.

8

Let them be spiritual practices for the vision (darshanam) of Truth,
Worship (plural) of the Supreme with name and form.
Abidance in the true Reality, the Attainment of that Self-Being (or: Abidance in the True Reality, the attainment of the state ((conviction)) of That is the Self),
Alone is the vision of Truth (true vision). Thus know (understand).

9

All dualities [and] all triads,
[On] some thing (Reality) depending (on some thing taking support), shine.
(All dualities and triads shine for some thing ((some reality)) that is the support ((for some thing upon which they depend)))
[When] that is traced (sought), all are loosed and dropped.
For them who see the Truth (Being), there is no movement ever (at any time).
(Not to them who see the Truth is there movement ever.)

10

How can knowledge shine if there is not ignorance?
Without knowledge, does ignorance shine?
And "Whose are the two?" thus. Inquiring into the source (root),
Abidance in one's own (true) nature is the Knowledge of the Supreme Truth.

11

Can that knowledge that does not know the one who knows oneself (the Self)
Be Knowledge of the Supreme Truth?

(or: Can that knowledge which is of one who does not know the Self ((oneself)))
(or: Can that knowledge that does not know the Self, the one who knows,)
Of knowing and of knowledge (or: the to be known), the support, oneself,
The one who knows shall destroy the two.

12

Sleep is not knowledge. Perceiving (sensing, seizing, grasping, taking into the mind) is not knowledge.
One does not grasp (seize, perceive) anything in true Knowledge.
Different from the categories of sleep and perceiving is
Consciousness alone (indeed); Knowledge shines forth [and is] not a void.

13

The Truth is the Consciousness-Self. Various (manifold) forms of Consciousness
Are not established (accomplished) apart (different). True Consciousness is not divided.
(lit., The Truth is the Consciousness-Self. It is various ((manifold)) forms of Consciousness that are established [as] apart ((different)) [yet] true Consciousness is not divided.
(or: The Truth is the Consciousness-Self. Various ((manifold)) forms of Consciousness are not established as apart [or] divided [from] the true Consciousness.)
Can the change (transformation, modification) of ornaments exist truly
Without the gold, separately (apart), here in this world?

14

"That" and "you" have "us" for a firm basis.
Upon the destruction of that "us" from (by means of) the knowledge of the root (source),
Without the "that," "you," and "us" notion, the One
State (Abidance, Stand) shines, the innate Self shall be.

15

The past (the having been, the gone) and the future (the to become) are the present (being) in [their] own time.
Relinquishing the Truth of what is presently existing (the present),
Will it not be laughable, repeatedly thinking over (discussion) [what is] gone [and] will be,
Like counting without the number one, in the world?

16

Where shines (appears) talk of space (direction) and time without us?
The play of space and time, here, is if we are the body.
Nowhere we shine (appear), at no time we shine (appear),
But we everywhere and always shine.

17

In the body being the Self, the wise (the knower) and the ignorant (the unintelligent) are alike (the same).
(or: In the state of the body-self, the wise and the ignorant are the same).
For the one, in the body, in the heart, the Self illumines,

Including (encompassing, spreading over) the body and the universe, the Perfect Fullness.
For the other, the Self is discernible as only the body (the Self is only the measure of the body).

18

For the ignorant and for the wise, the universe is (exists).
For the former, the seen universe, indeed (alone), is the real (the true).
For the other, the seen the resting place has become; the One,
The Real (the Truth), the completely Full, shines as formless.
(or: For the other, the One that has become the resting place of the seen,
The Real, the completely Full, the Formless, shines.)

19

The talk (controversy) of fate and of effort (striving) shall be for
Them who do not know the root of these two.
For those who know well the root thing of fate and effort,
There are not, indeed, fate or one's own activity (free will).

20

That seeing of the Lord [that is] the seer
Not seeing, that shall be mental seeing.
Not other than the seer is the Supreme, indeed. Of Him
The seeing is in one's own source (root) the absorption (lit., having been absorbed, dissolved) and abidance.

21

See the Self, see the Supreme;
Thus, the Agama (the scripture's) declaration. This is not an easy bhava (state, meditation, contemplation). (or: This is easy, not a way of thinking.)
If the Self is not, indeed, the seen, how can there be talk of the Lord? (how to seek the Lord?)
Oneself becoming His food is that seeing (is seeing Him).

22

In the mind, the Light the Supreme grants (gives) (lit., having given),
Oneself (Himself) within the mind (or: interior to the mind), He shines hidden.
The mind is to be turned back within (interior to) the mind, here.
From the union (absorption) is the seeing (wisdom) of the Lord, not otherwise.

23

The body does not say "I," thus. In deep sleep,
No one says, "I did not exist," thus.
Upon the rise of that (which), all arise. Of that
"I," with the mind (intelligence), investigate (make clear) the birth place.

24

The body does not know. Being (Existence), is not born.
The body measured (limited to the body) another arises in the midst (between, in the middle),
Ego, knot, bondage, subtle body,
Mind, bhava (mundane existence, samsara), jiva (the individual) named.

25

[Its] birth (springing from) is of form, based on a mass of form.
[It is] a feeder on form, one that has given up and grasped form,
Itself formless. Upon (at the time of) inquiry into itself,
It runs [away], this ego-ghost.

26

On the becoming of the "I," all this shines (appears).
On the dissolution of the "I," not anything, indeed, shines (appears).
Therefore, of the form of "I" is this completely.
That search is the way (path) (Or: the search for That is the way) for victory over all.

27

The Real State (True Abidance) is where "I" does not arise,
And that, without the fervent search (inquiry) for the place of emergence,
Is not destroyed (will not perish). If that is not destroyed (does not perish),
How may there be abidance, of the nature of Oneness of the True (own) Self?

28

Just as in a well of water into [which one] has dived deeply, just so, within
One must dive (plunge) with intellect highly (extraordinarily) sharp,
Prana and speech to be controlled (lit., having controlled), inquiring (reflecting on);
One shall find the nature of the root of one's own ego.

29

By silent diving by the mind [into] the true (one's own) root:
[This] inquiry (consideration), indeed, (alone) shall be true Self-inquiry.
"This I am, this is not my true (own) nature,"
Thus, [this] correct idea (understanding, knowledge) is a limb of (unessential to, secondary to, inferior to) true inquiry.

30

From (by) the search is to be attained (reached) (lit., having attained, having reached), within the Heart, That.
The "I" consciousness shall fall, head bowed.
Then, another "I" shines forth, preeminent (superior).
It is not the ego. That is the Supreme alone (indeed), the Perfect Fullness.

31

[He] who shines, having swallowed (consumed, caused to disappear) the ego,
For him, what is left remaining to be done?
He knows not anything other than the Self.
Who is able to conceive of his state?

32

Aha. The Veda has made clear (clearly opened) "That you are," thus.
So, still, abidance as the Supreme Self is not to be completely attained.
More inquiry is weakness (feebleness) of the mind (weakness of conviction).
That always, as one's own Self, indeed, shines.

33

"I know not me," or "I know me,"
Thus, expressions of man are to be laughed at.
From the difference of the seer and the seen, is this Self divided in two (twofold)?
The Oneness of oneself (the true Self), indeed, is the understanding (knowledge) [that there are] no differences.

34

Not having attained (obtained) the abidance in the established Self (true) Existence
(or: Not having attained ((obtained)) the abidance in the accomplishment of the true ((Self)) state),
The attaining of (reaching) the Heart, the true abode, in the innate True Nature (in one's own innate nature),
A play (echo) of maya (illusion) are "real, unreal, with form,
Without form, many (separate, different), one;" [they are] proclamations of the mouth.

35

The Knowledge of the established Truth (Being) alone is accomplishment.
Comparable to (resembling) a dream, indeed, are other accomplishments.
The dream of one who is awakened, how can it now be true?
Does one who abides in Truth (Being) again approach illusion?

36

The "He am I" inquiry, when in the "body is the Self" state (conception),
Is helpful for the search for (the path to) the Supreme.

In the true Self (one's own Self) Oneness
Accomplishment, that again is purposeless (useless, meaningless),
Just as the correct notion (conception) of man-ness (manhood) of a man.

37

"Duality in inquiry, but in the Knowledge of the Supreme Truth,
Nonduality," thus. This is not good (holy) speech (doctrine, advice, proposition).
Prior to the search, when the tenth [man] was lost,
And after, when found, the tenth-ness is one (that one only, the same).

38

"I do karma (action)," thus a man considering (regarding)
A bound one becomes and enjoys (experiences) the result (fruit) of karma.
If, by inquiry in the heart, doership is removed (cast off)
The triple karma perishes (is destroyed). That alone is Liberation.

39

With the being in the conception of bondage, is the anxious thought of Liberation.
But bondage of whom? Thus, by the inquiry,
In the accomplishment of himself (of itself), in one's own (true) Self, one is ever-liberated.
(or: Is established of itself, in one's own Self, the ever-liberated.)
Where is the anxious thought of bondage, and where is the anxious thought of Liberation?

40

Having a form, having no form, and of the nature of both kinds,
Liberation is of three forms, thus, the knowers say.
The complete destruction of that "I"-notion (conception of individuality) that examines (ponders) this triad
Is the Supreme Truth of Liberation.

41

Saddarsanam composed in the Dravida language,
By Maharshi Sri Ramana pure,
The composition excellent (highest, best), in the immortals' language
Spoken afterward by Vasishta Muni was composed.

42

Giving honestly (straight-forwardly, sincerely) the Essence of the Truth of Being (Existence),
Giving joy to the world of seekers of Liberation,
The divine (not a man) Sri Ramana's (delightful, agreeable) voice ,
The rays of Light, as a wall-like surface (as a fragment), the Muni's speech (words) shines.

An Inquiry into the Revelation of Truth and Oneself

Om Om Om

(Silence)

The revelation of Truth is the eternal Knowledge of the Self's own Being. As this is eternal Knowledge, it does not, therefore, belong to an individual, for an individual is not eternal. Indeed, the assumption of individuality is not real. The revelation of Truth is eternal Knowledge, for it is Being's own Knowledge of itself, which is not something in time. The Knowledge is not something that is not present at one time and attained later. Rather, it is of the nature of Consciousness, which is the very self-luminosity of Being.

Being is absolute. It is pure Existence, and it is to be realized as one's own Self. With the revelation of That as one's own Self, one's own Existence, there are no more differences, no further doubts, no questions and their answers, and no idea of something happening or someone for whom it would happen. There is just blissful Being, in all of its perfect fullness. The revelation of Truth is the non-conceptual Knowledge of Being's own nature, for itself, by itself, and entirely within itself.

The revelation of Truth is always the revelation of your own Being. For this revelation, we have the Maharshi's luminous guidance, which is the revelation of the Truth, of Self-Knowledge, by the Truth, itself. There can not possibly be any better guidance. His instructions are the clearest of the clear. If we comprehend even a particle of them, the Truth stands revealed. That is the highest good and the greatest peace. Indeed, it is an understatement to say, "It is supreme Bliss."

In the attempt to pursue the Maharshi's instructions, it is essential that you recognize that they are about you and not about something else, for the idea of something else is built upon the imagined stance of being an ego-entity. Rather, the instructions are about you; they are about your very Existence. To keep the mind turned inward, pointed at its very source, immersed in the inquiry to know who you actually are, is the right way to understand his teachings. So, he has taught no topic, but he has revealed the Truth, and the Truth that is revealed is always the nature of the one by whom it has been sought.

It is most important to have this Saddarsanam, this darshanam, or vision, of Sat, of Being, of Existence, for yourself. It is not difficult, for you, yourself, are the Self. The Existence of the Self is always, and the Knowledge of this Existence is never apart from the Existence. There is no obstruction. There is no difficulty. All that is necessary for the revelation of Truth is the abandonment of imagination, of whatever ignorance or delusive concepts that seem to superimpose limitation on the innately unlimited, that superimpose objective appearance on that which is forever nonobjective, that superimpose birth and death upon the unborn and the imperishable, a body upon the bodiless, a mind upon that which is free from thought, and an "I" upon the innately "I"-less, or egoless. If such imagination ceases, Truth is revealed to itself, all by itself.

Saddarsanam is the revelation of Truth, the vision of Reality. In the revelation of Truth, who reveals what and to whom? Of course, we can say that Sri Bhagavan reveals the Truth of the Self to the earnest seeker of Self-Realization, but who truly is Sri Bhagavan? What, in truth, is the Reality that is revealed? Of what nature is this revelation, and for whom is the revelation?

As for Sri Bhagavan, although any amount of description be given, it is impossible to adequately describe him. He is That before whom words and thoughts turn back, unable to grasp. He is That, the Truth, itself, which is the Self, and he never has any misconception regarding himself. He has no illusion and no delusion and, consequently, no limitation and no form.

As for the revelation of Reality, it is always the revelation of Truth to itself, the Reality of Consciousness knowing itself, without the division of knower, knowing, and known. Such differentiation is common in illusion, but it is nonexistent in Reality. The revelation of Truth is always beyond the realm of words and thoughts. It is always most immediate, and it is the revelation that is self-luminous, or self-known. It can never be known by an "other." So, in the revelation of Truth, it is not correct to conceive of it as some aspect of the non-Self, such as the individual, the mind, and so forth and so on, becoming aware of the Truth. Truth, Brahman, alone is capable of knowing itself. Nothing else can possibly do so. If the revelation of Truth is to be a matter of direct experience for you, the very definition of "you" must be inquired into to such a depth and extent that there remains not a trace of the non-Self in the definition of you. Upon such profound inquiry, only the Self remains as your identity, and, for that, there is the perpetual Sat-darshanam, the perpetual revelation of Sat, which is Truth, or Being.

Truth is not something in time, and it is not something in space. It is quite obvious that it is not something bodily or sensory in character. It transcends all mental modes, is quite beyond mental conditions, and is not limited to, or within the context of, any state of mind, such as waking, dreaming, or sleeping. The revelation is always the innate Self-Knowledge of Being, the Self, which is the very nature of Sri Bhagavan. This should be known as our only nature.

The Knowledge of Truth is not distinct from That. There is no such differentiation. The Reality of Being-Consciousness, itself, is the Knowledge revealed, the one to whom it is revealed, and alone the one who reveals. This is understood as self-evident fact for all those who inquire within, and, utterly effacing the notion of being an ego, remain in their real nature.

Meditate upon the teachings elucidated by the Maharshi in *Saddarsanam* by maintaining a constant inquiry into who you are. This is a constant inquiry into the nature of your very Being. In this manner, you comprehend the true sense of the Truth revealed, and you comprehend it by direct, immediate experience. It is immediate in the sense that nothing is mediate and intervening between the experience of Truth and yourself.

We should approach the sacred teachings by the Maharshi, such as are contained in *Saddarsanam*, with an understanding that they are final teachings. That is, they are the conclusive revelation of Reality as it is. Approaching with the understanding that they are conclusive, we should attempt to realize the same conclusive Knowledge, the Truth revealed, in ourselves. We should also approach them as final in another sense, and that is as if they were the only invaluably precious opportunity to acquire such instruction. The revelation of Truth is perpetual. Nevertheless, it is a very gracious opportunity to dive deep into the teachings.

The Sanskrit text is by Ganapati Muni, and it is a translation of the Tamil text composed by the Maharshi and arranged by Muruganar. In the Sanskrit, the first two invocatory verses are marked off as prathana, which means prayer, but what a prayer this is! This is a prayer unlike any other prayer. Although it is considered a prayer or an invocation, what actually is invoked? The very nature of Reality is revealed. He begins the invocation by setting forth the very nature of Existence. The Maharshi commences the text by a direct exposition of the nature of Reality, the nature of pure Existence, and how to know that Existence, that is, the nature of Self-Realization.

Saddarsanam

॥ सद्दर्शनम् ॥
|| saddarśanam ||

॥ प्रार्थना ॥
|| prārthanā ||

Prayer

सत्प्रत्ययाः किं नु विहाय सन्तं
हृद्येष चिन्तारहितो हृदाख्यः ।
कथं स्मरामस्तममेयमेकं
तस्य स्मृतिस्तत्र दृढैव निष्ठा ॥ १ ॥

sat-pratyayāḥ kiṁ nu vihāya santaṁ
hṛdyeṣa cintā-rahito hṛd-ākhyaḥ |
kathaṁ smarāmas-tam-ameyam-ekaṁ
tasya smṛtis-tatra dṛḍhaiva niṣṭhā || 1 ||

1

Can there, indeed, be the belief (faith, firm conviction, idea) of existence without that which exists?
In the Heart, free from (devoid of) thoughts, this is called the Heart.
How to think of (remember) (lit., How can we remember) that immeasurable one?
Remembrance of that, therefore, is, indeed, firm abidance (alone).
(Or: Remembrance of that is firm abidance therein alone.)

N.: Always, for everyone, there is the very firm belief, the unshakeable conviction, of Existence. This firm belief in, or conviction of, Existence manifests whenever you have the idea, "I know this," or "This is." In every experience, regardless of the form of the experience, be it subtle or gross, there is the underlying, firm conviction of Existence. The forms of the experience are illusory and are according to the conceptions of the mind, but the existence aspect has a deeper root.

Whenever there is an experience of any kind, behind it is the conviction, "I exist." Always, you feel that you exist. It is indicative of absolute, invariable, imperishable Being. Without this basis of Existence, or Being, the very idea, "I am," could not appear, and, without the idea, "I am," there could not be the idea, "This is." The existence of "I" and the existence of "this" depend on Existence. What is it that exists? We must know that and not merely the idea of existing. Examine your own experience. Always, there is this conviction, this firm, unshakeable faith that there is existence. It is not "nothing," but existence. What is this existence?

Sri Bhagavan begins to describe the Existence as free from or devoid of thoughts. Both interpretations are correct. Existence is inconceivable. Being is innately free from thought. Being is formless and indivisible, and so it is innately devoid of thought. If we assume that thought has any kind of existence, the Self is free from it, and an inquiry as to who you are reveals your thought-free nature. Your nature is pure Consciousness and not a thought; your nature is pure Existence and not the conceived. You are free from thought. It is delusion when, through imagination only, you connect yourself with a thought. Thought alone constitutes bondage. Thought alone constitutes illusion.

The problems with thought and the nonexistence of thought are brought out clearly in the *Ribhu Gita*. Ribhu expounds this point to the extent that there cannot be a thought that remains about the matter. If we transcend a thought of Existence and abide just as the Existence, itself, we find that Existence is devoid of thought. What actually is it that we call thought? What is its nature? What is its substance? If we assume that thought exists, do we assume that by way of another thought about it?

Without thought, there is no duality. Existence is nondual. Similarly, without duality, there can be no possibility of thought. The Self is free from thought, and the Self is devoid of thought. Without thought, where is illusion? Where is bondage or limitation? Without thought, where is samsara?

"Free from (devoid of) thoughts, in the Heart, it is called the Heart," signifies that Existence, which is beyond thought, is your quintessential Being. In your Being is to be found the Truth about Existence, and your Being, itself, is the Truth regarding Existence.

Sri Ramana poses a question, "How, then, to think of, or to remember, that immeasurable One?" Which one? The pure Existence, the One that is called the Heart; that is, your own Self. How are we to think of it if it is devoid of thought? Or, how are we to remember it, if it is beyond thought? We cannot really forget the Self, because that Existence is always present, underlying the firm conviction in it; nor can it be remembered as if it were an object. The Self can neither be forgotten nor remembered. It is not an object, and it is not apart from the one who seeks to know it.

Then, how is one to think of it or to remember it? All want to know it, because to do so is to be awake to Reality. Not to do so is to dream in illusion. To dream in illusion is to fabricate bondage and suffering. To be awake to Reality is to be blissful and at peace. All want to know it. All want to recall it or to remember it. It was originally there, so we want to remember it. It is always there, but interior to, and beyond conception by, the mind. So how can you think of it?

Consider this deeply in your own inquiry. Do you expect to apprehend with the mind what the Self is? If you do, the Maharshi poses the question regarding how this is going to occur. Quite naturally, there is the desire to know the Self. All those who are wise seek to know the Self because of its Bliss and peace, but how is this going to be accomplished? It is the immeasurable One, so it is not to be conceived by the mind. Infinite, it is beyond thought's grasp.

Sri Ramana says, "The remembrance of that, therefore, is, indeed, firm abidance therein, alone." To abide as That, as pure

Being, as that very Being which is free of all thought, is the proper way to know it. It is the only way to remember it. We can interpret the last line as, "Remembrance of That is firm abidance therein alone." The meaning is the same: to abide in That as That.

What is the abidance? It is pure Knowledge. Knowledge is never what you think. What is the Knowledge? It is your sense of identity firmly and irrefutably established as just the Existence. This Existence is what we always are. It is eternally the same. Only imagination gives rise to contrary conceptions. Those are the limited views of being something else, such as an "I," an object, and the assumption that somehow the Existence is divided. To have the darshanam, or vision, of Truth, you must, therefore, know your Self. Your very sense of identity, your very sense of existence, should abide as, or be absorbed in, that Existence, which is absolute. No longer think of yourself in any manner whatsoever. No longer imagine yourself to be limited by, or defined by, anything conceived in the mind. You are the Existence. You are the Heart. You are the immeasurable One. Let there be no mistake about this.

In one sense, with this one verse, the Maharshi has begun and concluded the teaching. He has masterfully summed up, in a very pithy form, the whole essence of the Realization of the Truth.

Some of the terms employed in this verse have multiple nuances of meaning. The first line of the text is: "Can there, indeed, be the belief of Existence without That which exists?" The same word for belief can be interpreted as faith, firm conviction, or an idea. Can there be the idea of existence, the faith of existence, or the conviction that there is existence without That which exists?

Always, you feel that you exist. Always, you know that you exist, with a conviction, a faith, or a belief that cannot be broken. This conviction is continuous. How could there be the idea of, or belief, in your existence, however conceived, unless there is Existence? Whether apparently wise or deluded, there is the firm conviction of Existence, always, regardless of the state or condition of the body or the mind. The Maharshi begins his spiritual instruction by posing a question. Can there be such conviction of existence without That which exists?

We can interpret the belief, or idea, of existence to mean the existence of all things, as well. Can there be the belief or idea that something exists, whatever may be your experience of it at any time, without Existence? The conclusion should be obvious. Every idea of "This is," and every idea of "I am," is utterly dependent on That which exists. You could not even have the idea that "something is," if it were not for that Existence.

The marvel of marvels is that, in illusion, although that Existence is the single most important thing, the only real thing that there is, it is overlooked, and the ideas, "I exist," and "I exist like this," seem predominant. Could any of those things that appear to exist even appear to be without the Reality that exists? Could there ever even be an idea? Could there be an idea of "you" without That which exists, which is the Reality? The conclusion to draw is that the Reality is ever present and never at a distance. Even if we say that it is veiled from view, so a revelation, or darshanam, is necessary to unveil it, still, it is not at a distance but is ever present. "Can there, indeed, be the belief of existence without That which exists?" Could the ideas of "I," "the world," "God," or anything else be, without That which exists?

"In the Heart, free from thought (devoid of thought), this is called the Heart." In the first phrase, the Maharshi shows that the ideas of existence, however interpreted, subjectively or objectively, are utterly dependent on That which exists, apart from which, such ideas cannot stand at all, not even in imagination. Now, he says, that That which exists is free from thought. We may also interpret this as devoid of thought.

The declaration is indicative of two aspects of the Knowledge of Reality. The first is that, by inquiry into your nature, you should know yourself as free from thought. That is, thought does not determine your nature. It does not provide a definition for you in any way whatsoever. The second aspect of this is that we should understand that thought has no existence, and so That which exists is devoid of thought. Generally, the understanding of your Self to be free from thought would come first, prior to the comprehension that there is no such thing as thought.

The Heart should be understood as the core of your Being. It is the Center, to which there is nothing interior. "In the Heart, free from thought," realizing that it is devoid of thought, is where we should abide. This, your very Existence, is, thus, called the Heart.

How can you possibly be bound by what is thought of? How could thought ever be a definition for your own Existence? The ideas depend on Existence. Existence, which is the Self, does not depend on ideas. How could ideas, or thought, in any form, be a definition for what you are? If thought is never a definition for what you are, what remains to be called "your Existence"? What boundary does it have? What form does it have? What division does it have? It is none and has none of such things. In this Existence, where is the space for thought? Where is the cause of thought? Examining your own nature, know that it is unthinkable. You are the inconceivable Existence. How is it possible for thought to arise for you, in you, at all? Examine your own experience to perceive what it actually is that you refer to as thought.

If you, as Existence, abide free from any idea, free from thought, as the Existence that you are, this, he says, is called the Heart. You are, then, no longer one who abides in the Heart, for you are the Heart, itself.

The idea of an existent object, the idea of an existent perceiver, the idea of "I" without the subject and object division or attributes, and the idea of the existence of the Supreme Self are entirely dependent on the one Existence. The one Existence, which is, indeed, the Self, and which is the only "I," transcends all of the ideas.

Q.: You mentioned that this spiritual remembrance is not something associated with thought. All of my identifications are with thought, and it is apparent that I approach things through thought.

N.: If you do not identify yourself with a thought and abide in the certain Knowledge that what is thought cannot possibly be who you are, what happens to your approach? You are already where you want to be, correct?

Q.: Yes. It does not make sense to approach through thought. It seems that gross misidentification is the consequence of approaching through thought. When I come to satsang or attend spiritual events, though, that changes, and I realize that such an approach is a mistake.

N.: All right. It could be said that misidentifications take the form of thoughts, and the thoughts, themselves, are the very form or substance of which the misidentifications are made. When a thought is formed, what actually happens? In the space of Consciousness, how does the thought form?

Q.: It seems that the apparent reality of a thought is only the belief in it. The belief in it creates it.

N.: From where does the belief derive?

Q.: The belief always derives from the same place, which is the solidity of the Self.

N.: You have the belief, "It exists." Sri Bhagavan explains this in the first line. In this case, it is of the form, "The thought exists." The Maharshi points out, "Could there be the belief, 'It exists', without there being Existence?" The answer is obvious that such could not occur. The instruction of Sri Ramana does not mean without thought existing, but, rather, it means without Existence. Without Existence, can there be belief or thoughts about something existing? Without Existence, can there be the belief that a thought exists or that belief exists?

Q.: I understand that belief comes from Existence. All power, all solidity, and all reality come from Existence.

N.: That is clear. Yet, that does not mean that thought exists. He refers to that very same Existence as being devoid of thought. Though you may regard thought as that which constitutes all the forms of misidentification, do you not first have to imagine yourself in some manner other than the Self, in order to believe that thought exists?

Q.: Yes. Exactly. It occurs only when there is imagination. Once that imagined separation from the Self occurs, thought appears to have an independent reality. Before that is imagined, thought does not exist.

N.: So, the only difference between the two times is that one is with imagination and the other is without. (silence) How did there come to be two different times?

Q.: One is the Absolute. There is no such thing as time. It just does not exist. The other is circular and is just bubbles upon bubbles that go in a circular pattern.

N.: To say that illusion is a set of circular bubbles is a very apt description.

Q.: Each bubble is based upon the previous bubble.

N.: Each one is dependent upon the other in that circle, but there is nothing solid therein.

Q.: When one goes to a sage, he pops one of those bubbles in that chain. Then, the whole thing goes. They challenge that bubble.

N.: All right. Again, this is a very apt description. For yourself, where is there a difference between you, or your experience, and the Absolute? The idea is that first there is the Absolute, and then there are the so-called bubbles of illusions. Does the Absolute change its nature? Does some change occur to this Existence?

Q.: It seems that the difficulty is lack of focus on the Existence.

N.: Focus for whom? Is the focus for the Existence or for some other?

Q.: It seems that the focus is in the forefront and seems to be obvious. Maybe focus is not the right word. It does not seem to be missing.

N.: All right. Whether we call it the "forefront," "nothing missing," or "obvious," it amounts to the same. For whom would it not be obvious? For whom would it become the background only? For whom would it be out of focus? The Maharshi says that the Existence is in the Heart. That means it is right where you are, in your very Being, and it is the Heart. "It is called the Heart." It is your Being, which is the very core, or the very center.

Q.: Such can only be for this fictitious, nonexistent thinking process that occurs occasionally.

N.: However, the Maharshi says that absolute Existence is devoid of thought and free of thought.

Q.: Well, I am not going to try to disprove that. (laughter)

N.: No. That would not be advisable; nor would it actually be possible. There can be no disproving of the Maharshi's revelation of Truth because it is the Truth. We can prove it to ourselves, but we cannot disprove it.

Q.: I was thinking that, if I would try to disprove it, I would suffer.

N.: The existence of the one who would try to disprove it would be further proof of it, because there could not even be the idea of such existence without the Existence. So, in this sense, all of your illusions have only proved the Reality and nothing more. At this depth, we can understand this. To any other perspective, what was just said will seem incomprehensible, for how would illusions prove Reality? At this depth, we can understand.

Q.: This understanding comes from the depth. The understanding comes from direct experience.

N.: From "the immeasurable One," it is understood. One means undivided. Immeasurable means nothing can divide it, nothing can differentiate it, nothing can limit it, and nothing can conceive of it. From that One, which is the Existence that you are, all is comprehended. Then, all of creation reveals no-creation. The entire illusion only indicates Reality, because there is only the undifferentiated One, and you are that One. That One is pure Existence, your own Existence, which you have always known and which you always are. There is no one who is apart from this.

Q.: I am considering the application of this teaching, but, perhaps, at this level, there is no application. It would be that, at any time that I believe there is thought, to inquire as to could there ever have been thought?

N.: Know the Existence from the Existence, itself. Could there have been illusion? For whom would it have been? (silence)

So, how can you think of yourself? The entire purpose of spiritual practice, in all the forms that it takes and, most especially, in the inquiry to know your Self, which is abidance in That, as That, itself, is to have the vision of Truth. It is to see Reality, which is seeing one's own Self. One starts to realize this by first recognizing the Self's freedom from thought.

You are the immeasurable One. You are the unconceived One. Distinguish clearly Existence from thought, be such a thought of the world, a thought of the body, a thought of some attribute of the body, a thought of some activity in the world, or a subtler or abstract thought. Distinguish clearly what is merely a thought and what is Existence, because the Existence is free from thought. If you are to know your Existence, you should disentangle the pseudo-connection between your Self, which is your identity, and whatever is thought of. Whatever may be the thought, it is not you. In Truth, you have never thought of yourself, and you never will. You will know yourself, but you will never think of yourself.

Every limitation, every kind of suffering, and every seed for suffering is a thought, and only a thought. It is just an idea. It is not reality. It is the stuff of which dreams are made. Such is not the Truth. Such is not Existence. That you feel that all of whatever you have thought of in life exists is proof of the Existence underlying that. It is not proof of what you have thought of, but is proof that there is an invariable Existence that does not diminish, no matter how much you lend its reality to whatever you think. It is quite beyond thought. Not one of your ideas applies to it. To abide divested of the misidentification with thought is to know the Truth of your own Existence.

One need not be concerned with whether the thought is or is not. In your inquiry, let the focus be upon distinguishing your identity and freeing your identity from whatever is conceived. That accomplished, the Unconceived remains, which is Self-luminous. It remains as itself. This is the abidance referred to by the Maharshi: Existence just by itself.

Another Q.: Right now, what is being experienced is the self-luminous Consciousness. It is very tangible here. If I am somewhere else, I do not feel it as potently as I do here. I don't feel the Existence of the Self-luminous Consciousness elsewhere. That cannot be correct, for it is everywhere. Why is it that one feels the Consciousness so much more potently here?

N.: There are several answers to your question. The first has to do with the value of satsang, being in the association, or in the company of, the wise who have realized the Truth. The Maharshi says that those that have realized the Truth abide as the Truth, itself. The same is indicated in this first verse. The effect of that is immeasurable, so it is difficult to explain, yet there are scriptures that have described it. Wherever such Truth shines, that becomes known in this world as a holy place or a temple. The effect of being in such a place is known by those who are there. In addition, what is it that they experience when they are in that place or in such holy company? They experience something that goes beyond the boundaries of time and space. It is not really something in this world. Worldless, timeless, and spaceless, the pure Existence is what they experience. To experience something timeless, spaceless, worldless, and formless, you, yourself, must be timeless, spaceless, wordless, and formless. So, right here, "here" and "there" disappear.

Q.: Then, one must assume that she is not in that timeless, spaceless, worldless, and formless Consciousness if she does not experience That.

N.: If that would be so, the question would arise, "Why not?" There would be a call for the examination of that with which you are misidentifying or to which you are attaching yourself.

Q.: If one is not experiencing the fullness of what is experienced right here, it definitely is misidentification.

N.: The advice given in various scriptures and by sages and saints is that one should never abandon that which supplies such experience. That could be the holy place, the holy company, the Self, or any combination thereof. It depends on the one who approaches.

Q.: If one is an individual, one should never abandon that. However, if one is not an individual, no such question would arise about abandoning that.

N.: It would no longer be possible.

Another Q.: If there are a few thoughts coming, this indicates that I still consider myself to be an individual, but I do not seem to be able to trace these thoughts to find the misidentification that is apparently generating those thoughts.

N.: Who is the one who is observing them? You need to examine his identity.

Place emphasis not so much on whether there are few or many thoughts but on the identity of the one who could say, or think, "This thought exists," and who becomes caught up in the idea of that thought. Inquire into his identity. If his identity is not inquired into, there may be few or many thoughts, but the same dualism prevails. For Existence, which is absolute, there can be no thought, or question of a thought, at any time, or any change of nature. It cannot be modified into something else, and it does not have a changeful experience. It just is as it is forever, for it is absolute Existence. If something appears to happen, such as a thought, the question is, "For whom does it happen? What is his identity?" It is not of great significance whether it happens occasionally or frequently, or if it is a sparse occurrence or a very cluttered occurrence. For whom does it happen? What is his nature? Do you see what is being pointed out?

Q.: Yes. I see that there is the Existence, which is clear. There also appears to be something other. There is Existence, and then there is some apparent manifestation. I am missing the part—well, no, I am not actually missing that part. It is just a matter of looking for it and not drifting off into the thoughts, and then adding more thoughts while trying to figure out those thoughts. I should ask, "Who is thinking?"

N.: The absolute Existence is void of thought. For Existence, there is not a question of thought or of anything else. The question in your inquiry is, "For whom is the thought?" Everything that appears to exist is utterly dependent on this Existence, which is absolute, but this Absolute Existence is devoid of any such modification or change, devoid of duality, and devoid of thought. If something seems to rise, it is based upon some kind of differentiation from that Existence. This split styles itself as "I," even without the word, "I." It is the notion, the mere supposition, that there is "I." Whether he has many thoughts or very few thoughts, you need to find his identity. If you find his identity, he ceases to exist as such, and all that remains is the Absolute Existence in which nothing ever happened.

Another Q.: It is becoming evident to me, when I know myself from my Self, through my Self, simply, alone, I am. When I know myself, or I know my existence, from the seer, the assumed "I," I appear as the seen, or the world. Only then do I appear as the seen or the world. When, however, I know Existence from Existence, that split does not take place. It is a matter of where I am looking from that makes the apparent division between the seer and the seen.

N.: Therefore, the inquiry is always the inward, nonobjective examination of the subject.

Q.: It is for the destruction of that imagination.

N.: Thereby, the seer and the seen are known to be only that Existence and have no different existence whatsoever.

Q.: All that is required is the abandonment of the imagination. If something seems to arise, the simple instruction is to deeply inquire into the nature of the one for whom there is this arising. The inquiry dissipates his apparent reality, as dawn the imagined ghosts in the dark house.

You are making it clear that there is no connection at all between thought and Existence, and that, but for Existence, thought does not have even a scintilla of independent existence. Abiding as the core of one's Self, the Heart, is the Silence in which all questions, all doubts, and all thoughts are dissolved.

Another Q.: I am trying to understand that there is no connection at all between thought and Existence and that thought is not even existent. The inquiry, "For whom can this thought be?" is that from which all the questions should be asked. I can't start with thought and ask the question. If I do, I entirely miss the truth.

N.: You start with Existence because, as the Maharshi has taught in the opening line, can there, indeed, be the belief of existence, be it of the body existing, something existing, or you existing, without That which exists? Reading through to the second line, we could read this as: "Can there, indeed, be the belief of Existence without That which exists in the Heart?" Without your Self, which is the Existence, without That which exists as the very core of Being, can any idea ever appear? Then, the second part of the second line would be: "This, which is devoid of thought, is called the Heart." So, the first point is that all the ideas depend upon the Existence, or the Existence in the Heart, and the second point is, free from thought, this, your Existence, is being called "the Heart."

Q.: It seems clear that the Self isn't conditioned by thought at all. Misidentification, though, seems to condition the experience of the Self.

N.: Yes, but whose experience? Does it condition the Self's experience of itself?

Q.: No. (laughing)

N.: Then, it would have to condition someone else's experience of the Self, and who would that someone else be?

Q.: It would mean the same unreal person in an unreal world, with an unreal mind and all such things.

N.: So, an unreal person entangles himself in an unreal mind, which projects an unreal world, and then conceives of conditioning. For purposes of instruction, it is said that the misidentification conditions the experience of the Self, or conditions the Self, but the Self is actually forever unconditioned. The Self never changes its nature. Therefore, the ideas condition themselves and never the Existence upon which they depend.

Q.: That is very clear from your opening remarks. It is impossible to ever get to the Self, as the Self is always present.

N.: Exactly so. If we feel that we are trying to reach the Self, the endeavor is noble, but it is accomplished by realizing that the one who is supposed to reach the Self, is, himself, the Self that he is trying to reach. If, in the mind, we conceive of the idea, "Yes, but we must start somewhere," why not start with the very Existence? Why attempt to start in the place that you really cannot start at all? If we say that we must perceive, or proceed, from where we are beginning, yes, yet where is the beginning? Could you even have an idea of a "beginning" existing, without Existence?

Q.: That is a very amazing point that the Maharshi has made.

N.: Yes. When you comprehend the full significance of it, it is incredibly profound. The entire conception of inquiring, meditating, or aspiring from some other location, from some other nature, and passing through the barrier of thought to get to the Self is very partial. It is not a complete picture. Sri Bhagavan says that That which is called the Heart, the core of your Existence, is free of thought, or devoid of thought.

You cannot get away from your Existence. So, you start with your Existence. Where you start is where you end. For that Existence, there cannot be a barrier of thought, because, he says, "cinta-rahitah," that is, without thought, or devoid of thought, is your very Existence. It is already free from thought. Your Existence is already untouched and untainted by any idea. This is your very Existence and not an existence.

Q.: I must abandon laziness. I need not force myself to stand as the Self, but I simply must abandon the illusion that I am other than the Self. I need to stop imagining the illusion.

N.: Yes, full intensity, full purpose, and full perseverance should be applied to what you regard as your very identity. By whatever name it is called, such as "habitual," "lazy," or "wrong thinking," there is no valid support for it. There is no valid cause for it. It does not stand on Truth. In truth, you cannot be other than the Self. So, inquire as to what makes you assume otherwise. The inquiry should be directed centrally along the lines of, "Who am I?"

Q.: I can interpret the question in two ways. When I inquire, "Who am I?" the thought arises, "Who can make this conception?" It seems to be a misconception.

N.: Yet, that misconception cannot stand apart from the Existence. Can there be any idea of existence, right or wrong, unless there is Existence? If, in the inquiry, you initially trace yourself to the first basic misconception, which is the assumption of an individual, simply continue the inquiry. What is the existence of the individual? If you so inquire, you will realize that there is just pure Existence, which has no individuality to it at all.

Q.: Tracing is noticing where the misconception occurs and then tracing further to where Reality stands, which is where the misconception holds no weight, no reality, whatsoever.

N.: It holds no weight, and you are free from thought. The misconception is really for no one and does not exist, in which case you are devoid of thought.

Q.: Sri Ramana starts the first verse off with a bang.

N.: He starts with Silence, which is louder than any bang (laughter, followed by silence).

The verse continues with, "How to think of (remember) that immeasurable one?" How can you think of that undivided, absolutely one Existence? How can you stand apart from it to think about it? When you think about something—well, I just said it—you think about some "thing." There is an objective portion of your thought. How could there be an objectless thought? The object need not be gross. It can be a subtle object, such as an abstract idea, but there is always an objective portion of the thought, without which, the thought is not a thought at all.

The Maharshi asks, "How to think of that immeasurable one? How to remember it?" Instructed to remember your own nature, how are you going to do that? It is immeasurable. How are you going to determine it? It is inconceivable, so how are you going to think of it? It is far too formless and limitless to be retained in memory. Since it is infinite, you cannot stand outside it or apart from it to think of it.

All wise sages give this instruction to meditate on the Self, contemplate the Self, think of the Self, and remember the Self. Therefore, the Maharshi has posed the question regarding how one can remember it. The line of this verse does not deny the validity of such instruction, but it causes you to go deeper as to what is signified when you are told to remember the Self. Remember the immeasurable One. How is this going to be done?

Q.: Does all thought always contain a misidentification with "I"? You were just pointing out that all thought is objective. It pertains to the "I," does it not?

N.: The "I" is implicit in every thought and is integral to it. Without the notion of "I," however defined—as a perceiver, as a conceiver, as an experiencer, as a rememberer, as a thinker—could there be any false notions of, "this thought exists," and "this object of this thought exists"? The entire illusion of differentiation in the undifferentiated Consciousness is utterly dependent upon this first assumption of "I." Without the "I"-notion, there is no such differentiation. The inquiry reveals that the "I"-notion has not yet been born.

Q.: So, that is how the inquiry works. The "I"-notion, defined as a thinker, a perceiver, etc., is implicit in every thought.

N.: Yes. The Maharshi has given the instruction to inquire, "For whom is this thought?" If pursued, that dissolves the entire objective portion of thought, without which the thought cannot stand, and all is returned to the "I."

The "I" truly is pure Existence and not the assumed "I"-notion or ego-entity at all. It is not quite right when a person says that he focuses on the "I"-thought and sees the "I"-thought." It is unclear what he is actually focusing on or what he is seeing, since an "I"-thought has never actually been born. If we really focus, that is, if we inquire into the nature of the "I"-notion, we discover that there is no "I"-notion, that is, there is no individual. There is just the "I"-less true "I", or "I"-"I," which is the real Self.

We come to the final portion of the verse. We can read it with two slight variations in meaning: "Remembrance of That, therefore, is, indeed, firm abidance alone;" or, "Remembrance of That is firm abidance, therein, alone." The variation depends on how we wish to treat the word "tatra," which means "therefore" or "therein." If we understand the word to mean "therefore," the meaning is causal. How to remember the immeasurable one? The answer is obvious: you cannot remember it. So, remembrance, so-called, of that, therefore, is firm abidance alone. Or, if we take the word to mean "therein," the meaning is non-causal, thus: Remembrance of that is firm abidance therein, alone. "Therein" means in the Self, in the Heart, which is pure Existence. Either way, the essence is abidance, and abidance alone.

Since the Truth of the Self cannot be conceived or remembered, what is it that constitutes Self-Realization? What is it that constitutes the remembrance of the Self, the recollection of one's actual true nature? It cannot be a thought. Sri Ramana says, "nistha," which means "abidance." It signifies the establishment of your very identity in That as That, and in That as That alone, without the addition of any adjunct to it.

What is the abidance? It cannot be just the movement of some mental attention, some permutation of thought, or some form of concentration. It must be something much deeper and more interior, something not subject to changefulness, and something that does not waver. Firm abidance is that which does not change as the body changes or as the mind changes.

Therefore, the entire inquiry and the resultant Knowledge are of a thought-transcendent nature. They are of the same nature as the Heart, or Existence, which is devoid of thought. By inquiry, you must arrive at the continuous experience of your identity as being the Self, without a trace of misidentification, which is the consideration of yourself to be somehow mixed with what is actually not the Self. This is the "remembrance" of your Being.

Realizing your Self just as it is, you see quite clearly that you have been That always, and, in the profoundest sense, that you have always known That. The individual, being nothing, knew nothing. His ignorance was not real, and Knowledge was not for him. Knowledge is inherent in the Self. It is the most interior and formless Knowledge and not a thought-produced knowledge. This is not a matter of thinking, "I am the Self," for no matter how much one would think something, it would not be stable. It is in the very nature of thought to move and to change. The Maharshi has revealed firm abidance. This is the Knowledge that truly, and once and for all, recalls one's Being as it is. Therefore, again and again, inquire to determine what your nature is, what your identity is, what your actual Existence is. Dwelling as that Existence, pure, without the superimposition of any idea and without any misidentification, is the firm abidance to which the verse alludes.

Another Q.: Does remembrance also imply that I actually know?

N.: We can take it as such.

Q.: To remember, one must have known it at one time. He is saying that I return to what I actually know and not to what I really do not know.

N.: The term can signify, "to think of," "to consider," "to remember," but "remember" seems, in our language, to fit the meaning best, because, we can never really think of the Self. So, in the form of the question, it can signify, "How to think of the Self?" or "How to remember the Self?" When he gives the answer, it is a remembrance but not a remembrance in the usual sense of memory. It is a recalling of a Knowledge that you actually always had about Being, which you always were, and in this way, we reclaim the Bliss that was actually never lost. Nothing new is attained, but something that did not actually come to be is lost.

Q.: It is almost as if he is saying, "Remember that you exist," and, with that, "It is agreeable to all."

N.: It is agreeable to all. Sri Ramana has indicated firm abidance, that is, to be free of differentiating, through imagination only, a separate identity apart from the core of Being, which is the real Existence. Firmly abide as That. Put an end to the imagination through inquiry, and do not start imagining again. When, through Knowledge of your Self, you see how self-evident the nature of your Being is, the possibility of such imagination has ended.

Another Q.: For me, firm abidance implies a sense of action, but there is no action. In another sense, though, it is remaining still.

N.: Yes, it is being still in the deepest sense, yet no action is implied. Pure Knowledge is implied, but this is Knowledge that is identical with Being. It is not a mental knowledge, because how could mental knowledge grasp the immeasurable one? Whenever we have the idea of action, "I do," whether in a gross form with the body or with the senses, or in a subtle form with the mind, the "I" is always in there, and that "I" is always unquestioned. Self-Knowledge is questioning that very "I."

मृत्युञ्जयं मृत्युभियाश्रिताना -
महंमतिर्मृत्युमुपैति पूर्वम् ।
अथ स्वभावादमृतेषु तेषु
कथं पुनर्मृत्युधियोऽवकाशः ॥ २ ॥

mṛtyuñjayaṁ mṛtyu-bhiyāśritānām
aham-matir-mṛtyum-upaiti pūrvam |
atha svabhāvād-amṛteṣu teṣu
kathaṁ punar-mṛtyu-dhiyo'vakāśaḥ || 2 ||

2

For those who have taken refuge, out of fear of death, in the Conqueror of death,
The "I" thought (notion) is the first to attain death.
Thereafter, in them [who] are naturally (by their own nature) immortal,
How again can there be space for the thought of death?

N.: The "Conqueror of death" is a well-known name for Siva. What is this Siva? What is that which can conquer death? It can be nothing of the false appearance. It must be something of the very nature of the Existence described in the first verse.

If we do not know ourselves, we seem to fall into illusion. The illusion is characterized by transience. If we are to be free of the transience, which runs contrary to our nature, we must seek to abide and find refuge in something that is eternal. What else can be eternal but this very Existence, pure Being, which is absolute? If we take refuge there, though, the first thing that will die, proclaims Sri Bhagavan, is the "I"-notion, which is the false sense of individuality. It will be the first to die because it will die before the body perishes. It will be the first to die because such is the focus for one who is truly seeking refuge, which is one who is seeking to know the Self.

In some of the illustrious commentaries composed by others on this sacred text, it is said that the first verse represents jnana, or knowledge, and the second one represents bhakti, devotion, and implies surrender. Plunging deep into the significance of both verses, there is really no distinction, and so we need not divide the verses between knowledge and devotion. These verses are statements of what is and of where to abide.

"For those who have taken refuge, out of fear of death, in the Conqueror of death, the 'I' thought (notion) is the first to attain death." Once you are in the sphere of illusion, you naturally want to be out of it. Your nature is immortal, but, having been confused with what is mortal, you fear the end of that mortal existence, and you are subject to mortality. If the Existence can be distinguished from the mortal part, the fear will disappear entirely, once and forever. To disengage the immortal from the mortal, one should inquire and know oneself.

"Thereafter, in them who are naturally (by their own nature) immortal:" that is, by their own nature, by the very fact of their own Existence, they are immortal. Who are they? They are those who have abandoned the false identity with the notion "I." All that remains is absolute Existence, and that is innately immortal. What, then, has become of the fear of death? The Maharshi says, "How again can there be space for the thought of death?" There is not even any room for it in the absolute, undivided Being.

No one wishes to go out of existence. Intuitively, everyone knows that happiness is connected with existence. We do not wish to go out of existence because we do not wish to lose our happiness. This desire to remain happy and to exist lies at the very root of the fear of death, which occurs when you mix up the Self with what is not the Self. If there is an "I," there is that which is transitory. If you are "I"-less, there is no death for you, no fear of going out of Existence, and no fear of losing your happiness. Let this notion of individuality be the first to die in you. Seek your sanctuary, your refuge, that is, your peace and your freedom, in that which is alone capable of conquering death. If you place your faith in something that will perish, of what good is it? Put your faith and your conviction in that which is inherently immortal, the Eternal. Find refuge there. Do not depend on anything else or regard such as being important. Do not count on anything else for your happiness or for your peace. Indeed, do not attempt to hold up anything else as your identity, but take refuge in the Conqueror of death. That One who is known as Siva, Mrtyunjaya, the Conqueror of death, is your own true Existence. Inquire so as to know this Existence as it is, and you will find that there is no room for an "I," let alone room for fear, fear of death, and so forth and so on.

The first word in the Sanskrit text is "Mrtyunjayam," the Conqueror of death. It is a name given to Siva. What is it that can conquer death? Obviously, only That which is deathless can be considered the Conqueror of death. How does this conquering of death come about?

No one wishes to cease to exist. This is because there is the intuition that happiness is identical with Existence. If unhappiness were identical with existence, everyone would want to go out of existence, but everyone wishes to remain without ceasing, because there is this intuition that Existence is, indeed, happiness. In delusion, though, the Existence is misidentified with something that perishes. As soon as there is misidentification with any form, there is correspondingly a fear of death, a fear of going out of existence, for every form has a creation and a destruction. If the misidentification is with the body, there is the commonly known fear of death of the body. If the misidentification is with something subtle or a thought form, there is the fear of that thought form being destroyed. Thus, there is fear of destruction, which is the fear of death.

Where can one who has fear of death find that which is a refuge from death? It is only in that which is unchanging by its nature, which is only in that which has neither birth nor death. Those who have a fear of death seek a peace that will not be destroyed and, so, seek freedom from the perishing. The freedom from the perishable is freedom from name and form, freedom from the body and the mind, freedom from the individual, and freedom from everything that is changeful.

So, fear of death becomes the motivating factor. It appears as such even in the case of the Maharshi's recounting of his own Self-Realization, or "death experience," as it is often referred to. In the recounting, he says that the fear of death struck him and that he felt he had to get the answer to it, then and there, by himself, within himself. He most certainly found the answer. Not only did he find the answer, he became the answer. He, himself, became the Conqueror of death, not only because he raised himself above death, but that very One, Siva, the Absolute Consciousness, which is the eternal Conqueror of death, he became. He became That by realizing himself to be eternally That.

If you fear death or destruction of any kind, seek refuge in the changeless One. Seek refuge in that which has the power to transcend death and, therefore, to conquer death. That One is the innermost Consciousness, the immortal Being within you. That is Siva. That is the real Self.

Sri Ramana says, "For those who have taken refuge, out of fear of death, in the Conqueror of death," signifying those who have sought refuge nowhere else, but they have sought peace and happiness in That alone. For those who have done so, the "I"-thought, or "I"-notion, is the first to attain death.

Q.: I do not understand the experience of the eternal.

N.: What is the definition of the one who does not understand the eternal? Where is his abode? Where does he dwell?

Q. He dwells in a time-bound body.

N.: He seems to dwell in a mind and in a body. The mind and the body are not the conquerors of death. The body is born, and the body dies. The mind that is created is destroyed. Do not seek refuge there. Do not place your identity there. Do not place your hopes there. Do not place your hopes to find what is real, to find your happiness, and to find out who you are in the body and the mind. Seek refuge only in that which, being innately immortal, can conquer death. What is said about conquering death is also true about conquering time. If you are in the mind, you are in time. It becomes obvious, even painfully so, that, if you are misidentified with the body, you are in time, but are you the body? Are you the mind? Where do you really dwell?

Q.: How to make the inquiry most effective? When I do something that I think is inquiry, I know the answer to the question before I ask it. If I truly knew the answer to "Who am I?" I would not be asking it. I find it helpful to assume that I do not know who I am, and ask the question from there. But I know that I exist; I cannot not know that.

N.: Yes.

Q.: What I find to be effective when I inquire, "Who am I?" is to assume that I just really do not know the answer to that and really try to find out.

N.: It is because you then rely on experiential knowledge rather than an image or an idea. The idea, "existence," is far, far, far removed from actual Existence.

Q.: It is so far removed, it is not even close.

N.: This is generally true of everything of a spiritual nature. The idea of bliss is not the experience of Bliss, and the experience of Bliss does not care one bit for the idea about bliss. Likewise, the idea of consciousness has nothing to do with Consciousness. All of your inquiry, and that which is truly Knowledge, is purely experiential. If, in your mind, you think, "I know this," and you are not immediately, then and there, having the experience of the perfect fullness of Truth, you do not really know. It is just empty echoes in the mind. When you start with your existence, as you described, you start with your experience, and when you question, "Who am I?" you pursue experiential real Knowledge. When you say to yourself, "I know that," but you do not really have a clear Knowledge of who knows that, further inquiry is worthwhile. The approaches are not even related to each other. Can you see this?

Q.: Yes, one is the looking for a "what," which is spiritually useless. The other one is looking for who is looking.

N.: Yes. So, the first one leaves the "I" solidly intact. It is an illusion, but it is being left solidly intact. In the other, the "I" is the first to die.

Q.: It is totally different. Instead of accumulating something, in terms of more objective knowledge, you are eliminating the very core.

N.: There is dissolution of the very knower who would be involved in the accumulating.

Q.: We are getting rid of the accumulator.

Another Q.: In different places, one reads of the practitioner encountering Yama. To me, this sounds like a very clear explanation of that process.

N.: Yes, there is the story of Markandeya, whom death comes to snare and take away. Markandeya holds to the Siva-lingam, which indicates his adherence entirely to Siva as the monolithic, infinite, eternal Reality. Thereupon, Siva repels death and destroys death. He who is absorbed in Siva exists solely as the eternal Siva. Death dies. Immortal Siva remains.

The purpose of these stories is that you also become deathless by losing that which is perishing. What is it that dies first, even before the body dies, for one who adheres to the Absolute? The "I"- thought, which is the ego-notion, perishes. To attain that perishing is a wonderful attainment. It is not fearful, but it is the destruction of all fear.

Ego-loss is always blissful. There is no such thing as fearful ego-loss. There is fearful ego-clinging. Where there is ego clinging, there is fear; where there is the ego, there is duality. The Upanishad says, "Where there is a second, there is fear." A "second" refers to someone other than the Absolute, that is, the ego, and a "second" refers to dualism, which is dependent entirely on the ego. If the ego and dualism are present, there will be fear. If the ego subsides, fearlessness is one's natural state.

The Existence, which is the Self, cannot have the fear of going out of existence. Who is it that has, or generates, the fear of going out of existence? If that very one, who is seemingly a transitory individual, seeks his source and his refuge in the Immortal One, which is his real Being, his individuality vanishes, and so does the fear of death, which is his fear of a loss of existence or the fear of a loss of happiness.

The Maharshi says, "Thereafter," meaning after the dissolution of the "I"-notion, after the utter relinquishment of the assumption of existing as an individual entity. "In them who are naturally immortal," "svabhavad," born of their own nature, existing by itself, "amrtesu," in the immortal, "how again can there be space for the thought of death?" If you are the individual, there is plenty of room for fear, unhappiness, suffering, and bondage. With the demise, or utter dissolution, of the individual, there is just this space-like, pure Consciousness. Consciousness is space-like in its formlessness, yet it is packed full with the perfection of its own Existence, so much so that there is not a gap, not even a particle-sized space, for anything else to be. So, Sri Ramana says, "katham punar-mrtyu-dhiyo'vakasah," "how again can there be space for the thought of death?"

The very notion of going out of existence is absurd for you who are the Self's own Existence. This must be realized experientially, vividly, by a profound inquiry into your own nature to see what you actually are. What are you in your own Existence? The Self, your own Existence as it truly, naturally is, is what was proclaimed in ancient times, and now also, as the Immortal. Can the Immortal fear mortality? Can that which is Knowledge, itself, entertain ignorance? Where will there be the space for ignorance in Knowledge? Where will there be space for the thought of death in your immortal Existence?

The message is clear: Seek your peace and sanctuary in That which can conquer everything in time and everything that is transient. Finding That within yourself, abiding as yourself, remain as the Timeless, the Eternal, the Deathless, without the least doubt and without the least wavering. In this, life's purpose is fulfilled. Before the body exhausts its allotted time, the "I"-notion should die. That is the only death necessary.

Another Q.: About twenty years ago, I had an experience during which I was looking up in the sky and felt awareness everywhere. There was no form. There was no person. There was just awareness. I remember it so well that it is outside of time. Would this be like after death?

N.: If you want to know how it is after death, you will want to find out what your Existence is now, which is the same as it was before you were born. As long as there is some association of the Self with the body, it is difficult to get beyond the notion that there are different states. Obviously, from the bodily perspective, there is a living state and a dead state, the state in which the senses are operative and the state in which the senses cease. This is an example of difference. If you, in your own nature, have no connection with the body and with the senses, what, then, is your experience? By speaking of what you are "even now," the reference is to your eternal Existence and not a particular moment in a particular lifetime. Does that awareness still exist?

Q.: Yes, but it should not be attached to anything, to any form, yet there must still remain some association with form, now.

N.: Inquire deeply into what the presumed associations are, because those various associations cause you to believe that you are in a given state, when really you are the One who is beyond all states. The associations cause you to think of being mortal and then passing into another state, but pure Consciousness is not encased in such limitations. It is not in a state that is going to pass into another.

Q.: Yet there remains the tendency to misidentify with the body.

N.: Then, there are concerns brought in because of that misidentification. The Maharshi said to take refuge in the Conqueror of death. The Conqueror of death has to be the Deathless and cannot be anything less. Because a body dies, the Conqueror of death cannot be the body. Since the senses perish, the Conqueror of death cannot be anything perceivable by the senses or a sensing entity. As the mind dies, the Conqueror of death cannot be the mind. If every thought dies, sooner or later, the Conqueror of death cannot be something contained in thought. It cannot be a product of thinking, and it cannot be comprehended in thought. There must be something beyond, but what is entirely beyond is innermost. Sri Ramana declares that it is your own Existence, which is your own nature.

Q.: The experience twenty years ago has remained so vividly present, as a moment in time, yet I can go right back to it. It is that sense of limitless Awareness without a sense of a person perceiving it.

N.: If it is impersonal, illimitable Awareness, is there life or death for it?

Q.: No. The experience that I had is reflective of Reality.

N.: Yes, and it might be better to consider it along these lines. The Awareness continuously exists, and the one who says, "I had that experience," is the illusion. It is this "I" that has come and gone, back and forth, while the Awareness exists. This shows you the proper orientation and, also, what should be relinquished by means of knowing where you really abide. Is this clearer?

Q.: Yes.

N.: In the opening line, Sri Ramana mentions "those who have taken refuge, out of the fear of death." Those who wisely pursue the Truth observe the basic facts of life and death. They aim to transcend life and death to remain as immortal Being. In the course of practice, they notice the presence of life and death, and they do not ignore such facts. In samsara, people usually do not like to think about these things. Then, when it stares them in the face, so to speak, as their own imminent death or the death of someone close to them, they think about it. When the situation passes, their memory of such fades, and their thinking about it also rapidly fades. Perhaps, it is because they do not have an answer for it or they do not know that the answer is really within. It is wise to observe that life and death are with us all of the time and to take the proper steps to realize the Truth, which is immortal and blissful. If you keep this in mind, your practice will always be very intense. Consequently, you practice inquiry to know the Truth as if it were the very last thing you were going to do.

Another Q.: In the beginning of this verse, he mentions that one imagines loss of existence or happiness, yet one knows intrinsically that it is meant to be there, that happiness and bliss are both the natural and the eternal state. That is where the natural discrimination lies for someone spiritually oriented, even though one may not cognize this. Is it a matter of cognition?

N.: No one wants to go out of Existence. Everyone rightly supposes that Existence is one's happiness. Whenever there is a reminder of the transience of what they are regarding as their existence, such as the body, which is not the Existence, itself, which remains unseen, there is corresponding suffering. It is worthwhile to consider, if your body dies, will you suffer? If the body of someone you know dies, will you suffer over the loss or disappearance of that body?

Krishna's instruction to Arjuna in the *Gita* commences with, "Neither for the living nor the dead do the wise grieve." Why not? What do the wise know? What is the wisdom that makes them wise and enables them to be free of suffering regarding any of the living and the dead? What do the wise know about the nature of the Self, to the extent that they are absolutely convinced that there is no one lost at any time?

If we go along thinking that things will remain more or less just the way they are, we are in a very precarious situation. If we are very cognizant of the changes of life and death, and seek the answer in the Conqueror of death, Siva, as the Maharshi has indicated, we arrive at a state in which we know the unmarred perfection. For that perfection, there is no flaw and nothing wrong ever. With the realization of that, death loses its ability to make us suffer, which is not the purpose of death anyway. Moreover, Sri Ramana says that, realizing the immortal Existence as one's Self, there is not even room, not even space, for the thought of death.

Q.: I have always had the fear of death. I don't want this life to slip away. I have asked many people about their experience regarding death. Some of them say that they do not actually have the fear of death.

N.: Why do you think that is?

Q.: I was wondering why that was so for them.

N.: Two people could say that they do not have the fear of death. For one, it might be because he never thinks about it and prefers not to do so. He does not want to deal with it. For the other, it may be because he has thoroughly known the Truth of the Absolute and has identified himself with it. Their words would be the same, and they may seem equally nonchalant about death, but their states would be very different.

It can also be the case that the identification is, at that moment, in the mind, with something else more than with the health and welfare of one's own particular body, as, for example, with the care over a loved one, a child, or someone else. Such a person may say, "I have no fear of dying, but if my son or daughter would ever get even close to death, it would be a great tragedy." This is a case of a person not examining his own experience.

Q.: That can be seen as lack of inquiry and of misidentification with the body.

N.: Yes, it is due to lack of inquiry. Also, a person may experience this same fear as a sense of loss and suffering, as well as fright.

Q.: It is not very common to ponder this.

N.: Even though they are surrounded by it all the time.

Q.: It is not too common for one to ponder one's death. One suppresses the thought of death by thinking, "Oh! I will just be fine."

N.: That orientation is again an intuition. It is true. "I will be fine." Unfortunately, the "I" is mixed up with some form, such as the body, and how fine the "I" really is is not clearly discerned. Regardless of whether or not there are people who do not have a fear of death, for whatever reason, in the verse, the Maharshi addresses his instruction to those who cognize that they do have a fear of death and wish to find the answer. The answer lies in the realization of Existence, which is the very same as was mentioned in the first verse. So, if you meet people who say, "Death means nothing to me," such is fine. Do not worry them unnecessarily. For yourself, though, if you notice your mind's agitation over the possibility of death, dive within and realize the Existence, which has neither gain nor loss, neither beginning nor end. Know yourself to be That. Know That, which is misperceived as everyone, to be the only One. Then, there can be no loss for you. There will not even be space for the idea that there could be loss.

Q.: I often reflect on being an ant upon which a big shoe is coming down.

N.: Can it come down on you? If you are in the body, there will be an out-of-the-body experience shortly thereafter. If you are not in the body to begin with, in and out do not pertain to you. Where do you exist even now? Do you exist in the body?

Q.: No.

N.: Knowing for certain that you do not exist in the body, is there anywhere for you to go when the body vanishes from your experience? The illusion, or the delusion, is to think that you are embodied and that, when the body's life expires, somehow the Essence is snuffed out. Really, the Essence is pure Consciousness, existing in and out of the body, or beyond the body-consideration entirely, and it is the body that appears and disappears, while the Essence, the pure Consciousness, always is. Look in this way.

Q.: That could pertain to the prana, too?

N.: Yes. The prana can be said to enter and to exit the body. One may regard the prana as increasing and decreasing, or one may say the prana remains the same and it is just that it is entering or exiting, being particularized or joining with the greater amount of prana. There are different ways of looking at this, but do you go in and out? When the body is alive and prana seems to be animating it, are you in that body? If you find now that you are not in the body, that there is clearly a distinction between the body and you, and between the prana and you, that very "you" is going to remain as it is after the prana no longer animates the body. This should become so totally your identity that you are completely free. What the Maharshi is speaking of is not theoretical. It is not even something meant to be only believed in, while you retain an experience that is otherwise.

Another Q.: It is not a counter-measure.

N.: It is only in the sense that it destroys the first measure. (laughter)

Q.: I meant, in the sense of an "interim." It is not something to hold something at bay. It is meant to destroy the entire notion.

N.: Yes. Siva does not merely hold Yama at bay, but Siva causes Yama to disappear.

Q.: Recently, I had a fear of dying when I was flying. I was flying an airplane that was fairly new to me. Part of the process, after take off, is to raise the flaps some, but not completely. If one raises them completely, there is too much lift, the plane stops flying, and it comes back down, which would not be a bad thing if what were underneath the airplane were the runway. Shortly after take off, I started to raise the flaps, but I raised them all the way, instead of just partially. The airplane started to fall back to the runway, and I was running out of runway. There were houses and trees ahead. We weren't flying anymore; we were coming down. I was not flying at full power, for this plane does not require full power to take off. I then applied full power.

N.: While simultaneously the people in those houses—one does not know why those houses were built so close to the airport—were praying ardently? (laughter)

Q.: I would not live at the end of a runway. It was frightening. It took only a couple of seconds for the airplane to regain enough air speed to start flying. I am reflecting on what it is that I thought was going to happen. I do not know that I would have died, but it surely would have made a mess of the airplane and of the other fellow and me who were in it. Looking carefully at the experience, I see that the one who was afraid was not the Existence. The Existence did not shift. It knew all about what was happening and would have watched all the way to the end.

N.: It would have been watching even after the end.

Q.: Yes, there would not have been any end for That.

N.: Identify with just that Existence and not with the form of anything else. That is what is so vitally important. In considering such an experience, you should also clearly distinguish between the natural motions for survival, the workings of your adrenal glands, and similar physical responses, and the fear of death, which is the fear of going out of Existence. You can simultaneously have the same abilities to respond, for those are physical matters, and know your Self as the Truth. Nature's way of attempting to preserve the bodily form as long as it can may continue as normal, but your inner peace as Existence remains transcendently detached from all of it. The one who is supposedly in between, claiming the identity of the Existence, on the one hand, and the limitations of the bodily form on the other, and who says, "I am undergoing this experience," is the one to be destroyed first, and he is destroyed by the Knowledge of his own nonexistence. Is this making sense to you?

Q.: It is making sense. I am dissecting something that I have not really dissected before, so it is not really clear. It is clear that there is my existence that was not affected by the experience. It was that which made the whole event come out the way it did, so that there was clarity in my actions as the response, and I did the right thing to correct the problem.

There is the Existence. There is the body and its natural response to survive. There is this one in the middle that is fearful, and that does not help at all. That fear did not make my hands work better and did not help me think better. What the correction was due to was a lot of training, not necessarily training for that specific incident, but the knowledge that, when I start to come back down, I must put on the power, and, at the same time, lower the nose of the airplane. I cannot fly away from the ground; I actually must fly at it to get some more speed.

N.: Does the knowledge, training, and application of those physical skills require an ego-entity who believes he is half-Existence-and-half-a-body? Cannot all those things be accomplished quite well without the ego?

Q.: It is obvious the ego does not help, because the fear and the panic just cloud the correct response. Is the ego of any value at any time?

N.: How could there be value in an illusion? That is like asking, "Is the mirage water good for any kind of irrigation?" (laughter) "Can we water these crops, or can we swim in it?" (laughter)

Q.: No. The mirage does not have any value.

N.: It does not produce anything, and it does not do anything. It is just a conjurer of illusion. Similarly, one would not measure your abidance as the Self by the physical responses.

Q.: No. They do not define it.

N.: Abidance does not mean that the body always has the perfect physical response in each situation. It does not mean that you will not respond. An idea that abidance as the Self means that one is non-responsive, that is, that the body is always in a state of inertia, is not true.

Q.: It is freeing to see that. There have been times when I have used fear of something to drive myself to do something. Most of the time, it is not useful. I have asked myself, "Who is it that is afraid of something? Who is this entity that is afraid of whatever?" It is obvious that it is the ego. Existence never has that experience.

N.: When you are afraid, is it not because you think your happiness will perish, or be taken away in some manner or another? Yet, is it so?

Q.: It is not so.

N.: Can actions be done without fear, in the fullness of happiness, from beginning to end?

Q.: Yes. I think that is the case, and I am thinking about if the ego really helps. The deeper my practice becomes, the less fear and the more bliss I have.

N.: Yes.

Q.: When I first started this practice several years ago, there was a great deal of suffering, and there were not many breaks in the suffering. Now, it is the other way, for there is a much happiness, bliss, and freedom.

N.: Does not that bliss act as a continuous drawing to you to realize it conclusively, so that there is no interruption in it?

Q.: It is actually more effective than fear for me at this point.

N.: Maybe, the motivation is not different.

Q.: The motivation is to be free continuously without a break.

N.: To be free continuously, and to thus be happy, or blissful, continuously without a break, is the motivation that, when you did not know better, manifested as fear. The wise know how to make good use of the experience without placing emphasis on only the objective portion of the experience, so that we do not think of it as solid or as a thing in itself. Notice that the instruction is about where to seek refuge from the fear of death and how one finds the answer in one's own Existence. If the answer is found, the fear of death will then, obviously, vanish by itself, without even the space for the thought of it. Notice that Sri Bhagavan does not advocate suppression of the fear of death, such as merely not thinking of it or some other silly approach.

Q.: And he does not advocate trying to make it worse.

N.: No. Death is already universal. We do not need to make it worse. Everyone born dies. The instruction of the wise takes up the apparently present experience, turns your mind inward, and drives you to the essence of the pure Existence, without any emphasis whatsoever on the belief in the so-called present experience. By the conclusion of this verse, Sri Ramana has revealed how there is no more room even for the thought of the fear of death, but the fear of death has been made good use of, for purposes of pointing out the Immortal. Do the same for yourself with all experience. If even the fear of death, as intense as that can be, can be made use of so wisely, as the Maharshi has amply demonstrated and taught in this verse, certainly everything else can be approached in the same way. Every other suffering can be regarded as a minor reflection or version of the same.

Q.: From this conversation, worry seems to be the fear that, sometime in the future, I am going to lose my happiness.

N.: Yes, and since you are thinking of the future in the present, you suffer right then and there. You do not wait. It is merely a minor version of the same thing.

Q.: This really helps to clarify fear and suffering, where it comes from, and what the obvious solution is.

N.: The Maharshi has very graciously and wisely summed that up in one verse. Not only has he set the example, but, in one verse, he has concisely, fully taught it.

(Silence)

Though these first two verses of the Maharshi's instruction are considered the invocation, the prayer, if the significance of what has been imparted and implied in these two verses is comprehended deeply within yourself, this, in itself, will be adequate to meet all of your spiritual needs.

Now, in his Grace, and in his all seeing Eye of Knowledge, he will expound the Truth further and more fully, for it is Sat-Darshanam, revelation of Reality. If you understand your own deathless Existence, without which there could not even be the idea of something existing, let alone something actually existing, and thus recall what your real nature is, what more need be accomplished? In this way, before he actually commences the instruction of the text, he has already revealed the Truth, just as, before he spoke, in his Silence, the Truth was already revealed. (Silence)

Text

सर्वैर्निदानं जगतोऽहमश्च
वाच्यः प्रभुः कश्चिदपारशक्तिः ।
चित्रेऽत्र लोक्यं च विलोकिता च
पटः प्रकाशोऽप्यभवत्स एकः ॥ १ ॥

sarvair-nidānaṁ jagato'hamaś-ca
vācyaḥ prabhuḥ kaścid-apāraśaktiḥ |
citre'tra lokyaṁ ca vilokitā ca
paṭaḥ prakāśo'pyabhavat-sa ekaḥ || 1 ||

1

By all, an original (first) cause (original essence) of the universe (world) and of the "I"
Is to be said, the Lord (who is the powerful Master), someone with boundless power.
Variegated here (in this) (In this picture here), the seeing one (the seer) and the seen, and
The screen, and the Light, only (also) He, the One, became.

N.: That the universe and "I," the experiencer of all that is experienced appear seems to be the common experience of all. Sri Ramana says that, because this is so, there must be an Origin for this "I" and for the universe and that the Origin must, necessarily, have all the power to lend its reality, its light, its substance, and so forth and so on to the "I" and to the universe. This is the Lord, the all-powerful Master, the One with boundless power.

"I" and "this," the experiencer and the objects of experience, seem so vivid and solid. From where do the vividness and the solidity come? The "I" and the universe both seem real. What is the source of their seeming reality? When one considers all the living beings, and one considers the vastness and duration of the universe, it is a very powerful Lord, indeed. The Lord is of the nature of the unmanifested and is neither "I" nor "this." "In this picture," or having become "variegated" in some way, there is this one who sees the seen. The Maharshi says that, like a movie being projected, the screen, and the light, all this He, the Lord, the One, became. Only One it is that becomes, or appears, as many, as "I," as "this," as the "seer," and as the "seen," and the illumination by which the "I" perceives "this." One "thing" became the knower, the knowing, and the known.

Whether we comprehend that all this is really One or we comprehend that the One has become all this, the emphasis is not on "all this," but on the One. One Reality appears as you and as the universe. One Reality appears as your apparent ability to know and to cognize the world, or universe. What is that One? It is supremely powerful. It has none of the limitations of the subject or the object. Look for this One within you; it is not a thing. Sri Ramana refers to it as the all-powerful Lord. Look for the all-powerful Lord within you, in the depths of your own Consciousness. It is a Lord of unlimited power, for everything derives its light and its reality from That, but That does not derive its Light or Reality from anything else. It does not depend on the world. It does not depend on the ego, or "I." It does not depend on anything else. Rather it, itself, has become all this, without changing its nature, for if its nature would change, it would not be all-powerful, and that which changed it would be all-powerful.

One has become all this, and all this, therefore, is only that One. What is that One? Referred to as "the Lord," you must know That as it is, within yourself. It is the Reality in all that appears to exist. It is the Being in all of the apparent experiencers, or seers. It is the Consciousness in all the knowing, perceiving, and cognizing. It is the only thing that there is. In the first invocation verse, the Maharshi considers the same Existence in its utterly transcendent nature, free of all thought, and, therefore, free of the possibility of anything else. In the second invocatory verse, the Maharshi points out the Lord's, or Self's, "I"-less nature, its egoless nature, and its deathless nature. In this verse, taking for granted the appearance of all, for the purpose of instruction, the Maharshi reveals that only one Reality is being experienced all of the time. Only One is all this.

If there is a manifested universe, there must be a cause for it, or an original essence, which is something before which there was nothing else. If there is an "I," there must be a source or a cause of it, and for that which is before the "I," there was no "I." If we consider the universe as existing or appearing, and if we consider the "I" as existing or appearing, there must be a cause, or essence, that appears as these very things. The cause appears as the effect. The effect is only the cause in that guise. If the original cause, which is before all, is undifferentiated and one, what is the nature of the effect? As Reality was originally, so it is now and always. This, then, is said to be the Lord. The word for Lord used here is "prabhuh," which means "a powerful Master," and Sri Ramana clarifies the significance by saying, "someone with boundless power." What power is it that creates the "I" in everyone? What is the power that can bring forth the entire universe?

"In this picture here," signifies the picture of the manifest universe. The term "citre" can also mean variegated, so the meaning would be "in this variegated experience." "The seeing one," is the seer, the subject, and "the seen" is all that is objective. "The screen" is the substrate upon which all this, that is, the subject and the object, appears, and "the Light" is that by whose illumination the subject and object can appear. Sri Ramana declare that all of these "only He, the One, became."

He, the Lord, God, which is only One, appears as all this and as variegated. The One of which there is no picture became this entire picture. All of the forms, as an effect, rest in the cause, which is formless, but the effect can never be different than the nature of the cause. The effect is the cause appearing as the effect. The original cause, which is God or the Supreme Self, is, therefore, all this.

What is the nature of the seer and the seen? Sri Bhagavan says that One, alone, has become both the seer and the seen. The emphasis is not so much that the One has changed its nature, but the inquiry, "What is all this?" is the emphasis. In your experience, the subject and the object appear. By what power do they appear? By what Light are they known? Upon what screen are they displayed? The screen and the Light, that is, the ground, or substrate, and That which illumines, or knows, as well as that which appears as "I," the subject, and that which appears as the object, the entire universe, are all just one Reality, one Divine Essence. If we understand in this way, where is the room for believing that "the world is separate," "I" am separate," and "this is separate?"

Just One appears as all this. To know the Reality, therefore, we must know that One, and that One as it is, not just as that One appears in this variegated picture, which is the dream of this world. We must know the One's Existence as it actually is. To know the One's Existence, we need to know our own nature and realize our nature to be that very One, the One of boundless power, the powerful Master, or God.

When you have the idea, "I know this," "I experience this," what actually exists?

Q.: Just the knowing of it.

N.: What is the power of that knowing?

Q.: Just the Knowledge. The Self is the only active thing.

N.: That which is the Self is no small personal thing, but the Lord of boundless power. What does this say of the idea of individually knowing something? What does it say about the individual, or "I"? What does it say about the entire universe? Just One is all this, because, for the Self, there is no creation, no world, no this, no other, or any such conception. Sri Bhagavan has referred to that very same Self as God, Prabhu, the Lord. The same one Self is known as the Lord for those who are considering the universe, as the Witness, which is infinite Consciousness, for those who are meditating in the mind, and as the Self, which alone exists, for those who have realized Reality.

Q.: That is why you say, "It just is as it is."

N.: There can be no difference in That, ever. Whether we are speaking of Existence pure, or whether we are speaking of "all this," still, there is only one Existence. No change ever occurs for it. If you comprehend the meaning of this verse, you will never take the experiencer, the experiencing, and the objects of experience to be real. You will know them to be like images on a screen. You will know them to be illusions. You will know them to be artificial names given to the one Existence, as if it were divided among many things.

आरभ्यते जीवजगत्परात्म -
तत्त्वाभिधानेन मतं समस्तम् ।
इदं त्रयं यावदहंमति स्यात्
सर्वोत्तमाऽहंमतिशून्यनिष्ठा ॥ २ ॥

ārabhyate jīva-jagat-parātma-
tattvābhidhānena mataṁ samastam |
idaṁ trayaṁ yāvad-aham-mati syāt
sarvottamā'ham-mati-śūnya-niṣṭhā || 2 ||

2

With naming the individual, the world, and the Supreme Self
Principles (verities), all suppositions (doctrines) begin.
(or: Naming the individual, the world, and the Supreme Self
Principles is inherent in suppositions.)
This triad is so long as the "I"-notion will exist (be).
The best of all is abidance void of the "I"-notion ("I"-assumption).

N.: Certainly, when we consider various spiritual doctrines, we can see that they are concerned primarily with naming, defining, and explaining the individual, the world or universe, and God or the Supreme Self, and discussing their relation to each other. We should understand that all suppositions, of whatever kind, involve naming or identifying or, in some way, defining yourself, the world, and the Supreme Self in relation to such. Consider your suppositions regarding your own practice of inquiry. When you think about such, do you do so with the assumptions of an individual who is trying to realize, a world, which you are attempting to transcend, and the supreme Self, which you are trying to realize? All such suppositions fall far short of real Knowledge. Within the context of such suppositions, or doctrines, you have an idea of the individual, the world, and the Supreme Self. It is inherent in the very act of making such suppositions to define these things, but the Maharshi points out that the world, the individual, and the Supreme exist only as long as the notion, "I," exists. So, he proclaims, "The best of all is abidance void of the 'I'- assumption."

The only way of knowing what it is that is really your self, what really is the Supreme Self, and what is really the nature of the universe is abidance devoid of the "I"-assumption. Once the individuality is assumed, there are other things. If there is dissolution of this false assumption, what is left? Without the "I," what is the world? Without the "I," what is left of "you?" Without the notion, "I," what is your view of the Supreme Self? What has become of these? The three are no longer three. What remains of them, and what has happened to their distinction? Knowing, or "naming," any of the triad cannot compare to abidance without the false notion "I," because, without the false notion of "I," pure Existence knows itself. It is not three-fold. It is not manifold. It is not two-fold. It is that which is ever undivided.

We can say that the meaning of the passage is, "With naming the individual, the world, and the Supreme Self principles, such is inherent in suppositions," or "With naming the principles of the individual, the world, and the Supreme Self, all suppositions begin." Or, we can interpret this to mean that inherent in all doctrines is this naming of these principles. By "naming," the attempt to explain is included.

Vedanta, which is the final, highest Knowledge is, therefore, not a doctrine and not a set of suppositions, for it does not begin by naming or explaining the world, the individual, etc. It begins with Existence. It begins where we end. It does not attempt to name or explain things that are supposed to exist, but rather aims at an inquiry into the very nature of Existence. What is it that is called the individual? However the individual is named or explained, so, in accordance with that, the world and the Supreme Self are explained.

Sri Bhagavan declares, "This triad is so long as the "I"-notion will exist." If there is the notion "I," individuality is built up, and the qualities of the individual are conceived. Just as the qualities of the individual are conceived, so are the qualities of the world conceived, and, when considering the Supreme, or the Supreme Self, that is also viewed in accordance with the perspective of the individual. Examine your own approach when you attempt to know what the world is, what the Supreme Self is, and what the individual is. Is it as if you were approaching a topic of study, with naming, analyzing, and explaining? Certainly, wise sages, have given names to these three things—the individual, the world, and the Supreme Self—but what has been the purpose in their naming and explaining? Their purpose is not to give the impression that these are objective, concrete realities. They have been named or explained only for the purpose of negation, of sweeping them aside, so that the real singular Existence is revealed. The triad is so long as the "I"-notion exists. As long as the "I"-notion exists in you, you treat the Supreme Self as if it were some object, "the Self," and you treat the world as if it were something objective to you, "the world." This includes the characteristics, traits, qualities, and the tendencies accruing to the individual, which are then treated as if they were objectively existing things.

The Maharshi says, "The best of all is abidance void of the "I"-notion." However we would name and explain, from dual to nondual, the principles, or tattva-s, of the individual, the world, and the Supreme, even if we give them exceedingly eloquent names with eloquent explanations, none of that would compare to abidance void of the "I"-notion. He says that this is the best of all because whatever is built on the basis of an "I"-notion is only as real, or as unreal, as the "I"-notion, itself.

Do you attempt to figure out what something is, or do you attempt to know yourself? A supposition is a guess at what is, and a doctrine may be regarded as a collection of such suppositions. Truth transcends doctrine and is not realized through suppositions. It is realized by direct inquiry that yields true Knowledge, which is Knowledge that is identical with the Existence known.

"Mati" means notion, assumption, or supposition. If the "I" is assumed, what do we know about these things? If the "I" is no longer assumed, what remains of these things? What do you know about the world? From the ideas that correspond to the sensory impressions to your feelings and perspectives about it, what do you really know about the world? What do you know about the Supreme Self?

Q.: It seems that there is no in-between state. There is only the one Reality. You are eliminating any possibility of a separation between God and the Self. If I abide as an "I," there is confusion. Deeper than thought, absent the thought of "I," there is none. There can not be teetering in the middle.

N.: The reason you cannot "teeter," or even "totter" (laughter), in the middle is because there are not two to begin with, between which there could be a middle state. What Sri Bhagavan describes is not a change of states, but what actually exists. From the false assumption and its consequent perspective of an "I," you may seem to conceive of the three: the world, the individual, and the Supreme Self. The text is intended for those who are inquiring, so he uses such terms. Without the "I"-thought, the illusion is not. Between the apparent states of "with an 'I'" and "without an 'I'," there is actually no separation, since they are not actually two existent states. The "with the 'I'- notion" is totally illusory. Without it, there is just the Innate. If you are seeking an "in between" state for the purpose of spiritual progress, it is found in the dissolution of that "I." The dissolution of the "I"-notion is the spiritual progress. So, Sri Ramana says that this "is the best of all." However you would define the world, as heaven or hell or anything in between, however you would define the individual, as being full of merit or demerit or anything in between, and however you would define the Supreme Self, in whatever glorious terms, none of that can compare with abidance free of the "I," in which the Reality is known directly by oneself.

Q.: To postulate those three, therefore, is simply to be in the mind.

N.: It would not make a difference what kind of supposition you conceived or what doctrine was conceived on that basis, it still would be within the context of the "I"-assumption, which is the root of all delusion. The Maharshi's teaching is based on Knowledge of Reality, by the Reality, itself. So, it would not be right to call his teaching a supposition, a doctrine, or anything similar. It is entirely of the nature of transcendent wisdom.

Q.: Yes, because it does not involve the mind at all.

N.: It is not a setting forth of ideas, even well-arranged ideas. It is the revelation of the Knowledge of the real Self, by the real Self, for itself. So, it does not include any of the dualism, or any of the triads, that one wants to dissolve. The triads are as he has already explained. In this case, dualism is thinking that there is a triadic state and a non-triadic state. Sri Ramana's instruction deals directly with Reality. If we want to speak of progress, it is completely in terms of the depth of realizing that "I"-less Knowledge.

Q.: So, the depth would be constituted of less misidentification with an "I" or any of its components and less grasping to the same. The experience of freedom would be the result.

N.: The dissolution of the "I" that conceives of this world, of "myself" as an individual, the jiva, and of the Supreme Self is the liberating Wisdom.

Q.: Because once ignorance is eliminated through Knowledge, the Self alone remains? The dissolution of ignorance is Self-Knowledge. The root cause is Knowledge.

N.: Yes, yet Knowledge, in its depth, does not have a cause. It is inherent in the Self.

Q.: Because nothing else exists. It seems from this side. . .

N.: Which side? (laughter)

Q.: I guess that I can ask the question only from this side. Otherwise, one would be Dakshinamurti. (laughter)

N.: Being Dakshinamurti is certainly not a bad thing. (laughter) He does not have any doubts or questions. (laughter) He sees from behind you. Take up his perspective. [ed., in addition to the spiritual meaning of this answer, the questioner was positioned directly in front of the Dakshinamurti altar.]

Q.: I can see more and more that the postulation of an independent "I" is the ignorance.

N.: So, when they are in the spirit of inquiry, the raising of questions serves to dissolve the "I" and whatever suppositions are built upon that "I." The reason for the doubt, which the questioning seeks to resolve or destroy, is always this assumption of "I," and all the suppositions come out from there. Whether they be elaborate, well-formulated doctrines or just wild, individualized suppositions, all of them come forth from this one "I"-notion. Undisputed Knowledge of the Reality is necessary and not a supposition. There is nothing to figure out regarding Reality. Real Knowledge is not the end result of a long thinking process. There is no engineering trick needed for Self-Realization.

Another Q.: It is reverse engineering (laughter).

N.: (laughing) Yes, it is reversing the engineer so that he goes back to where he came from (laughter), and the problem is solved. See the distinction between suppositions and real Knowledge. It is the difference between doctrine and the true teaching. The true teaching is found in abidance in the "I"-less state and not in defining illusions. Knowing more about illusions is not wisdom or real Knowledge. Knowing the Self is real Knowledge. Knowledge of the Self is directly realized by the elimination of the "I" that would suppose, or could conjure up, any idea or any kind of illusion.

Another Q.: Realization always seems to be in the direction with less definition of all kinds. I become hooked on trying to define less definition (laughter). Nothing can be said about something that does not exist. I keep trying to say something about it. In other words, "neti, neti" is not a definition. It is abjuration of definition. I keep thinking that there is some form of definition, a negative definition, that I can define. It is absurd, but I cannot seem to get over that.

N.: If you make all these definitions, what good comes of it? If you start making these definitions, soon you have definitions even about the formulation of definitions, and even a definition for the negation of definitions. Then, what do you do?

Q.: I need to inquire experientially instead of thinking about it.

N.: That gets rid of all the suppositions, and all your self-created doctrines fall by the wayside. Whether you go through all that cogitation or directly inquire, either way, in the end, you must come to actually inquire into your nature and arrive at the dissolution of the "I"-notion, as the Maharshi has said.

Q.: But one's nature is definition-less.

N.: So, you come to that in the finality, anyway.

Q.: The question for me is how to come to it. Siva said to Parvati, "I am Awareness, pure and simple." I am thinking of what "pure and simple" means. It means without definition.

N.: Yes. May we print that as a commentary? (laughter)

Q.: (laughing) Silence. (laughter)

N.: Oh, progress is being made, for, even as he speaks, he becomes silent. (laughter) Do you see that, no matter which way the mind turns, there really is no obstruction? In the end, you must come to know yourself. Knowing yourself is not a matter of making definitions, conceiving of ideas, or of giving names to things. In the Knowledge of your Self, the individuality, which is falsely assumed, dissolves. There, all the doubts are dissolved, as well, and all the questions are answered, with one resounding Silence.

Q.: Whether you are speaking or silent, it seems to be the same thing. That is something for which to be grateful.

N.: All of us can never be too thankful to Sri Bhagavan. All that is true and good is his Grace. (Silence)

Another Q.: The verse seems to address relative knowledge.

N.: Yes, but, if that knowledge be traced inwardly, what is its nature?

Q.: There is nothing objective about that nature. Tracing it inward, I cannot separate the knowing and the knowledge. You mentioned that one cannot separate the known, as well. Certainly, in meditation, that is the experience.

N.: If the Knower, or the knowing Essence, is assumed to be an individual knower, everything that he knows is just a pack of suppositions and deluded guess work. Whatever he thinks that he knows about the world, or any aspect of it, and whatever he thinks he knows about the Supreme Self are just supposition. If we say to ourselves that we know the Supreme Self to be such and such, the belief or conviction is good as far as it goes, but for real Knowledge, though, we must abide free of the "I"-notion. Then, the Absolute, or the Supreme Self, knows itself.

Another Q.: Looking from an ego point of view, I put myself at the center of some universe that is based on a center that is not really there.

N.: Yes, and from there, one imagines that he knows about the world, or the universe, both in gross forms and in subtle forms, his so-called "outer experience" of it and his mental impressions of it. He thinks that he knows about himself, what he is like, and what he is not like. With the ideas of "I am this," "I am that," "I am not like this," "I am not like that," "I have these qualities," "I have this history and this memory," and such, the individual is thus defined. Then, he enters into the field of spirituality. He hears about the Supreme Self, or about the Supreme Lord, and whatever ideas are fashioned from the perspective of that individual he takes to be the reality. It is better if all that effort is oriented toward what is nondual and deeply spiritual, in contrast to that which is merely worldly or dual, but the best of all, "sarvottama," Sri Ramana proclaims, is abidance void, "sunya-nistha," of the "I"-notion, "aham-mati."

Q.: It is not only best; it is really the only way.

N.: Anything else is merely dreaming.

Q.: I can see now that all the approaches that appear to work from an egotistic point of view regarding how one lives in a world will most likely be carried into his spiritual practice or how one approaches spirituality. One then will explain spirituality, behave toward it, and approach it in the same deluded way that he has approached something else that was only delusion.

N.: You have touched upon something that is very significant in spiritual practice, or sadhana. A truly spiritual approach questions and discerns the nature of the approach, itself. If we keep the same suppositions, which are named here, and merely accrue information within that context, what have we really done in the name of spirituality? While I would not criticize it, its benefit could certainly be questioned.

Q.: One would not really have approached the spiritual realm at all. He would have pulled the spiritual realm into a deluded reality, and it would be no different than any other part of that deluded reality.

N.: Unless you question and discern the very nature of the "I," and thereby unravel the conceptions of the individual, the world, and Supreme, no lasting benefit occurs. The true expansion from the illusion of duality to the Reality of nonduality does not occur, unless there is some means by which one abides devoid of the "I"-notion. Inquiry is that means. Otherwise, one will just have new names for the same suppositions that constituted the illusion, but the purpose of the instruction by wise sages, from time immemorial, is not to reinforce the same delusion that is already there. To the contrary, the purpose of the instruction is to show something that was not known before and to undo what was thought to be known before.

Another Q.: I am looking at my approach to the next phase of my life. I have organized it into a set of spiritual activities. It has became clear to me that I am taking the same old approach, but with spiritual terms applied to it, notwithstanding the admonition of sages that the true spiritual approach is not one of activity or any combination of activities but one of Knowledge, which is Self-Knowledge. I have the same wrong thinking, for it is still based on the wrong idea.

N.: You can organize a schedule of daily activities, but can you apply the same approach to your spirituality?

Q.: No. That is how I organize my body, and spirituality has nothing to do with that.

N.: Would much spiritual benefit actually occur by merely organizing a regimen of bodily activities, without proceeding further?

Q.: Not much. It would be better than watching the soap opera on television, perhaps.

N.: Undoubtedly, it would. In terms of lasting Liberation, it would not be fruitful, because it would still contain the same suppositions. That which yields Liberation is that which brings about abidance that is void of the "I," as the Maharshi has instructed. That which yields Liberation uproots the suppositions about the individual, the world, and God.

Q.: Instead of relinquishing the previous life, I need to relinquish the one who thought he was engaged in it.

N.: Yes. Abandon the previous conceptions, the root conception being the "I." Otherwise, one changes the activity, but the basic causes of ignorance or delusion are still there.

सत्यं मृषा वा चिदिदं जडं वा
दुःखं सुखं वेति मुधा विवादः ।
अदृष्टलोका निरहंप्रतीति -
र्निष्ठाऽविकल्पा परमाऽखिलेष्टा ॥ ३ ॥

satyaṁ mṛṣā vā cid-idaṁ jaḍaṁ vā
duḥkhaṁ sukhaṁ veti mudhā vivādaḥ |
adṛṣṭa-lokā niraham-pratītir-
niṣṭhā'vikalpā paramā'khileṣṭā || 3 ||

3

True or false, this is consciousness or inert,
Suffering or happiness, thus to no purpose (vain) is the dispute (quarrel).

The world is not seen, no "I"-belief (no going toward the "I")(clear ascertainment of no "I"),
Abidance without differentiation (without doubt), the Absolute (the Supreme), is agreeable for (dear to) all.

N.: There is no purpose in such disputes. Discussing the matter with others in polite spiritual quarrels and arguing within your own mind in a mental dispute are both entirely quite vain. Actual Knowledge of your Self is necessary for Self-Realization.

In the state of Self-Realization, the Maharshi says, "the world is not seen." It is not seen means that it is not experienced at all. So, there can no longer be any doubt regarding whether it is real or false, made of consciousness or inert, or is a place of suffering or a place of happiness. All such disputes, or thinking, depend upon the idea that the world exists. Sri Ramana says, "adrista loka," meaning "the world is not seen." That is the seeing that there is no world. In that state, all the concerns, doubts, and disagreements about what "this" is cannot be, for the obvious reason that there is no "this" to begin with.

In that state, there is no belief in an "I" who would entertain any such ideas or who would experience such a world. The state of true Knowledge is characterized by an absence of "this" and an absence of "I." It is the "clear ascertainment of no 'I,'" Sri Bhagavan says. It is that in which there is no "I"-belief, in which there is not even a "going toward the 'I,'" and in which there is no motion to create an "I"-notion. That in which there is neither "I" nor "this," no notion of "this," no definition of "this," no notion of "I," and no definition of "I," which is the same discarding of definitions alluded to in the previous verse, is the true state of Knowledge. It is abidance, "nistha," without differentiation, "avikalpa," and without doubt. Indeed, the differenceless state is alone the doubtless state. Where there are differences, there are doubts. Where there is no conception of difference, we no longer have any doubt regarding the Reality. We know it to be the Self.

"Abidance, without differentiation, or abidance without doubt, the Absolute, is dear to all." This is what is "agreeable for all." The final phrase indicates where our bliss lies and where our peace is. What is dear to us is so because of its nature of bliss, that is, of happiness, peace, and love. What is it that is completely agreeable for you? That which is completely agreeable is only abidance in the Absolute, as the Absolute. If there are differences, the experience is disagreeable. It is disagreeable within your own mind and, eventually, disagreeable with others. That in which there are no differences is perfectly agreeable. That in which there is no world and no "I," that is, seeing no world and the clear ascertainment that there is no "I," is the right state. This is the state of being the Absolute. Knowingly or unknowingly, that which is dear to all living beings and which is dear to all spiritual seekers is the abidance in That, as That, itself.

In your meditation, therefore, do not quarrel within your own mind. Sri Ramana says that all such disputes, as described in the first two lines, are to no purpose. That is not what is to be done in meditation. Do not have a quarrel within yourself. How should you meditate? How should you proceed spiritually? Abide in the state in which the world is not seen. Inquire and abide in the state in which there is no "I"-belief and in which there is neither a seen nor the seer. Now, what is left? The Absolute alone remains, without an "I" or a "this," without an "I"-notion and the world. There is no differentiation. In the differenceless state of your real Being, there is no doubt. Reality comprehends itself with a doubtless Knowledge. All the assertions of the mind cannot compare to it. If you abide in this way, you have found that which is exceedingly dear, in which you are content, and, so, which is agreeable for all.

From another perspective, let us say that you are discussing spiritual matters with a friend. The presentation of different points of view on certain topics may arise. The topics have differences. The "I"-less state has no differences. In the "I"-lessness, you are in perfect agreement. In the differenceless, there is no contention. Differences arise after the "I," and they are differences among things considered as "this." "I know this, you know this, and our this's don't match." In the "I"-less state, wherein there is no "this" at all, all are in perfect agreement.

Whether we consider something as true or as false, as inert or as Consciousness, as happiness or as suffering, and whether these ideas pertain to something in the world or to the world as such, they are still a consideration about "this," built upon the supposition of "I." What is the use of these concepts?

In the scriptures, we read the sayings of wise sages. Some say that this entire world is false, so that we realize the Truth of Brahman. Without actually contradicting themselves, those same sages say that this entire universe is true, for the Truth of Brahman, alone, constitutes all of this. Likewise, those same wise sages say that all this is inert, so that we realize that which knows, which is pure Consciousness and which is not of this world. On the other hand, they also say that this entire universe is nothing but the infinite Consciousness, and there is nothing inert anywhere. Similarly, it has been pointed out that this world is a place of suffering. This prompts the aspirant to seek Liberation in the worldless, egoless state. For those who have realized the Truth, though, that Truth is everywhere, of the nature of Bliss-Consciousness, and there is not a particle of this universe that is without this Bliss-Consciousness.

Sri Ramana says that there is no purpose in dispute and quarrel is in vain. It is purposeless to dispute which perspective is right. It is a waste of time to verbally dispute, and it is also a waste of time to dispute in the mind, because our focus should be the Knowledge of the Self and not an attempt to determine what "this" is without first knowing "I." If we attempt to determine what "this" is, without first knowing the "I," the best that we can hope for is one of those doctrinal suppositions mentioned previously. While that might be regarded as useful for some people as some kind of stepping stone, it would be a stepping stone to actually inquiring into the "I" and knowing the Self as it is, for in that way, alone, does one know Reality. This is so because the Reality, alone, can know the Reality. The unreal cannot know the Real. The ego is unreal, and as long as we take up our position, as it were, in the ego, our knowledge of things is unreal. If we want to know what is what, we must know who is who.

The undifferentiated, doubtless state is that which has abandoned the objective outlook. What is it that it is dear to all? What is dear to all is that which causes the highest Bliss. What is it that is agreeable for all? What is agreeable for all is that which is truly happy. What is the highest Bliss? What is the profound happiness? Profound happiness is abidance in that state in which one is just the Absolute, with no separate identity, no "I"-notion, no being drawn toward an "I"-notion, and no conception of an objective world. The worldless, "I"-less Reality is your true nature, and that alone is completely satisfying. It is agreeable to all. It is the dearest of all.

"True" and "false" are concepts about Being. "Consciousness" and "inert" are concepts about Consciousness. "Suffering" and "happiness" are concepts about Bliss. Neither of the concepts of these dualisms can compare with the Being-Consciousness-Bliss realized as the no-creation ("the world is not seen") and the unborn ("no 'I'") nature of the Absolute. No-creation is the realization of Knowledge, in which Reality comprehends itself, and is not a sensory experience. Reality is the Self of all and is perfectly agreeable to itself. There is no existent other one to find it otherwise.

Q.: In the state of abidance, there is a certainty that the one thing that cannot know the Self, or the Truth, is the mind. This is so, not only because there is no mind, but because neither the "I" nor "this" is real. There is a certainty that "I" alone can know myself, and no "other" can, because there is no existent "other" to know me or not know me. That is clear in the state in which no differences have arisen. Differences arise when the mind, starting with the "I"-thought, pops up.

N.: The mind can tell you everything about everything, because everything is entirely in the mind. It cannot tell you anything whatsoever about the Self. If it attempts to look at the Self, it loses its form and is swallowed up in it. You are correct. You alone can know your Self; an "other" cannot do so. The mind is an "other."

Q.: In the realm of ignorance, we look for Truth using the instrument of the mind, which is the one method, or instrument, by which we can never succeed in finding it.

N.: What causes the mind to seek?

Q.: The Self.

N.: So, the mind is only an instrument.

Q.: Yes. The mind is the instrument.

N.: It is inert. So, it is not capable of seeking.

Q.: Yes. It is not capable of doing that. This is opposite to everything that has been taught since childhood. We go to school to learn the truth about this and about that, but the Truth of one's true Self can never be found if we keep trying to do so in that way. It is futile. One has but simply to inquire.

N.: Even if someone wanted to teach this to somebody else, how would it be done? How would one teach Self-Knowledge to someone else?

Q.: It could not be done. In Self-Knowledge, there is no one to whom to teach it. There is only Existence, and it can't be taught to "anyone else."

N.: It was because the Maharshi was immovable in the absolutely solid Knowledge that there is only one Self, without an "other," that his teaching is so successful, so fruitful, and so immense. All that we need to do is to plunge into it and find our Self.

Q.: From this perspective, that would be a condition precedent to even an attempt to teach this sacred Truth.

N.: One must abide as That, but if one abides as That, it is perfectly agreeable, and so there is no longer an urge to teach. There remains no "I" to teach, no "other" to be taught, and no world.

Q.: You are saying no desire to teach even arises? This is not my experience, but the motivation to teach, then, is only from compassion but not desire. Is that true?

N.: Desire assumes some motive to acquire happiness, and that cannot be for such a one who is full of Bliss. So, we say that Sri Bhagavan taught out of infinite compassion and out of his Grace. Of course, that is said from the position of being a disciple or devotee who still thinks that there is someone who needs compassion. If there is someone who needs compassion, Sri Bhagavan is the all-compassionate One. If we take up his teaching in right earnestness and question, "Who is it that is in need of compassion?" we discover just how illimitably compassionate this teaching is.

Q.: That would reveal the duality of the separation from the Self, right then and there.

N.: It reveals the nature of the recipient. If the recipient of the Maharshi's teachings, considering them compassionate, meditates on who it is that is receiving compassion, his "I"-ness vanishes, which is the greatest compassion. His state becomes "I"-less and duality-less. Even to discuss his compassion becomes impossible.

Q.: If the ego is dissolved in the inquiry, no one remains to receive the compassion?

N.: If you are the recipient of this compassion, you find that the compassion is in the form of the teaching to inquire, "Who is it that is receiving the compassion?" With this inquiry, the "I"-sense vanishes, which is simultaneously the greatest compassion and also utterly transcendent of any view of compassion.

Q.: So, with the disappearance of the imagined "I" that would receive the compassion, the very idea of compassion melts into and merges with the Bliss of Being, which is one's Self.

N.: This Self is utterly impersonal, the pure Brahman, the perfect Bliss, and never knew any ignorance, any bondage, or any suffering.

Another Q.: I suppose that Sri Ramana was silent much of the time because it was difficult to take the questions seriously. (laughter)

N.: As in the case of Dakshinamurti, the Silence is actually of an absolute nature. Where even a trace of the ego is not, how could the ego's doubts and questions be taken seriously?

Another Q.: I understand that experience has nothing to do with thought and that realization comes with the deepening of experience. The mind seems to be the enemy. Is it possible to create an environment that deepens that experience by producing more silence, turning down the stimuli, and not engaging in much conversation?

N.: Depending on the aspirant and the point of development in the aspiration, those things can be of help, but they are not the core or the essence. The real Silence must be found in that in which the "I"-notion does not appear. Better than quieting the mind is the dissolution of the mind. Certainly, it is fine to do those things that you regard as sattvic, which tend to support your spiritual practice of turning your mind inward. There is no point in your mind immersing itself in worldly topics and making as much noise as possible. So, doing those things that you find supportive of your spiritual practice means wisely governing, or directing the use of, your senses, your speech, your thinking, and such. The Maharshi's teachings and the Vedanta teachings make reference to this, but the essential key is the Knowledge of your Self, the dissolution of false identity, and the dissolution of the idea of an existent mind.

Q.: Isn't the mind the vehicle for Knowledge?

N.: Something deeper than the mind knows this Knowledge.

Another Q.: Let us say that one is going to do some selfless service. It is something that would call upon the holiest approach. I have the idea that some thinking is going to be involved, but I don't think it is the thinking as an individual. It is something different. There have been a few times when I have written or done some action with a very holy purpose in mind, and there was not a lot of thinking involved.

N.: If there is thinking, it does not represent a disturbance.

Q.: Yes. It is not a disturbance.

N.: The thinking must proceed from something else besides misidentification. Likewise is it with the action. When you are caught up in the inspiration toward that which is selfless, or egoless, the motive for the thinking and the action is very different from the motive in your attempt to pursue your happiness through that thinking and doing.

Q.: That is a very disturbing kind of thinking. It is grasping. It is a desperate kind of thinking.

N.: Yes. Worldly thinking is a desperate search for happiness, which is within. Knowing that it is within, devoting yourself to that which is within, your thought, your speech, and your action become inspired, motivated by that very same power within. It is not that the Self ever thinks, and, certainly, the Self never does anything, but the actions and the thoughts preceding them are streaming forth from this inspiration. So, the selfless activity is filled with a certain happiness to which the worldly attempt that is driven by a desire to secure happiness external to oneself can never compare.

Q.: I can see that there is no ego involved when one is doing selfless service in an inspired state, but I have to ask, "Who is doing that?"

N.: A single source with unlimited powers has to be accepted, Sri Ramana said in verse one. It is the Lord.

Q.: That, in itself, flattens the ego completely. Then, there is nothing to lose or gain in the process, because something else is in charge?

N.: Your body, speech, and mind are merely instruments. They are not instruments for worldly desire driven by an ego, but they are instruments in the hands of a higher power. Thus, you stand disidentified. If you abide entirely disidentified and plunge into the depths of your own Being, you stand as that which is utterly immovable. The inspired activities go on without your involvement in them. We may say that the Lord does them. That is the reason why some of the saints have jokingly said that they stand even higher than the Lord, because the Lord is doing everything, and they are just peacefully being immovable. The "I," in their statements, though, is solely pure Brahman, the pure Self, and not an individual.

Q.: I think that I understand what you have said. That would be the best way to spend one's time.

N.: Egoless and selfless in the activities? Certainly. When performing activity that is selfless, you make divine use of something that would otherwise be worthless.

Another Q.: If the Self is not doing any action, and if selfless action comes from inspiration, from where does inspiration come? What motivates that?

N.: We may call it the reflected light of the Self. If we know the Self, it is that in which there is no world seen, no seer in it, and neither an action nor an actor. If you ask, at the level of actions and taking for granted that a body and a world are present, the explanation is given that it is the reflected light of the Self. When one turns toward that, she becomes swept up in that and leaves the worldly shadows and illusions behind. If you leave them behind entirely and plunge into that in which you are becoming absorbed, you find that in which there is no "I" and no "world." Nothing is being done. If there is no world, obviously, there is nothing being done in it. If, though, you ask about actions, you already assume that there is some manifest plane of existence and require an explanation of it. Then, it is the One that has become this entire variegated picture.

Q.: No-creation is the highest Truth.

N.: In the Truth of no-creation, in which there are no suppositions, no doctrines, and no ideas of any kind, there is no question of action.

Q.: There is no seer, no seen, and no witness, yet we speak of the witnessing Consciousness.

N.: One Consciousness, when viewed from the perspective of the universe appearing or existing, is called God, or the Supreme Lord. When viewed in terms of everything being only within the mind, the same Consciousness is called the witness. When known as it is, it is called pure, nondual Consciousness. In relation to the universe, it is God. In relation to the mind, it is the witness, which includes being the witness of the whole universe. Not in relation to anything, it is the Unborn, the uncreated Consciousness. So, instruction regarding the "witness" is given to those who are attempting to transcend the mind.

Another Q.: Why is the dearness of the Self described as intuitive?

N.: A person has some sense that there is a state that is the highest good and that is free of the "I" and the world. Consider how dear and agreeable is falling asleep. If one misses it for some time, she longs for it. The subsidence of the "I" and the world make it dear. A state of dreams full of images of herself and the world is not appealing.

Another Q.: That would not feel like sleep. That would be the same as staying awake or a nightmare.

N.: More dreams like the present state are not wanted.

Another Q.: This is true. I never considered it in this way previously.

N.: If the dearness of sleep were just rest for the body, a horizontal position would suffice, and there would be no interest in sleep. A person who is lying in a bed and who cannot sleep, even though the body is in a horizontal position, after some time, may become agitated. She wants her sleep. She wants to get rid of this "I" and this world. Though waking and sleeping are a natural cycle, we should remain in identity with the Absolute Self, Paramatman, which is "I"-less, which has no "I" arising, for which there is nothing based on an "I," and for which there is no world. This realization should be even while apparently awake.

The Maharshi has emphasized that our inquiry and our knowledge should not consist of suppositions, however apparently conclusive those ideas may be, but the true Knowledge of Reality. Darshanam, the revelation, of Sat, Truth, comes by giving up the objective outlook, abandoning the ego-notion, and knowing one's Self.

Another Q.: In practice, I concentrate on getting rid of the "I"-notion and then proceed to abandon the world, which is objective to the "I"-notion.

N.: Sri Ramana says, "The world is not seen, no 'I'-belief." Why is giving up the objective outlook mentioned? It is because, when we have an objectified view of things, inherent in that view, or perspective, is some definition or set of definitions of the "I." There must be some definition of "I" so that the objective world can appear as it does to one. Those definitions should be abandoned. The best way to utterly relinquish the "I"-notion is to inquire to see if it actually exists. What you are attempting to negate, then, is not so much the word or the idea of "I," but the assumed individuality, the perspective of existing as a particularized thing, based upon which the entire samsara rests. Do you comprehend?

Q.: Yes.

Another Q.: Is there any value in looking at going to sleep and how easy that is? I love to sleep. It takes no effort. It just happens. There is a great trust that this happens, and it almost always happens, at least for a few hours. That is a lovely break. Could I trust inquiry, in the same way, knowing that such abidance is the best sleep?

N.: Find out.

Q.: I think I have already found out.

N.: This is like a person asking, "If I go to sleep, will it be as good as you say it is?" You would tell such a person, "Go to sleep and find out." How can one give an analysis of sleep without going to sleep? When you fall asleep, no struggle is involved, but there is a relinquishment of the bodily orientation, the worldly orientation, etc., and you do that even without the instrumentality of knowledge. You change the state of mind by going to sleep, and your existence still remains. The actual process of doing so cannot be chalked out in concrete steps. It is similar to inquiry, inasmuch as a set of concrete steps cannot be chalked out. The path is rather formless but very natural. When you fall asleep, you give up the world and the "I"-notion subsides. All of it is experienced as being very natural, and you do not wonder, after you fall asleep, "Where has the world gone? Where is my 'I'?"

Q.: Yes, I do not think, "Did I make a mistake? Should I have gone to sleep?"

N.: It is similar with inquiry. Inquiring into one's Self, one is not left wondering, "What about the world? Where is my I?" and such.

Another Q.: Is it just a matter of trusting the process of feeling the inquiry to be not a struggle but a respite?

N.: You could bring in the element of trust, but even if you did not trust, you could inquire and prove it to yourself.

Q.: It just happens?

N.: The inquiry is not haphazard. Inquiry always works, because it is the Knowledge of Being. Sleep is only a pointer in the direction. We are not aiming for a sleeping state experience when we inquire.

Q.: The question, "Who am I?" seems to come through words. Experiencing it is still difficult.

N.: Do you have difficulty experiencing the fact of your own existence?

Q.: No.

N.: Does Existence depend on words to be or to be experienced? The inquiry is concerned with, and takes place entirely within, Existence. Do you need to develop trust in the Truth of your Existence? Do you need to develop faith that you exist, or is not that already inherent in you?

Q.: I still believe that existence is the body.

N.: Do you not have experience in which the body is absent?

Q.: Yes.

N.: But you still exist. Based on your own experience, based upon the nature of your own Existence, discern what the Existence is. The ability to know itself is intrinsic to the Existence. You are not dealing with something entirely unknown. Actually, you are dealing with that which is best known.

Another Q.: I approach spiritual practice with a plan. Yet, I understand now that spiritual practice is not laying out steps, doing those steps, and winding up where I think I am going to wind up.

N.: There is precision to the path, but there are not conceptual steps. The instructions, as given by the wise sages, include great detail regarding how to inquire and how to transcend the mind, the body, and the ego. When put into practice, they are of a very formless nature. Tracing out the steps by which those before you have become liberated, is, as an Upanishad has declared, "Like trying to trace the tracks of birds in the sky."

Your approach will not come to fruition based on what concepts are conceived along the way in the attempt to grasp spiritual Truth, but the Knowledge is revealed precisely in proportion to the concepts you relinquish. The fruit does not come with new names or new ideas for the world, for the Supreme, and for the individual, but with the abandonment of those notions, because you abandon, or question, the very "I" who has them. Always look toward the knower. In him lies true Knowledge. In the known is found only the mirror image of whatever conceptual definition is given to the knower.

Q.: Every concept I have about Brahman is never Brahman. Indeed, any conception of Brahman is so far from it that I cannot even call it different.

N.: The concepts of Brahman do not correspond to Brahman, and Brahman is utterly transcendent of all that. Similar is the case with the concepts about anything else, though the "anything else," too, is really only of the nature of Brahman.

Q.: That swallows up everything but Brahman.

N.: So, Sri Ramana said that the best and the most agreeable is abidance, without differentiation and without doubt, as the Supreme, the Absolute, which is Brahman. All the rest is vain disputation in your own mind.

Q.: All spoken for the supposed benefit of something that is not there. The ego speaks for itself, in some vain attempt to understand itself and the cockeyed world that it has made up.

N.: Fortunately, that ego has no life of its own.

सरूपबुद्धिर्जगतीश्वरे च
सरूपधीरात्मनि यावदस्ति ।
अरूप आत्मा यदि कः प्रपश्येत्
सा दृष्टिरेकाऽनवधिर्हि पूर्णा ॥ ४ ॥

sarūpa-buddhir-jagatīśvare ca
sarūpa-dhīr-ātmani yāvad-asti |
arūpa ātmā yadi kaḥ prapaśyet
sā dṛṣṭir-ekā'navadhir-hi pūrṇā || 4 ||

4

With-form idea (belief) the world and the Lord [are]
So long as the with-form idea the Self is (the with-form idea in the Self is) (in oneself is).
If the Self is formless, who is to see?
That vision (eye, wisdom, beholding) is one (single), limitless, [and] certainly perfectly full.

N.: The Existence of the Self is self-evident. It shines as the Truth revealed, as soon as any vestiges of the assumption of existing as an individual vanish. Existence is absolute, invariable, and One without a second. It is not in relation to anything else whatsoever. For the Self, there is nothing else whatsoever at any time. Undifferentiated Existence is the Reality. It is this very same undifferentiated, absolute Existence that is revealed by the Maharshi in his teachings, such as those in *Saddarsanam*.

Individuality should vanish, but does individuality exist? All of the wise agree that the ego should be eliminated. Does the ego exist? Questioning within yourself, "Who am I?" to see what it is that seems to be an individual being, trying to get to the very root of that, is the sure path to Self-Realization. Getting to the very root of this individuality is the certain way to make it disappear.

That which you are always is the Self, which is the undifferentiated Existence. You can never actually be other than That. It is only ignorance when you imagine otherwise. If you imagine there is an "I," multiplicity appears. The multiplicity is the triad of jagat-jiva-paramatman, the universe, the individual, and the Supreme Self, and these three appear as if differentiated from each other.

Sri Ramana says that the best is abidance devoid of the ego assumption. Then, those three are no longer three. They were never actually three, but they seemed to be three. All duality, triads, and multiplicity are a seeming appearance that has made no difference to the differenceless Reality. In your experience, though, this makes the difference between illusion and reality.

When you experience illusion, the Reality does not change. When there is the illusory ego, it is only imagined. The real Self has not been transformed, and a second self has not been added to it. If you assume yourself to be an individual, upon which is based supposition upon supposition, all the suppositions have the triad woven in them. If you seem to be engaged in illusion, trace this to its source. It is obvious that all illusion is for the "I." The "I"-notion comes first. Find the root of this "I"-assumption, or "I"-notion. Trace your own sense of existence, seemingly individualized, to its core, and see what is there.

Who are you? If, in Truth, you have always been and always will be the undifferentiated Existence, the real Self, your supposed bondage has never been real. If who you are is this real Self, of the nature of Being-Consciousness-Bliss, all that has been apparently experienced by you, has, indeed, not been experienced by you at all. Your real Being has remained ever still, completely detached, ever formless, and without state or condition. Has someone else come into the picture? Inquire. If you inquire, the seer and the picture both vanish.

What form do you have? The world appears to have a form. The Supreme is also assigned a form. Perhaps, it is a visualized form, or it may be a form only abstractly conceived. It is something regarded as other than the one undifferentiated Being. Anything "other," even to the slightest degree, has some form by which the differentiation is marked out. The world seems to have a form; hence, we call it "a world." God, too, seems to have some form, however abstract that might be, as long as the Self is thought to have a form. The Self never has a form, but, if you believe that the Self has a form, you will believe in an existent world with form and a Lord with form.

Only so long as the Self is regarded as with form do such delusions appear. If that belief ceases, what remains of the Lord? What remains of the world? If the world is without form because the Self is without form, what kind of world is that? If, because the Self is without form, God also is seen without form, what kind of experience of God is that? The Maharshi says, "If the Self is formless, who is to see?" Where there is form attributed to yourself, there is seeing and something seen, be it God or the world. Where the Self is known as formless, there is Being, not seeing, and all this universe and God, also, are only my Self.

Thinking that you see the world, who actually sees what? What is it that we call, in illusion, "this universe"? Who is the seer of it? What is it that we call "God"? Who sees God? "If the Self is formless, who is to see?" If there is no seer, as implied in his rhetorical question, there is only vast, illimitable Being. Who sees what? No one sees anything at any time. You are, and that "are" is all, in all, at all times. That vision, or that eye, the one that sees, that beholding or that seeing, is really only Being. So, Sri Ramana describes it as one, that is, singular, for it has no duality, no divisions in it, and there is nothing apart from it. Limitless, there is nothing beyond it or outside of it. It is certainly perfectly full. Realizing it as it is, all is complete.

When you think of yourself as having form, there is limitation. Then, there is something outside. Then, there is something "other." Then, there is some kind of division. When, upon inquiry, you know yourself as formless, there is nothing else, divine or worldly, seen at any time. When you know yourself, the formless, as you are, there are no parts within you, there are no things outside you, and there is nothing to divide your experience. Rather, your experience is continuously that of the one Self, which is just Being. Being never becomes anything. It is not born as a seer, and, therefore, it is not born or created into "this." If the Self is imagined to have a form, the very same Self that is misconstrued as a seer is also mistaken to be the seen. It appears as the "I" and the "this" in one's experience. Search the "I." What form does it have?

As long as the Self is falsely defined, then, according to those false definitions, the world and the Lord appear. How could we ever understand what God is, unless we know ourselves? All that we would have is a human conception of God, and not a Knowledge of God by God.

Similar is it with the conception of the world. The world has form as long as the idea that the Self has form exists. If the Self is formless, who is to see, whether such is seeing God or seeing the world? If the seer is formless, do seeing or the seen exist? If the experiencer is formless, what remains of the experiencing? What remains of the object of experience, the entire world and even of the experience of God?

The text says, "atmani," which means "in the Self." The form idea of the Self is only in oneself. The ideas of a form of the world and a form of God are only in oneself. The idea of the external is not, indeed, external. If within is the Self, and if the Self is formless, who sees what? Similarly, the inquiry "For whom is this?" returns the reality and identity to within, and the inquiry "Who am I?" reveals the nature of this Self.

That vision, in which one abides as the Formless, "is single, limitless, and, certainly, perfectly full." With the rise of the notion of "I," the assumption of individuality, at that very moment, through delusion only, there is an illusory deficiency. The moment that the "I" subsides, the Reality shines just as it has always existed. It is the perfect fullness. There is no deficiency in it, and there is not anything beside it, for it is limitless. That means that no one and nothing can stand apart from it—not God, not the world, and, most certainly, not the individual.

"If the Self is formless, who is to see?" Inquire and examine the definitions of the seer. Know the seer. Whatever form the seer has, subtle or gross, identified with the mind or with the body, the seen will correspond, whether the seen is the world, in the attempt to know what "that" is, or the seen is God, in the attempt to know what "That" is.

Sri Bhagavan instructs: if you abide as the formless Self, without the assumption of "I," who is to see and what is to be seen? Only the infinite, perfect fullness exists. We may call that "the Self." We may call that "Brahman." It is the Reality. This is without an "I"-sense, and this is without an objective outlook. This is nonobjective true Vision.

Q.: I am not really certain that I know what form actually is. I have accepted it as something there, but if I try to catch hold of what I think a form is, I really do not know what I am talking about. It appears to be completely made up.

N.: Yes. The form is always of the nature of the attribution of some quality, some definition, to the seer, which is yourself. According to whatever quality or attribute is superimposed through imagination on the seer, the seen, or object part, appears likewise. The definition of the seer determines the definition of the seen. The seer being with form, with some kind of definition, the seen appears likewise. For example, if in delusion, the seer is determined to be limited to the form of the body, rather than to be the limitless Self, the corresponding seen object will be the form of the world, which appears as if external to the body. Yet, what actually is there? We can ask, "What do we mean by 'there'?" "There" is some sense of Existence plus time and space projected onto it. The Maharshi begins the invocation by asking if there could be any idea, any belief, or any conviction in existence, unless there is Existence? Existence does not have a form. It is the "there" in your experience, and it is also the "here."

Q.: The Existence is not nothing.

N.: No, it is not "nothing." If we would have an idea of "nothing," the reality quality attributed to that "nothing" would be derived from the very same Existence. So, when someone says, with apparent conviction or certitude, "There is nothing there," he is very convinced of "there," and he is very convinced of his own existence, the one who is making the declaration. The Maharshi's teaching starts at that point, questioning, "Who is it that exists?" We could say, "What is it that exists?" but, generally, Ramana has stated, "Who is it that exists?" and "Who is it that sees?" because the way for Self-Realization is nonobjective. Such inquiry avoids the pitfall of one not looking at himself. It avoids the error of thinking this is an objective topic and an existence apart from oneself.

Q.: Everything I try to hold only further proves the Existence. When I say that there is nothing there, the "there" that is truly there, becomes even clearer.

N.: What form does that have? If we say, "The Self is there," "God is there," "The world is there," or "The universe is there," what is the "there"? What actually exists? In the context of the forms of those things, by which we would differentiate them one from another, what is it that we see? What actually is there? To know that and thus to know what actually exists, we must cast away from the knower whatever definition or form seems to be appended to him. The way is always inward and not outward. Therefore, Sri Ramana poses the question, "If the Self is formless, who is to see?"

Q.: By that, he is saying that we must have form to see some form?

N.: That is correct. Even if the form be as vague as "there," as some "thing," there must be some seer of it. If, though, you are formless, what happens to "there?"

Q.: "There" loses its reality.

N.: Whether we regard "there" in terms of the universe or in terms of God, what happens to "there?" If they lose their form, what actually exists?

Q.: I can describe it only as Existence. I cannot say anything more about it than that.

N.: This is wise: Sat-darshanam.

Q.: I think that I can just follow his lead.

N.: Yes. Originality does not count much in discovering Reality. Is the truth regarding form and formless now clear for you?

Q.: The Existence part is clear. I am unsure about the form and the formless.

N.: Continue to inquire into the Existence, and see if this Existence has a form. See if the very Existence that you know as your own existence has a form. To know the seer, remove what is objectively known from it. Determine whether the seer has a form. That will make everything abundantly clear.

Another Q.: I understand that what is taken to be one's identity is all-important. From and as this body form, I was looking at this bouquet of flowers. From the stand of a body, I notice that this bouquet, as are all physical forms and perceptions, is tinged with conceptions. For example, I see this bouquet of flowers in front of me. By changing the definition, I would see but a single flower or a stamen or, if under the lens of a microscope, I would see other infinitely smaller forms, phloem cells, for example. Similarly, with the portrait of Maharshi on the wall, I see a picture frame, a beautiful face, and a being.

N.: If you had a powerful enough microscope, you would see more space than matter.

Q.: Yes. The experience of the physical realm of forms and content is clearly dependent upon how the mind defines it. If I go deeper within, and stand as the true "I" that is formless, the Infinite, there cannot be anything apart from That. From that stand, if anything seems to appear, it cannot have any separate existence.

N.: The form of the seen depends upon the instrument used to perceive it.

Q.: Yes.

N.: Not only the instruments of a microscope and telescope, but the senses and the mind are the instruments being used. The mind is composed of its conceptions, and the senses are limited by the sense organs. Viewed more subtly, senses are merely a function of the mind. A particular way of thinking is experienced as sensing. These are the instruments being used. The form corresponds to those instruments. A change of those instruments will change the form of the seen. The form of the seen is dependent entirely upon the form of the seer perceiving through those instruments. Therefore, you have not seen or experienced anything but the form of those instruments. That is, you experience the forms of your senses; you experience the forms of your mind. You have never experienced anything sensed; you have just experienced the sensing.

Q.: That is true.

N.: You have never actually experienced the sensing. You have experienced only the state of mind that composes those senses. All of that has just been in the mind. The entire objective scene, even if thought to be external and even the thought that it is external, is also part of this instrument of the mind. Who sees the mind?

Q.: The immediate answer is "I."

N.: The Maharshi instructs: if the Self is formless, without instrument, without form, without shape, without definition, and without a seer, what actually is existent? That which actually exists is without difference. It is absolutely One. He teaches that it is certainly perfectly full and it is limitless. There is no space for anything else, other, or outside. There is no division, such as the seer and the seen. Only he who knows himself as he really is knows what a flower is.

Q.: Oh! The flower is just Being; the flower is just Existence.

N.: Otherwise, one merely thinks of what one sees.

Q.: The flower is certainly more than its scent. It is inseparable from Existence. It is not that I do not see a flower; I see that there is no flower. Present timelessly, Existence alone is what is.

N.: That Existence does not wilt.

Q.: Yes. That Existence most certainly does not wilt.

Another Q.: In Self-Knowledge, there is no conceiver who creates the perceived or the perceiving. That is based only on lack of Knowledge or wrong knowledge. True Knowledge removes that "I." Simultaneously, it removes, thereby, the notion of being separate from God or of a separate world "out there."

N.: In this verse, the Maharshi reveals that, as long as you possess some misidentification, some form, there will be a world and a God with whom you seem to be involved or with whom you have to tangle. Tangling with God can be rough. (laughter) The sure way to find refuge from such entanglement is in the immortal One that he described in the earlier verse. The immortal One is formless. The formless One is your true Self. If you abide in the Knowledge that your own Self is formless, the very individual who would perceive a different world and a different God with whom to tangle does not exist. That assumption dissolves, and the world, and whatever else there may be, returns to its Origin.

Another Q.: Is that formlessness the same as the substrate?

N.: Speak from your own experience. Does the substrate have a form?

Q.: No.

N.: How many "formlessnesses" can there be (laughter), and how would we differentiate one "formless" from another "formless?" In relation to all the forms that seem to appear in maya, the very same formless Reality is spoken of as the substrate. It is also the Light that illumines. It is, as Sri Bhagavan said in the earlier verse, the screen, the light, the picture, and everything. If we know it as it is and not in relation to some supposed other thing, it is no longer true that it is a substrate, for there is nothing for it to be "sub" to. It is that which is, and there is nothing to play upon its surface. It is like infinite space, which does not have a surface. This space-like, undefined, illimitable Being-Consciousness is referred to as the "Formless." It is not a mere disappearance of things in contrast to the appearance of things, as when we see births and deaths of bodies. It is not merely an unmanifested mode of things in contrast to their manifested modes. The whole universe is said to become manifest and unmanifest at different times. Rather, by the "Formless" is meant that the very possibility of any state, mode, condition, or any manifestation is quite impossible. The "Formless" refers to the one undifferentiated, ever still, ever undivided Existence. If you see a play occurring, look to the substrate and know that as your Self. Finding the substrate to be formless, however, you find there is no play. There is nothing on the surface. There is no illusion.

Another Q.: Is the word, "vision," in the last line, used in the same way we use the word Knowledge?

N.: He has used the word drstih, vision. It may mean eye. It may also mean wisdom. It may mean perceiving, as in beholding something. That is the literal meaning. We should comprehend the spiritual significance of it. Though it is a vision, it is not a physical vision, because the Self is formless, bodiless, senseless, and without a mind. So, what kind of vision is it, if it is without a mind, without the senses, without a body, and without a form? It is limitless, and what you see is what you are.

यत्पञ्चकोशात्मकमस्ति देहं
तदन्तरा किं भुवनं चकास्ति ।
देहं विना पञ्चविधं तदेतत्
पश्यन्ति के वा भुवनं भणन्तु ॥ ५ ॥

yat-pañcakośātmakam-asti dehaṁ
tad-antarā kiṁ bhuvanaṁ cakāsti ।
dehaṁ vinā pañca-vidhaṁ tadetat
paśyanti ke vā bhuvanaṁ bhaṇantu ॥ 5 ॥

5

The body is of the nature of the five-fold sheaths (lit.: Which five-fold sheaths forming the nature is the body.)
Without that does the world shine?
Without the five-fold body, that, this here (now),
Who at all see the world? Let them speak.

N.: "The body is of the nature of the five-fold sheaths" means the physical body, the prana, the mind, the intellect, and the causal sheath, which is called "the bliss sheath." This last sheath is the very seed-substance from which manifestation springs. In order to experience yourself as a body, you first must wrap yourself in all of those sheaths. Then, you can say, "I am here and now." When you think, "I am here; I am now; this is where I am;" what actually is occurring is a misidentification. The first aspect of this delusion is the misidentification with the causal basis of ignorance from which all other attributes spring.

Then follows the misidentification with an intellect, with what you are thinking, especially the more abstract forms of thought and your associations. Then, there is misidentification with the mind, which is in charge of all cognitions related to the senses. Then, there is the misidentification with the prana, which is the animating life-energy. Thereafter, there is misidentification with the material body. Only if you gather all those sheaths together and endow them with your own identity and your own reality can you say, "Here I am."

In Self-Knowledge, those sheaths are cast off. It is thus easily understood why someone who casts off those sheaths for the purpose of Self-Knowledge would not take a significant interest in the concept of "here and now." It is because that is just an imagined state due to being wrapped in those sheaths.

Sri Ramana declares, "Without that, does the world shine?" Remove the sheaths, and how does the world appear? For the world to appear or for the world to be experienced, must you not be endowed with a body? Must not the body be alive? Must not something activate the senses? Do you not need a mind to cognize those senses and that of which they supposedly take impressions? Do you not need an intellect that decides, "Here is the world," after the cruder mental functions of cognition of the senses have occurred? Must not all that rest upon a basis of ignorance that sees in terms of duality, in terms of a world that is an object and of an "I"? The Maharshi instructs, "Without that does the world shine?"

"Without the five-fold body, that, this here (now), who at all see the world? Let them speak." "Let them speak" may be understood in two ways. It is in the plural because Sri Ramana is speaking of the group of sheaths. So, "Let them speak," that is, let the inert sheaths speak, if they could, and declare their own existence or the supposed existence of what is objective. Or, we may interpret this thus: when people stand misidentified with the sheaths, with the bodies, there is a multiplicity, apparently, of selves due to that illusion. For those who are so misidentified, the instruction is, "Let them speak." Let them say, if, without such misidentifications and without such sheaths, they are really "they" and the world is really "the world."

Sri Ramana begins by saying that the body is of the nature of the five-fold sheaths. In order to have the experience of a body, and, certainly, to have the so-called experience of being embodied, of being a body, or of being a possessor of a body, all five sheaths are required, from the causal sheath, which is the basis of ignorance, to the intellect, to the mind, to the prana that animates, and to the physical matter called the annamaya kosa, the food sheath. Implicit in the Maharshi's instruction is the truth that the Self is transcendent of the five sheaths. So, in what way can there be a connection between the body and the Self? The Self is interior, that is, more subjective, than the five sheaths. It is not interior in the sense of being cooped up within them, but it is interior in the sense of being more subjective. The body is the end product of the five sheaths. Where is the connection between the body and the Self? In order to consider yourself embodied, first you must take up a position of ignorance, then engage the intellect, then the mind with its cognitions, then identify with the prana, or animating energy, and then come down to a level of thinking matter is one's Self.

Q.: Identity and reality were mentioned. The third aspect is happiness. Does this have anything to do with the bliss sheath? When there is a mistaken notion that produces the entanglement of happiness with form, is this an expression of ignorance within the bliss sheath?

N.: You may make that interpretation, provided you use such an interpretation to trace where the Bliss really is.

Another Q.: Is superimposition a two-way street? The nonexistent, objective realm cannot superimpose itself upon the Real. The ego, being nonexistent, cannot do it. The Self would not do it, because it just is and does not do anything.

N.: The idea of doing, such as creating a superimposition, or the idea of producing the illusion, is born of the causality that is, itself, part of the illusion.

Q.: I see. So, superimposition is no more real than anything else in the movie.

N.: It is only a means of describing the unreal. If you ask, "Who creates the ignorance?" the answer is that the ignorance creates the ignorance. The causality of an individual creator, doer, projector, or superimposer is, itself, part of the superimposition, projection, or misidentification.

Q.: So, all dialogue and instruction from the Master has for its purpose our being pushed inward to investigate the "I" to discover its absence.

N.: All of the instruction is based upon that "I," the destruction of which is the purpose of that instruction.

Q.: Oh! That makes sense. I understand that now.

N.: But about Reality, itself, all are silent.

Q.: Now, I am hearing what you have said so many times. The destruction of the assumed entity is the revelation of one's true Self, which alone is and about which nothing can be said. There can be no other, there never has been, and there never can be.

N.: That is it, but, about that Self, no one has ever said anything. (silence)

Q.: Because it cannot be said?

N.: If you want to know why, you need to take up the matter with Dakshinamurti. (laughter)

Q.: Yes, or inquire. (laughter)

Another Q.: You said that when the Self is known, it becomes impossible to imagine maya, or illusion, any longer. That would imply that, at one time, it was possible. So, if, at one time, it was possible, and then it becomes impossible, it seems that it could become possible again.

N.: As long as the root is left in tact, it can sprout. For those who are in ignorance, the ending of ignorance is proclaimed, and Liberation is described. If you do not find yourself in ignorance at all, who would bother to speak of such things? If bound, you seek Liberation. If you inquire, "Who is it that is bound?" no bound individual is found. Then, it is said that he has vanished forever. Such is called "Liberation." It is Liberation from merely imagined bondage.

Q.: So, that the imagining never really happens is what you are saying.

N.: If there is an individual, there seems to be imagination. There are occurrences and recurrences, as described by you. If, in Knowledge, one realizes there has never been and there never will be any individual, what can be said about bondage, imagination, and such?

Q.: I guess that one would know that it is simply imagination.

N.: Liberation has absolute finality. Self-Realization is absolute in nature. It is not an occurrence, but the abiding Reality, of the nature of pure Existence. If the individual, or jiva, is assumed, all kinds of things occur and recur. That repetitive cycle of recurrence after occurrence is called "samsara." In the samsara, the ego seems to be born and to die again and again. On a larger time scale, his body seems to be born and to die, again and again. So, the thing to do is to dissolve the individual. The individuality dissolves by ceasing to lend reality and identity to him. Identity and reality are the qualities of the real Self and not of what is assumed. If you follow the guidance of this verse, you can simply strip off the sheaths and see what remains of the individual. Remove the body. Remove the prana. Remove the mind and the intellect. Remove the very basic cause, the "I"-ness that gives rise to so much multiplicity.

Q.: The experience was fairly steady yesterday, and it is starting to become steadier as we go further now. The experience is that, after I inquire deeply, my identity as Existence becomes fairly clear. When the "I" starts to arise, by knowing my Existence, I can just dismiss it as unreal, and it goes away. Can you tell me a little more about what is going on?

N.: What do you want to know?

Q.: Is there a short cut? When that happens, I think I know clearly what is going on.

Another Q.: Isn't he describing Knowledge, itself? It is the Knowledge that is eradicating the belief. You cannot believe it. You know better. Knowing its unreality, it goes away.

Q.: Fairly clear. So, it goes away by knowing myself, which is a result of inquiry.

N.: If you know this, what is your question?

Q.: I don't know who was asking that.

N.: It vanishes by inquiry, by Knowledge. You know better, so you see it even as it seems to arise. What causes it to seem to arise?

Q.: I do not think that there is a cause.

N.: Become very certain of that.

Q.: I don't think there is a cause. If I can't find where it arises from, how can there be a cause?

N.: Yes, but be very certain of this. Let there be this better Knowledge. If we know better, but still assume ourselves to have an individual identity, it does not suffice. You must be certain. There can be nothing theoretical about this Knowledge.

Q.: Yes. What I just said was theorizing actually.

N.: Does Liberation come from theory?

Q.: Theoretically. (laughter)

N.: Let me put the question in a different way. (laughter) How do you become liberated from theory? (laughter)

Q.: I guess, I should get rid of the theoretician. (laughter)

N.: Yes. Questioning him is diving in with the better Knowledge.

Another Q.: I have the same question as I had yesterday.

N.: Can I give the same answer? (laughter)

Q.: It is about removing things that are not there. I think that what you just said is the answer to that. We need to dive in further, being very sure that they are not there to begin with. You have referred to this as "swallowing itself." It is an operation in imagination, but also an operation in what one already knows.

N.: Yes. Everyone already knows the Self in the deepest sense. We speak of "ego destruction," but it is the destruction of an illusion. That which is real cannot be destroyed. You were speaking of removing something that was not there. Obviously, if it truly is there, it cannot be removed. The Reality will not go elsewhere. We remove only that which is not there to begin with, and the manner of the removal is the deepening Knowledge that it is, in truth, not there, that is, nonexistent. This applies to the world seen through the five sheaths, to the "I am the body" conception, and to the very notion, or supposition, of "I." We remove something that is not actually there. Knowledge is said to do so. The thing that is not really there is only ignorance. Knowledge alone destroys ignorance.

Q.: And that we already have.

N.: You have it, and you are it. Loosely, we could say that That, for which there is nothing else to obscure it, reveals itself again. (silence) With the deep certitude regarding what your real nature is—the ever-shining, the ever-existing, real Self—be thorough in the removal of the ignorant notions that there is anything else and that you can be anything else. When Existence remains just as it is, just Being, there is nothing more that can be done; nor is there anything left undone.

Q.: And that really is what we already know. You remind us of what we already know. Is that not true?

N.: Whether we recognize that we always already know That or we do not, the thing to do is to realize the Self. "We know it; we don't know it." What could be the use of such discussions? What is dear and agreeable to all is the egoless state. This may sound familiar. (laughter). Nothing can be newly added to what the Maharshi has already stated.

Another Q.: Do the five sheaths even exist? It seems as though they are the product of maya.

N.: Does maya actually exist?

Q.: No. Neither do the five sheaths, do they?

N.: If the sheaths are considered the product of maya, and maya does not exist, what kind of question is this? How can a real effect come from an unreal cause?

Q.: Looking into what appears as the "I" and where the "I" emerges, the net result is that it does not emerge. What I take to be the "I" comes from nowhere and goes nowhere. It comes from what I think are my perceptions. Yet, they are unreliable.

N.: How could the "I" come from perceptions? The perceptions must be for someone, who is usually styled "I."

Q.: I thought it was very good when, at the end of one of the meditations, you said "All right." (laughter)

N.: It is a casual American version of purnam, the perfect fullness. (laughter) The sheaths are in relation to someone who has them.

Q.: Are they even that?

N.: Who is the one who has them?

Q.: The one who does not really have them.

N.: Then, you have answered your own question. In this present verse, Sri Bhagavan instructs regarding the relinquishment of the objective outlook, that is, giving up the world vision in favor of a vision of Reality, which is the revelation of Truth.

It is only from the bodily perspective that one speaks of a world. The sheaths are instruments for knowing what is objective. They are utterly incapable of knowing the Self. Not even the subtlest intellect can discover the Self, let alone the mind or the prana, or the body, which is inert. The sheaths are instruments for the objective. The objective is said to be that which is to be relinquished in order to know Reality. The sheaths, therefore, are for knowing what is unreal. For knowing Reality, Reality, itself, should be relied on.

Has anyone ever seen the world without a body? Is anyone the body? Has anyone ever perceived the body without the other sheaths? In this verse, Sri Ramana addresses two points with emphasis: the fact that we are not the body and that the world has no actual existence. The supposed existence of the world is a misperception from a position of misidentification with the sheaths, especially with the body. "Without that, does the world shine?" Have you ever experienced the world aside from the body and the sensory impressions connected with the body? He will deal with the senses in more detail in the verses that follow. He even invites them to speak. Who sees the world without the body?

Q.: It is all imagination from top to bottom, is it not? That it is "all right," I am glad to hear.

N.: It is "all right" because the Self is ever existent and is ever real. That is the "all right." If we assume the misidentification with the body and thereby regard the world as real, our experience is never all right, except when we take a brief respite from it, such as in sleep. Then, we drop off the body and most of the sheaths, and everything is much better. Of course, inquiring into the Self, because it is in the Knowledge of Reality, is far subtler than falling asleep. What they have in common is the abandonment of the bodily orientation, but Knowledge of the Self is subtler because it is not a change of state. It is of the nature of continuous Reality, and no change of state occurs, whereas sleep is a change of state for the mind and must come to an end.

Has anyone ever experienced the world apart from the sheaths constituting the experience of the body? Without the five-fold body, can we experience "this," "here," "now," or the "world"? When someone has the conception, "I am here, now," what is he actually experiencing?

Another Q.: It appears to be a downstream projection of the same ignorance. There is this objectified thinking that one is the body and that he is in it. Then, everything outside of that has to be the world. It is entirely dependent on that basic, mistaken identity.

N.: Every supposition based on that misidentification is as false as the misidentification, itself. So, if the misidentification is with the body, there are the corresponding conceptions of one's experience as "this," "here," "now," and the "world."

Q.: And when the body is active, one thinks one is active.

N.: And what the senses perceive one thinks to be the determination of Reality.

Q.: Then, I think that I know I am here.

N.: Yes. You may recall that earlier it was mentioned that, unless there is a change of one's orientation, or of the perspective, a change of terms is not really spiritual. So, if the person has the conception, "I am being this, here, now, with the world," that is actually the identical perspective the person had prior to giving it some spiritual embellishments or ornamentation in his language. It is the same perspective; it is just being lauded more, while the common person simply says, "I am here, now, doing this," and not making a big deal about it. It is still from the perspective of a body, through the five sheaths, and the world is thought to be the reality. Sri Bhagavan, though, says, "Who at all see the world?" The world is a misperception of pure Existence, which is absolutely worldless, and that misperception is rooted in the "I am the body" conception.

Another Q.: The "I am the body" misperception is rooted in the misperception of what I think the body is. All of these misidentifications are rooted in misperception.

N.: Or, perhaps, it is the other way around. All the misperceptions are only misidentifications.

Another Q.: They are equivalent, are they not?

N.: Depending on how one views oneself, one perceives accordingly. If there is a false definition, a misidentification for oneself, who appears as the subject, the object will correspond. The notion of the object depends on the notion of the subject. They rise and fall together, but, of the two, the object depends upon the subject.

Q.: That is true, but they both depend on whatever I think perception is.

N.: One can have misidentification with the fifth sheath, which is the causal, and have no perception whatsoever, as in deep sleep.

Perceptions must be for someone. The perceptions do not create the misidentification. The perceptions are the misidentification in another form, objectified. So, we need not so much address the perceptions. We have only to examine them enough to discard them, as Sri Bhagavan shows, by the recognition that they are part and parcel of, or utterly dependent on, the misidentification. We address the question of identity directly, which is a nonobjective vision. Otherwise, you would go off on the search for the accurate perception, and you would never arrive at the end of that illusion, would you?

Q.: I have to disregard perception all together.

N.: Yes. That is what Sri Ramana said. "The world is not seen," that is, no perception exists and there is no "I." He has uttered it in the same sentence. Is this clear enough for you?

Q.: I have just one more question.

N.: (smiling) Just one more question? Oh, good. After all these years. (laughter) I am just joking. Please go ahead. Ask freely.

Q.: (remains quiet)

N.: That is how it is. The final question is always answered in Silence. It happened for the four disciples of Dakshinamurti. Now, it is happening for you.

Another Q.: The world is inert. The perceptions are not the difficulty as much as the desire to procure happiness from the things of the world. It is the interpretation of the world.

N.: Yes. If we leave the objective view intact, we can then say that our interpretation of it, our desires, and such are the denser forms of ignorance. If we eliminate the desire for it, by knowing the real Bliss inside, we are still left with the "this," the perception. If we further inquire, we realize that the object portion is only the perception, and there is no "this." The perception is only a conception within our minds, so that the "this" is entirely conceived, and no one has ever experienced "this." In other words, the object of one's desire is no more external to your mind than the object of desire in a dream.

The world has no existence whatsoever. Its apparent, or supposed, existence, inclusive of all the objects in it, the events, etc., is utterly dependent upon this body-orientation. Without the body, has there ever even been a "this," let alone a desire for "this"?

There is no sense in blaming the objects of the world, blaming the body, or blaming the senses. All we need to address is the actual delusion, which is the misidentification. If we were to blame the objects and start pounding them to pieces, we would just have many shattered objects, but illusion would still be firmly intact. If we were to blame the body and try to destroy the body, in an attempt to renounce it, rather than renouncing it by true Knowledge, we would wind up with a sore, aching body, but no reduction in delusion. The "I am the body conception," would still be intact. This is brought out in the Yoga Vasistha story with Cudala and the king, her husband, Sikhidvaja.

If we would try to merely train the senses, while there might be some yogic application for such, Liberation would not be forthcoming. If we would merely try to refrain from seeing, hearing, touching, smelling, and tasting various things, the delusion that mixes up ourselves with the senses, so that we think we are a sensing entity and that the senses will procure the happiness from the outside, would still be intact.

Q.: That is the root cause of the problem.

N.: The root cause is addressed through Knowledge that destroys ignorance. Everything else that might be done spiritually that is of a bodily nature or of a sensory nature, in various ways, if done for the sake of God, for the sake of the Self, because of its purpose, has worth, but the worth lies in the Knowledge-Essence. The activities are the accoutrements, while the Knowledge-essence is the substance.

Q.: The deeper this Knowledge is, the better.

N.: Yes. For Liberation from bondage, Self-Knowledge is necessary. Inquiry, which is of the nature of Knowledge, yields the realization of Self-Knowledge. No other means could possibly do so. Nothing bodily could bring it about. Many may wish to know what brings Enlightenment. The answer lies in the Self of the one who desires it. It is not something so much brought about, as it is realized to be ever-existent. It should be obvious to all that, to realize the Self, there must be Self-Knowledge, and nothing else can do so.

Q.: One's spiritual activities might continue as before but with deeper Knowledge, as in the case of Nisargadatta Maharaj caring for his altar.

N.: Yes. As one proceeds deeper, the essence becomes very obvious. There are no hard and fast rules regarding one's spiritual activities. To say that we should do such and such activities is not entirely correct; to say that we should not engage in these spiritual activities is pure foolishness and silly. To understand the Knowledge-essence that is the core of these things, which dwells in us, is what is so important.

Let us listen to and meditate on the Maharshi's instruction.

शब्दादिरूपं भुवनं समस्तं
शब्दादिसत्तेन्द्रियवृत्तिभास्या ।
सत्तेन्द्रियाणां मनसो वशे स्यात्
मनोमयं तद्भुवनं वदामः ॥ ६ ॥

śabdādi-rūpaṁ bhuvanaṁ samastaṁ
śabdādi-sattendriya-vṛtti-bhāsyā |
sattendriyāṇāṁ manaso vaśe syāt
manomayaṁ tad-bhuvanaṁ vadāmaḥ || 6 ||

6

[Of] the form of sound and others is the entire world.
The existence of sound and others is a mode of the senses made to appear (brought to light).
The existence of the senses in the mind's power (control) is.
Full of the mind (Composed of the mind) is that world, we say. (or: Full of the mind, therefore, the world is, we say.)

N.: Sound is given as an example and implies the entire series of senses. Sri Bhagavan proclaims that the experience of the world is only the sensing of it and not otherwise. One does not actually experience a world, but only the sensing of it, and the senses are known through the mind's cognition. We do not know the sensing of it; we know the mind's conception of it. The Maharshi says that sound and others compose the entire world. Consider meditatively: what do you know of the world? Do you know anything but the five senses—seeing, hearing, touching, and the rest? In the mind, these together form a picture. You refer to that as "the world," and it appears as if external to the senses, when, actually, it is composed of the senses. We may understand this by considering the senses in terms of the experience of sensing, rather than the particular sense organs, such as the eyes, ears, skin, etc. All that you know of the world is the sensing of it. We cannot truly say sensing "of it," but just "sensing," because we do not know the "it" but only just the sensing.

"The existence of sound and others," that is, the sensing, "is a mode," a sense object, "of the senses made to appear." Some thing shines so that the senses seem to be active. Something makes the senses appear. What is it?

"The existence of the senses in the mind's power (control) is." According to the mode of the mind, so is the mode of the senses and, therefore, the corresponding objects. We see this very vividly and markedly in the contrast between the waking and dreaming states. A waking state of mind has a waking set of senses, and a dreaming state of mind is endowed with a dreaming state of senses. From the vantage point of the waking state, we know that the dreaming senses are entirely just the dreaming mind. We should see the waking senses in the same way.

The waking senses apparently perceive a waking world. The dreaming senses apparently see a dream world. Of course, we know that the dream world, just like the dream sensing, is only the dreaming mind, and not otherwise. It is the mind that makes those senses work. We could say that it is a mode of the mind that appears as the senses, and it is a mode of the mind that appears as the sensed. The same is true of the waking state. All that you have ever experienced as the objective world is the sensing, and the sensing is only brought about by the mind. It is a mode of the mind.

Sri Ramana says, "Full (composed) of the mind is that world." The world exists nowhere but in your mind. So, where are you? If the world is in your mind, you cannot be in the world. Where are you? Any place and anything that appear in the world, which exists only in your mind, cannot be your abode. The limitations of the world exist only in the mind. Those limitations in space, time, and such, cannot be yours. "Composed of the mind is that world, we say." Who says? Those who have examined their experience and have come to know the Truth say so.

If the world is only in your mind, to what should you become attached? When you are attached to something in this world, it is only one part of the mind becoming attached to another part. When you grieve over something in this world, it is just one part of your mind saddened by another part. When you become confused by something in the world, it is just one part of your mind bewildered by another part.

"Of sound and others" refers to all of the senses and all of the sense objects. Sri Ramana mentions one and says, "adi," the others. "Of the form of sound and others is the entire world." Have you ever had an experience of the world that is not sensory? "The existence of sound and others is a mode of the senses brought to light." The sound, the sight, etc., are the seeing, the hearing, etc. We never experience the world. We experience only the senses. The actual sense objects are not experienced, but only the sensing. It is the appearance of the sensing that is the sense object, and, apart from the sense objects, there has never been an experience of the world. The existence of the senses is "in the mind's power." Therefore, it is not really true to say that we have ever experienced a world. All the objects of the world have just been what we have seen, heard, touched, smelled, and tasted. There has never been a conclusive experience of any sense object. There has just been the sensing, and, proceeding along the same line of inquiry, there has never actually been the sensing, but there has just been the mind's conceiving. We can say that one form of the mind's thinking is sensing and that sensing contains within it the objects, which are imagined to be external, according to the bodily orientation. The world is composed of just the mind.

Seeing the world within the mind, you know that there is nothing to which to be attached. Seeing the world within the mind, and standing apart as the Knower of the mind, you are not of the world. The attributes and definitions of the world are not yours. You are not in the world, and you are not of the world. When we see the world and the mind in this way, the significance of limitless Consciousness, or infinite Consciousness, which is to be known as your Being, strikes home.

As long as we think that we are in the world or in relation to the world, we are still caught up in those five sheaths of the body and in the delusive conception of the triads. If we know that the world is within the mind and nowhere else, we have gone beyond those sheaths, and we have dismissed the false differences of the triads. So, when you complete meditation, do you re-enter the world? If you think so, meditate again on what Sri Bhagavan says.

If, when you wake up in the morning, or in the afternoon or evening, you have the idea that the world is coming to you, or that now you have come to your senses, you have, indeed, come to the senses, which is a mode of the mind. You have not entered a world. The world was not waiting for you. It is only in the mind. One who knows for certain that the world is only in the mind cannot be disturbed by anything in this world. So, his peace remains imperishable. Similarly, he cannot be frightened by anything in this world, and his happiness remains fearlessly.

Q.: I am thinking not just of the immediate world but of galaxies far away. Even then, the only knowledge I have of those is because someone showed me a picture of one. So, I looked at something.

N.: Even if you could fly there, there would just be your sensory perception of it.

Q.: The history that has to do with the world and people is completely dependent on some sensory perception. When I read about it, I am reading about somebody's idea about some perception or about something that happened to some kind of object long ago.

N.: It does not make a difference if it is in the past or the future or the present. It is still just a sense perception. The Maharshi gives the very expansive view. "Samastam" means the entire, and "bhuvanam," the world, and "bhuvanam samastam" means the whole world. It does not refer to only this planet, as if the rest of the planets are to be considered as different. By "world" is meant the entire, objective sphere of experience, including the billions of years of time, the countless light years of space, all the matter, all the motion of that matter, indeed, all of it, however perceived in whatever manner, by ever so many beings who are known in their multiplicity through your senses. The senses, though, do not know of themselves. The senses are, in themselves, as inert as the sensed objects. No sense object exists apart from the senses. It is within the senses. Your senses are not traveling "out there" to perceive objects. The objects are conjured up within the sensory experience.

Q.: If I remove the senses, there are no objects. They are one and the same.

N.: Sri Ramana goes further. The sensing experience is conceived in the mind. It is under the mind's power. The mind must be in a certain state in order to create the senses within it.

Q.: So, for the waking state experience of those kinds of objects, one needs to be in the waking state experience. I won't see them, or I may see a version of them, in the dreaming state.

N.: In a dreaming state of mind, you have dream senses and dream objects with a dream history that stretches back a long time, but all of that is within the mind. One who knows that the world is only of the senses and the senses are only of the mind, knowing that it is all just of the mind, is no longer disturbed by any of the objects of the senses.

Q.: The mind is no longer disturbed?

N.: The one who knows that the objects are only the senses and that the senses are only the mind can no longer be disturbed by any of the objects. The gain or loss of any particular object, the circumstances, and the history will not disturb him.

Another Q.: The senses and the mind are so faulty. The world is dependent upon the senses. If I blink the eyes or fall asleep, all these things disappear.

N.: You cannot even think of the world without bringing in the image of sense perception.

Q.: Yes.

N.: The thinking of a particular sense perception is the image of the world, whether that takes place in memory, in dream, or in so-called perceptions in the waking state.

This is Sat-darshanam, the revelation of Reality. You want to know Reality for the sake of blissful immortality, which is the conqueror of death. In order to know Reality, you must dispense with what is falsely assumed to be real. You must negate the unreal, which is the delusion regarding it. Here, the Maharshi has swept through the entire world to the mind, showing that all this is dependent and not truly existent. It is so utterly dependent—the objects on the senses and the senses on the mind—that the support alone needs to be addressed, while the thing that rests upon it has no existence. The support of the objects is the senses, and the support of the senses is the mind. Upon what the mind rests Sri Bhagavan will reveal in a later verse.

Another Q.: In a dream, I was unfolding a blanket and noticed sparkles in it, which were diamonds, pearls, and other precious stones. I tried to collect them. I then realized that I was not going to get away with stealing all these diamonds and other things. I would have to return them. It was a very realistic dream, with very realistic perceptions, which I thought were true perceptions. (laughing).

N.: Yes, but all of it was your dream, so who would have been stealing from whom? They were shining?

Q.: Yes.

N.: By what light were they shining?

Q.: This is the thing to know. But it was a dream! (laughter)

N.: Yes. Yet the Light is still one.

Another Q.: Is there really no such thing as sense deprivation?

N.: You undergo sense deprivation every night.

Q.: Yes.

N.: You do not feel deprived.

Q.: I do not.

Another Q.: Relieved.

N.: Yes, relieved. (laughter)

Q.: Can there be changefulness of the senses?

N.: There can be according to where you direct your mind. At any one point, your mind is directed to one sense or another. Rarely is your mind equally and fully directed to all five senses. While you are listening and watching right now, you are probably not giving much attention to the tactile sensations in the middle of your back. So, you are deprived of a certain sense. At any one point, one sense is more acute, one is more present, and one is more absent. Sense experience is very changeful.

Q.: It is a conduit.

N.: Between what and what?

Q.: Between our perception and the world is all the sense perception.

N.: This is what the Maharshi is addressing. What you have stated now is the common view, namely that the senses are a conduit that brings information from an outside existent world to an inner perceiver. Sri Ramana has revealed that there is not really a conduit, and there are not two sides of this conduit. What is considered a conduit is actually the experiencing, and there is no object on the other side. There is just the experiencing. How does this experiencing occur? It is the dreaming or conceiving of the mind. If you are deprived of your senses, you may fall asleep. A person does not need to fall asleep just because he cuts off his senses. Yogis and meditators are accustomed to cutting off one or more of their senses without falling asleep. Let us say, though, that a person falls asleep and begins to dream. In a dream, one becomes endowed with dream senses, with dream objects that correspond to those dream senses. Are those dream senses conduits funneling in information from an existent object, or is it not all in the mind?

Q.: All of it is in the mind.

N.: The present waking state is very similar.

Another Q.: For me, now, there is very little new history being created. The recording mechanism is being eliminated, and that seems to be very tied to karma—at least my idea of karma—because when there is nobody perceiving the world and there is nobody doing anything, all of what used to comprise an identity and most of the mechanism is gone.

N.: If the individual who is the cause of the karma is dissolved, what could possibly remain of the effect? The karma must be for someone, whether it is karma being created now or karma accumulated from the past. If that someone is not there anymore, how could more karma be created and what happens to the collection?

The story comes to an end, just like a dream story comes to an end when one awakes. The entire story comes to an end conclusively because the one who apparently went through the entire story, lifetime after lifetime, did not have a start, in reality. Realizing the Truth in which there is no scope for the individual, the story is wound up or dissolved, and there is no return. For this reason, countless texts proclaim that, for the one who realizes the Truth, this is his last life. There will be no return to birth. He has realized himself as the Unborn, and the Unborn will not take birth. To explain to on-lookers, it is said that the story winds down due to the prarabdha karma. As for his own experience, there is just the Unborn, the Uncreated. All the karma is gone. However explained, all are in agreement that the story is at an end. When the story ends, Reality shines.

धिया सहोदेति धियास्तमेति
लोकस्ततो धीप्रविभास्य एषः ।
धीलोकजन्मक्षयधाम पूर्णं
सद्वस्तु जन्मक्षयशून्यमेकम् ॥ ७ ॥

dhiyā sahodeti dhiyāstam-eti
lokas-tato dhī-pravibhāsya eṣaḥ ǀ
dhī-loka-janma-kṣaya-dhāma pūrṇaṁ
sad-vastu janma-kṣaya-śūnyam-ekam ǀǀ 7 ǀǀ

7

With the idea (thought, intelligence, mind) rises, with the thought (mind) sets
The world. Therefore, of the mind's (thought's) light is this.
The abode (glory, splendor, light) [in which] the mind and world are born and decay (are destroyed, perish) is the perfect fullness,
The real thing (the true Reality), devoid of birth and decay (destruction, perishing), the One.

N.: The world is within the mind. With the rise of the mind, a world arises. That world may be defined by the very same mind as a subtle world or a gross world, yet the mind conceives a world within itself. The mind rising, the world appears. The mind setting, the world subsides. The mind rising, the waking and dreaming worlds appear. The mind subsiding, as in deep sleep, the worlds disappear.

"Therefore, of the mind's light is this." It is the mind that illuminates the world, not the world that illuminates the mind. The mind knows the world; the world does not know the mind. The world is simply the thought of it. When that thought is absent, no world appears. This mind and the world within it that is dependent upon it, rise and set in something very vast, all-luminous, and steady. This is the "Abode." It could also be described as "Glory, Splendor, and Light." This is the real Consciousness. The mind and the world are born and perish in something that is not born and not perishable and that is unchanging. That is the Perfect Fullness, and if you realize yourself as That, and realize That as the Reality, your experience is the Perfect Fullness, in which there is no stain, no taint, no division, nothing missing, and truly nothing wrong at any time. That, Sri Bhagavan declares, is the "True Reality," or the "Real Thing." Nothing else is real. Nothing else is true. The mind that rises and sets is not true, and the world within it that is dependent upon it is not real. The true Reality is devoid of birth and destruction. It does not rise and set. It is One. Being One, it is indivisible and cannot be other than oneself.

Examine your own experience. Understand that the world you appear to experience, in whatever manner you appear to experience it, is only in your mind, and then observe the rise and fall of your own mind. From what position are you aware of the birth and destruction of the mind? It cannot be the mind, itself. Something exists before the birth of the mind that sees its birth. Something exists after its destruction to know that it has perished. What is that?

With the mind, rises the world. When the mind sets, the world sets. The world is nothing but the mind, so the rise and fall of the mind brings about the rise and fall of the experience of the objective sphere of experience, which is the world. Sri Ramana says, "Therefore, of the mind's light, is this" The world is lit up by the mind, and not the other way around, much like your diamonds and pearls in last night's dream.

Q.: Are birth and destruction like waking and going to deep sleep?

N.: For any form, entering into deep sleep is its dissolution. Waking up is its creation. Consider the birth and death of the mind in this life. Before its birth, Consciousness exists. After its destruction, the same Consciousness exists. It is the place, or the abode, in which the mind rises and sets, or is born and dies. That is all-glorious and perfectly full. That should be known as the Reality, your real Self, without the least misidentification with the mind and the world that is its content.

By inquiry, comprehend what the Maharshi has taught in this verse. If you do so, it will be quite impossible to be confused by the mind and the mind's imaginings, its own ideas, inclusive of the entire appearance of the world, ever again. If we truly understand what Sri Ramana says, we transcend all that is transient of the world and of the mind. If we truly comprehend what he says, we do not regard anything that changes in the world as a change of our nature or our state, nor do we regard any change of any state of mind as our change. We do not think, "I am entering into this state," "I am awake," "I am dreaming," "I am in this mode of mind," and "I am in another mode of mind." It is quite impossible to be caught up in thoughts and the modes, moods, etc., that thoughts can construct, because we identify only with the Unborn, the imperishable Abode, the glorious, Perfect Fullness, that does not rise and set when the mind and the world rise and set.

Q.: You mentioned that, with the dissolution of the mind, there is something that sees the dissolution of the mind. When I enter deep sleep, I have no memories whatsoever in that state.

N.: You know that the mind is gone, and you know that memory is absent. What knows that? If the mind is absorbed in samadhi, what knows that?

Q.: In the last meditation, I was tired. I was still aware of the drowsiness.

N.: You were aware of the drowsiness. Can that which was aware of the drowsiness be drowsy? Why not treat every state of mind like that? That which knows them is unchanged by them and unconfined by them. It is not located in them. It is not destroyed by them. That never becomes drowsy or the opposite. At any time, why should you identify the infinite, perfectly full Consciousness, which is unborn and imperishable, with a mind that so obviously changes, flits about, slowly shifts, darts about, rises up, and then collapses and disappears, taking, with it its world? Why should you associate any of that nonsense with your Self? (laughter)

Q.: There is no good reason for it. I latch on to what is objectified. In meditation, it disappears.

N.: What disappears?

Q.: Thoughts. The mind loses its form, and it seems to become clear.

N.: With the mind's dissolution, there remains something that is extraordinarily clear. We do not need to wait for thought to disappear at its own level. We can know directly the nonexistence of the mind, the nonexistence of thought, and realize the singular Consciousness. The Unborn, the Imperishable, is "the One." It is indicative that there is no other, no mind, and no world.

Q.: When that is realized, the mind is dissolved.

N.: All right. So, when is that realized? Does someone have a calendar or a digital phone that we can put a reminder on? (laughter) The reminder message could say, "This is your Self-Realization day. You do not want to be late for it." (laughter)

Q.: I have always considered Self-Realization to be something that takes place at some moment.

N.: It is not a moment, at all. It is eternal. Moments are for a pseudo-individual and exist within the play of the mind. Beyond the mind is only the Eternal; That you are.

Another Q.: It is obvious that the mind is not who I am because I see it coming and going. I do not change with it. Sometimes, I think that I change with it. Sometimes, when the body becomes tired, I think that I am tired. That is really odd. I find myself not observing the mind. I do not even think, then, that I am in a mind. It just seems as if everything is real. The distinctions of subject and object seem to collapse into the feeling that I am not really having a good time.

N.: Unhappiness is associated with taking the mind to be real, identifying with the sheaths or the body, and taking the world to be real.

Q.: That is always an unhappy situation.

N.: How could one find deep happiness while still retaining the deluded notion, "The world is real," which means that one is limited to a mind that appears as a body in that mind. The very constriction of those limitations runs contrary to the limitless Bliss of infinite Being. So, of course, there is unhappiness in such a state, and it is that very unhappiness that drives you to turn your mind around, point it inward, and undo those false limitations.

Q.: I certainly follow what you are saying, and I wonder if it is useful to find out why? Is asking "why" not useful, for that brings about more "becauses"?

N.: It depends upon for what you use the reason, or the causality. If you use it to say that there is a legitimate reason for suffering…

Q.: Then, I should see a therapist. (laughter)

N.: Whatever good there may come of that is rather dubious. If, on the other hand, you perceive the cause of suffering simply for the purpose of removing it, by turning the mind inward, it serves a very good purpose. So, if a person recognizes that the suffering is due to ignorance and then sets about diligently, with intensity and all humility, to destroy the ignorance, his reasoning and determination of the cause of the samsara are worthwhile. It is not that the causality he has conceived is the final answer, but it serves a good purpose. Sri Bhagavan compares such spiritual methodology, or instruction, to a sharp implement, such as a needle or a sharp thorn, being used to prick out another thorn or splinter out of the skin. The thorn is used to remove the other thorn. Then, both thorns are tossed aside. It has served a good purpose. One does not remain cherishing the thorn. He uses it only for that purpose. If you can determine the causes of becoming caught up in delusion, or of the forms the delusion takes, you then use that determination to undo those very causes. It is good use of a thorn.

Another Q.: Could you say that again?

N.: We are discussing the ascertainment of the causes of suffering. If one uses his thinking along the lines of determining causes to validate the suffering and to make it seem more real, substantial, or reasonable, that is, to provide an excuse for the suffering, or to falsely lend some causality to some outer circumstance as if that made one's own suffering, it is entirely quite useless. If we reflect on these things, and such points us inward, so that we determine the causes of suffering lie in the form of attachment or delusions within our own minds, and if that prompts us to actually destroy those very delusions and attachments, such serves a very good purpose.

Since you have familiarity with the Buddhist tradition, you know well the "four noble truths." The first two deal with the recognition of suffering and the recognition of the cause of suffering. It is not to be understood from these that one just thinks that there is suffering and that there are many causes for his suffering, so what a sorry lot things are. (laughter) If that were the case, there would not have been a Buddha, an Awakened One, one who is awake to Knowledge, because everyone already knew there was suffering, and many things were being blamed as causes, right and left. There would not have been anything significant about that. There would not have been any truth to that, and such certainly would not have been very noble. There must be a deeper significance. There must be the cognizance of suffering as an experience being contrary to our svarupa, our true nature, and there must be a recognition of the cause of suffering, which must be a mistake regarding that very same svarupa, that very same own-nature. When we see the causes of suffering as being invalid, we approach Liberation and take the direct way to Liberation, which must necessarily be Knowledge of one's Self.

Q.: I do not think I have understood suffering except from your excellent present exposition. Until now, I have been clinging to it. I think that I have a great deal of panic about relinquishing the mind's suffering.

N.: Look more closely. What is it that frightens you? Are you really afraid of letting go of the suffering? That is probably not so, because no one likes to suffer.

Q.: It is about being completely alone. It is the fear of going crazy.

N.: Why would you become crazy if you relinquished suffering? If you demolish the causes of suffering, why would you become crazy, which is a state of intense suffering? If craziness were a happy state, you would be very eager for it. (laughter) So, what you envision is a state of intensified suffering, not freedom from suffering, and your nature recoils from that.

Q.: My mind is so attached to it.

N.: In what way is it attached to the suffering?

Q.: I am having such a hard time with this teaching. It is as though an earthquake has happened, I need to steady my feet somewhere, and I can't find my footing.

N.: What constitutes the earthquake?

Q.: The deepening of the experience and its intense truth.

N.: In what manner is it intense?

Q.: It is unrelenting. I am being left on the hook of nondualism. I go back into ignorance and dualism and have lost the silence.

N.: All right. Do you want to be in the Silence of continuous Nonduality?

Q.: Yes.

N.: So, you actually want the experience of the teaching to be more unrelenting and not less.

Q.: Yes.

N.: You need to get off the hook of duality and stay in the Nonduality, because that will make suffering dissipate, will it not? In fact, by that, the suffering will evaporate.

You are not really attached to suffering. You want to be free of the suffering and do not want to return to a more constricted state. Those who perceive this keep up an unrelenting inquiry. There is never a valid reason to relinquish inquiry. You are not having a difficult time with the teaching; you are having a difficult time with whatever you have dragged in behind you, (laughter) which are the worn out and limiting tendencies of the mind.

No one is ever attached to suffering. No matter what the attachment is, a person is attached for the purpose of securing happiness. The happiness may be conceived as peace or as love. They are the same thing. By confounding some object with the happiness, which is what is called attachment, one loses track of happiness and causes herself needless suffering. To put an end to the suffering, break the fetters of attachment.

One confuses herself by ignorance, which is composed of her own thoughts. Break the fetters of thought. Cease to regard what you think as being so solidly real, and know that which is beyond the rise and fall of the world and the mind, which does not rise and fall, which ever shines, your glorious true abode, your own nature, the singular Reality, with which Nonduality is completely concerned.

No one is afraid of leaving suffering behind. Some are afraid that they do not know how to do it. It is not difficult. You have only to look within yourself. When you cease to believe in the thinking of your own mind, there will be no danger of craziness. Craziness appears when you take your own thoughts to be so important that they overshadow everything else. Then, you may feel the need of someone who is trained in these matters to give various technical terms to the various permutations of such a difficulty. The condition, though, involves taking your own thoughts to be the center and controlling influence of all things, and that is simply not true.

Another Q.: Every time the mind is mentioned, it is as if a gong sounded. We do not know what we are talking about. Is that not the case?

N.: The gong would also be in the mind.

Q.: Yes, but we keep talking about the mind as though we knew what it was. This is very strange.

N.: It is like that with the world, as well.

Q.: Yes.

N.: No one ever said there was not something strange about illusion. "The Abode, or the Light or Glory, in which the mind and world are born and are destroyed, is the perfect fullness." The mind rises, and the mind sets. With it, the world rises in it and sets in it. Something does not rise and set. That is perfectly full. The perfect fullness is immutable, and it does not grow or increase and will not decrease or be destroyed. That is the "real thing," which is transcendent of the world and the mind.

That is the true Reality. That is the thing of which you should have darshanam, vision. It is devoid of birth and destruction. It is "the One."

We should realize at Heart that our true nature is the Light, the Abode in which the mind appears and disappears, taking with it the universe. You are not, therefore, in the world, at any time. Likewise, you are not in the mind, which means you cannot be anything that appears in the waking, dreaming, or deep sleep states. The mind rises and sets with its states, and, according to its state, a world appears.

An eternal, imperishable, utterly transparent, infinite Light shines. That is the Light of pure Consciousness. It is of the nature of utterly formless Being. For everything that has birth and decay, or destruction, has a form. The formless, alone, has no birth and no destruction. That which is formless is devoid of multiplicity. It is only by form that we say one thing is one way, another thing is another way, and that there is diversity. Sri Ramana has concluded the verse by saying, "the One," because it is utterly formless and without difference. It is the perfect fullness, without change and destruction, and it is such because it is without birth and decay. Understand yourself to be That. Do not take yourself to be anything of the mind or the world.

That which rises and sets cannot be the abiding Reality. That which truly is always is. It is the Light of pure Consciousness, or pure Being. That is the real Self. The mind, which rises and sets, cannot be real. Obviously, a world that appears only in the mind and nowhere else cannot be real. What is real, or the true Reality? The true Reality is that which is devoid of birth and death, which has no creation and no destruction, and which is absolutely, indivisibly One forever.

भवन्तु सद्दर्शनसाधनानि
परस्य नामाकृतिभिः सपर्याः ।
सद्वस्तुनि प्राप्ततदात्मभावा
निष्ठैव सद्दर्शनमित्यवेहि ॥ ८ ॥

bhavantu saddarśana-sādhanāni
parasya nāmākṛtibhiḥ saparyāḥ |
sad-vastuni prāpta-tad-ātma-bhāvā
niṣṭhaiva sad-darśanam-ityavehi || 8 ||

8

Let them be spiritual practices for the vision (darshanam) of Truth,
Worship (plural) of the Supreme with name and form.
Abidance in the true Reality, the Attainment of that Self-Being (or: Abidance in the True Reality, the attainment of the state ((conviction)) of That is the Self),
Alone is the vision of Truth (true vision). Thus know (understand).

N.: Always adhering to the Nonduality that he, himself, is, the Maharshi did not decry the great variety of practices, including worship with name and form. Such practices occurred at the Asramam, and they go on to this day. Only, Sri Bhagavan says that they should be aids or "spiritual practices for the vision of Truth." When we worship, we should know what we worship. If we give a name, we should know the nameless One to which we have applied a name. When we utilize a form, we should know the significance of that form, which is the Formless that is signified. Then, they become aids for the vision of Truth. By themselves, though, they are not sufficient for Self-Realization.

What is the vision of Truth or the true vision? It is abidance in the true Reality, the attainment of the Being of the Self, or the attainment of the conviction that That, which is Brahman, is the Self. That alone is the Sat-darshanam, the true vision. If we envision the Absolute, whether it be in meditation, contemplation, worship, or puja, and we see distinction, we have yet to realize what it is that we actually worship. One of the saints has taught that, with the sense of difference, we are not only worshipping God, but we are worshipping the distinction, as well.

Abidance in the true Reality is really seeing what we worship. The attainment of the state, or the conviction, of "That is the Self," is really knowing what you worship. The ultimate purpose of worship is abidance in that undivided essence, the undivided state, in which That is the Self. The purpose of worship is the firm abidance in That, as That. If there is such abidance, whatever is the name or form used for worship, or even if the external worship is neglected, the worship is complete. If there is worship with name and form, but this inner essence is not realized in the Heart, the worship still has further to go and is not yet complete.

Let your forms of worship and devotion support your inquiry. Let the inquiry, or the Knowledge, be the light of such worship. Then, you know what you worship, and you, yourself, become That which is worshipped. You become That by abandonment of the false identity with the individual, the jiva, and realizing the Self, which is yourself, to be only That. The attainment of That is the goal and also illumines all of these practices.

"Let them be spiritual practices for the Vision of Truth." Of what is Sri Ramana speaking in this verse? "Worship"—in the Sanskrit text, "worship" is in the plural—"of the Supreme, with name and form." Let any kind of spiritual activity and spiritual practice be for the purpose of worship. Consider them as such. The Knowledge-essence makes them alive for you.

Abidance in the True Reality is a matter of Self-Knowledge. That is "the attainment of Self-Being," or "the attainment of the conviction, the state of, 'That is the Self.'" The Knowledge of one's identity, therefore, is the supreme form of worship. It is the formless worship and the nameless worship. Notice that he does not decry worship with name and form. He places it in its proper perspective. It points the way. It gives expression to something that is formless, but the actual Realization is a matter of attaining the state of identity, which can only be in Knowledge, in which you know yourself as That, and only That, by the power of That, itself.

That, Sri Ramana says, "alone is the vision of Truth," or that "is the True Vision." Any other kind of vision is partial and temporary. The True Vision is an eternal vision. It is a vision of the seer, and the realization of the nature of the seer is only Being. This we should know. This is what we should understand. Upon this we should meditate.

* * *

For the revelation of Truth, you must know yourself as you truly are. Without knowing the Self, the objective outlook is merely an illusion. If you know yourself, by means of profound inquiry, you, yourself, are the Truth. If there is misidentification so that it appears that you stand apart from the Truth of the Self, to whatever degree, that is only an illusory stance, and an illusory stance cannot bring the revelation of Reality.

You must know yourself, and, knowing yourself truly, you find yourself as the timeless, spaceless, single, indivisible, absolute Reality. The Reality knows itself. The unreal cannot do so, for it is unreal. Misidentification, such as that of existing as an ego entity, existing as a bodily entity, and so forth and so on, is unreal. The unreal conjures up an unreal knowledge about unreal things. Knowledge of the Self reveals undifferentiated Existence, without duality and without a separate knower, knowing, and known.

Again and again, inquire. The Maharshi's consistent emphasis, in *Saddarsanam* and throughout all of his spiritual instruction, is that the first person, the "I," should be known, and that the attempt to know anything else, without actually knowing the "I," is futile. Therefore, rise above any orientation toward realizing the Self as a foreign object or as a new state different from you, and deeply, consistently, seek to know yourself. Who are you? What is your actual existence? You are not finite. You are not transitory.

What is the nature of your ever-present Existence?

द्वन्द्वानि सर्वाण्यखिलास्त्रिपुट्यः
किञ्चित्समाश्रित्य विभान्ति वस्तु ।
तन्मार्गणे स्याद्गलितं समस्तं
न पश्यतां सच्चलनं कदापि ॥ ९ ॥

dvandvāni sarvāṇyakhilās-tripuṭyaḥ
kiñcit-samāśritya vibhānti vastu ।

tan-mārgaṇe syād-galitaṁ samastaṁ
na paśyatāṁ sac-calanaṁ kadāpi || 9 ||

9

All dualities [and] all triads,
[On] some thing (Reality) depending (on some thing taking support), shine.
(All dualities and triads shine for some thing (some reality) that is the support (for some thing upon which they depend)
[When] that is traced (sought), all are loosed and dropped.
For them who see the Truth (Being), there is no movement ever (at any time).
(Not to them who see the Truth is there movement ever.)

N.: All dualities and all triads depend on some thing. They do not stand on their own. The duality of "I" and "this," which is the primal duality, and all the dualities that stream from that, such as real and unreal, form and formless, light and dark, bound and free, and sad and happy, as well as all the dualities that appear within this dualistic world, such as pain and pleasure, up and down, good times and adversity, and such, and all the triads, such as knower, knowing and known, the seer, the seeing, and the seen, the experiencer, the experiencing, and the experienced, the thinker, thinking, and thought and so forth as so on, as well as the other triads of the three states, three gunas or qualities, and such, however described, depend upon some "thing." Even now, as such may appear for you, they depend upon some Reality. They "shine," that is, they appear, based solely upon that dependence. Something supports them without which they can not stand at all. The knower, the knowing, and what he knows, the experiencer, the experiencing, and what he experiences, and the dualities of "I" and "this," life and death, and such stand on some support. They are utterly dependent on that support. What is that? The supported is not real, and the support is very real. What is the substrate? When that thing upon which they depend is traced, as you seek the Reality that does not so depend, but upon which everything, without exception, depends, "all are loosed and dropped." Their bondage vanishes. That they fall away means that they cease to exist. Until the One Reality is known, duality and the triads appear to be. When that "One Thing" is known, the dualities and the triads are nowhere in sight.

Some have interpreted the "one thing" upon which the dualities and triads depend mentioned in this verse to be the ego, because it is from the ego that one sees such divisions. Given the context of the other verses, and because Sri Ramana uses the same term, vastu, which means "Reality" or "thing," in an absolute sense in the preceding and succeeding verses, such an interpretation of this verse as pertaining to the ego may be less certain. Understanding it as pertaining to the solid Reality, which is the basis even of all these illusions, shines with certainty. It would not, though, be a wrong path to interpret the verse as pertaining to the ego, for one's comprehension in this manner would still bring him to the same conclusion. "When that is traced, or sought, all are loosed and dropped."

"For them who see the Truth," that is, for those who see Being, which is not dependent, not dual, and certainly not multiple, "there is no movement ever," at any time. Since the manifested motion of the world, phenomena, and the senses is only in the mind, as already described by the Maharshi, Sri Natarajan has interpreted this to mean, "all mental movement ceases forever." The verse says, "For those who see the Truth, there is no movement," or motion, "ever." They do not move because their identity does not move. There is no motion away from the Self. There is no rising of an "I"-notion, which would be the first motion, or any other further motions of that "I" into the mind.

"For they who see the Truth." Who sees the Truth? Who sees Being? They who see Being are Being, itself. The false does not see the True. The True knows the True. If you see Being, your sense of identity is consumed in it, absorbed in it, and you do not remain separate. This has already been expressed in the previous verses in the text. The true vision is the egoless state. The true vision is the seeing of Being, or abidance as the Truth. This means that the sense of individuality has been lost. That being lost, everything else is "loosed and drops away," which means bondage disappears. "Not to them who see the Truth is there movement ever," because they are Being, and, for Being, there is no movement. Not only is there no further movement into delusion, which is the primary meaning of the verse, but there has never been any movement, because, for Being, there has been no ignorance, no samsara, and no bondage.

The subject-and-object is the primary duality. All other dualities fall within the context of the subject and object. Or, we may understand experience in terms of triads, as a knower, a knowing, and a known or as an experiencer, an experiencing, and an object of experience. Sri Bhagavan reveals that such multiplicity, whether considered as dyad or triad, depends upon some thing. They are not real. They depend on Reality. On some Reality, they take their support, and, by some Reality, they shine. They do not shine by their own light, that is, they are not known by themselves. They do not have their own Reality. They stand upon some other substratum, which is the actual Existence.

The subject that you appear to be shines by some other Light. The subject is not the Truth of you. What you are is something deeper. The object does not shine by its own light. It is known by something. If we feel that the subject knows the object, there is something else that knows both the subject and the object. There is some solid, underlying Existence, upon which the subject and object appear and into which they disappear.

The dualities and triads are not only supported by this Existence, they depend utterly upon this Existence. So dependent are they that they can be said to have no existence of their own. Something that has a dependent existence does not actually exist as such. Only that which is self-existent can be said to actually be. Examining your own experience, what is it that is self-existent and does not depend on another to exist? What is it that is self-effulgent, shining by its own Light, and does not require something else to know it? It is not the object, and it is not the individual subject. It is not the experiencer, the experiencing, or the object of experience, however they appear. Something shines, and they appear to shine. Something exists, depending on which, they appear to exist. What is that in you?

That should be known as it is, free of the superimposed dualities and triads. "When that is traced," or sought, that which is not dual and not triadic, that which is self-shining, self-existing, and the unsupported support of all, is realized. "Galitam" means loosed or dropped, so we can include both "loosed and dropped." The bondage of such and the appearance of such disappear. It is not that the dualities, triads, and the multiplicity remain, yet just lose their binding qualities, but, rather, the binding quality is lost, and the very appearance of differentiation vanishes. It vanishes because it is unreal. It does not have self-existence.

Sri Bhagavan says, "For them who see the Truth," which could be translated as "For them who see Being," "there is no movement ever," that is, "at any time." If you perceive Being, which is the Truth, you who perceive it are the Truth. You are Being. You do not move from your Self. Being is indivisible. It cannot split itself. If Being is unknown, individuality is assumed. Then, there appears to be movement, movement in the mind, movement in the bodily context, and so forth. Being remains unmoving and forever unchanging. For those who see the Truth of Being, this Being is all that they are. As Being is unmoving, those who have realized it are unmoving. It is just a manner of expression to say "those who have realized it." The realizer is that which is realized and retains no other separate identity. Existence does not move. Existence does not change. It does not increase, and it does not decrease. It does not begin, and it does not end. Beginnings and endings, and increases and decreases, are completely in the realm of the illusory dyads and triads.

Inquire within yourself in order to know your Being as it is, which is unchanging Existence. That is the Truth, and the Truth realizes itself. It is not that some portion of a dyad or triad realizes the Truth. Such would be a separate, individual knower or experiencer. Rather, Truth knows the Truth. Truth is the Truth. Being is itself. Being is, itself, the Knowledge. Being is not the experiencer, not the experiencing, and not the object of experience. The division is false and is but an illusion dependent on some other support. It is an inert illusion that is without light of its own. The self-luminous, self-existent, ever-unchanging Being, which has no multiplicity whatsoever, is your nature. If you know this, there is no motion ever. You are not born. You do not perish.

Q.: In the light of what was just revealed, if there is the experience of permutations or movements of the mind, such would be an indication that the ego has not been destroyed. Am I understanding you? Any movements of the mind would be indicative of the presence of the ego. The destruction of the mind would be the end of movement.

N.: Therefore, the destruction of the mind and the destruction of the ego are the same thing. It is better to place emphasis on the movement as the shifting of one's identity, lest you frantically run after the apparent motion of thought and become like a cat chasing its tail.

Q.: Is the movement of the mind the shift of identity from one's true state to the imagined state?

N.: If the identity shifts, the mind is taken to be real. The mind then moves. You do not know where it is moving, but it seems to move within itself, as it were, and you seem to be caught up in the vortex of thoughts.

Q.: That is a "red flag" that signals that the identity shift has been made.

N.: Yes. For the purpose of Self-Realization, do not chase after the moving thoughts or try to bring about a cessation of, or a stoppage to, the moving thoughts. Rather, put an end to the apparent movement away from your own nature. Do not move away from your own nature of Being. Then say whether or not there is thought, or whether or not the mind exists. If we treat the mind as an existent thing and attempt to put an end to it, how will we put an end to that to which we are lending our own existence? If we deeply inquire to know who we are and utterly disidentify from the mind, its motions are over because its existence is over. Then, nothing moves. No one goes anywhere, because no "I" has been born. This is the abidance in the true Reality, the attainment of the Being of the Self, alluded to in the previous verse.

From another angle of vision, if you observe permutations in your mind, of the form of various thoughts, you may ask yourself, "Why is it that these thoughts move in a particular pattern?" Trace the reason to your own sense of identity. You will find that the thinking follows the form attributed to your identity. Then, question your identity.

Q.: That would lead me back to the assumed entity, the "I," which is the imagined sense of individuality.

N.: By such inquiry, destroy the "I" and dismantle whatever you habitually take to be the forms of that "I."

Q.: Earlier you asked how something vast, eternal, and changeless could be associated with something that is fundamentally unreal, transitory, and projected. The first thought that came up for me, at that time, was that it is petty minded to associate that which is infinite with that which is nonexistent. Then, in meditation, the experience of peace and satisfaction was interrupted by discomfort of the body. I realized, in that instant of time, that I was being petty minded and was somehow confining the absolute Reality within a form called the body, located inside an ashram. Inquiry is required to free myself of the discomfort that is destroying the peace. No matter how much I went inside to realize that I am not the pain or discomfort, the peace and satisfaction of the Self were not regained.

N.: All right. What made the intrusion on the peace? There is the discomfort or pain in the body, and pains in the body are unavoidable. Just as there are pleasures, so there are pains. There is birth, and there is death. What actually produces the disturbance of the peace?

Q.: When this body is in pain, the bliss seems to be a thousand miles away.

N.: Where exactly does it go?

Q.: Nowhere. It is certainly veiled.

N.: What creates the veil? Of what is it composed?

Q.: But for misidentification, the Absolute would not be touched by whatever seems to happen in this waking state. There would be abidance that is transcendent of the entire dream.

N.: That is all very well and good, and true, for the Absolute. Now, what about you?

Q.: At the moment in time, I am this body.

N.: How did absolute Being become a body just for the moment in time?

Q.: That's the petty mindedness. (laughing)

N.: Yes. The description of maya as being "petty minded" is nice, but you can see the importance of being free of it when you are suffering discomfort or pain. Obviously, greater pains can occur. You can see the importance of knowing your interior freedom. It can not be determined from the outside. If your body is in great pain, there may be calling out, writhing, and such. Still, you can be free within.

Q.: I have modest pain and discomfort that are not even enough to complain.

N.: The experiential Knowledge of the Truth must be so vivid for you that there is no suffering and no false identity with the body when the body is in pain or with sickness, etc. Such liberation from the body, even in life, is certainly possible.

Q.: At times when there is pain, I channel down into misidentification with the body and am no longer abiding in the Self. Physical pain is the challenge.

N.: It calls for a deeper, more consistent inquiry, does it not?

Q.: It really does. Then, the suffering would not be there? Pain would remain for the body?

N.: There may be pain in the body, at the level of the body, but there will be no impinging on the peace of your Self. Do not expect that, by virtue of the inquiry or Knowledge, the bodily discomfort will cease. It will cease to exist inasmuch as the entire world ceases to exist, but it will not cease to exist for the body. The body will go through its destined aches and pains.

Q.: The Self will remain untouched?

N.: Keep your identity as the Self, not with a corpse-like body. Keep your inquiry experiential. Keep the Knowledge deep, vivid, and continuous. If you approach in this way, while no one would wish that your body has pains, you will know how to use the pain as a kind of blessing, as a pointer to the Truth, so that, as with any other experience, the more that it occurs, the more it simply points out the Truth. Then, it has lost its sting.

Q.: I now know how to practice with this. Thank you.

Another Q.: I have had an inverted idea about the mind moving and me following it. Now, I see that my identity shifts, and then my mind moves with it. First, there is some ego, and, then, that wanders in the mind.

N.: You see this for yourself as from the center of your own mind?

Q.: Yes. I previously misunderstood.

N.: The mind's supposed existence is derived from you. It has no power in its motion except the power lent to it by you.

Q.: Just as, if there is suffering, it tells me that I am misidentified, so, if the mind appears to shift, it is another helpful indication. I must stop. The mind isn't shifting; I am shifting my identity. The mind is just an indication of the shift of identity.

N.: Even more than that, it indicates something that has not shifted. Motion is seen from some still point. If both you and the mind were in motion, you would never know it.

Q.: That's great!

N.: Sankara compares mistaking the movements of thought as the movements of one's Self to the traveling in a moving boat on a river and saying that the trees on the bank are moving. Obviously, the bank of the river is not moving. The boat is moving. One takes up one's stand as misidentified with the mind and then says, "I have moved," but the real Self remains unmoving.

Q.: Because the Self knows, and the Self is not moving. That's great!

N.: Your own experience becomes a curious kind of sastra. It gives a detailed description of maya, and tells you when some ego has crept into the picture, so that you know to reverse course.

Your own experience also points out something that has not moved and that has not been caught up in the maya, at all. So, I say it is a kind of sastra, because it points out the details of "all this," and also reveals something about the Supreme. Without due discrimination, though, it is not a reliable sastra, which is why one should rely on the other sastras and scriptures to direct that sastra.

Another Q.: What was that first sastra?

N.: It has yet to be printed. (laughter)

Another Q.: The first that was mentioned in this explanation is the sastra that points us to the other sastras. (laughter)

N.: What is being pointed out is that one's own experience is like a type of scripture, in the sense of being an instruction manual, which can be relied upon to point out the movements and aspects of maya, as well as the Supreme. The movements of the mind tell that the ego is in play and there are misidentifications. The same movements of the mind also point out, in one sense, to those who wisely discriminate, something unmoving that is not in or of the mind. Because it describes the illusion and also describes the Supreme, I said his own experience was a kind of sastra.

Q.: You are saying that illusion is not a reliable sastra.

N.: Unless you use adequate discrimination. It would be more useful to rely on the other kinds of sastras, such as the Vedas, to guide this sastra of experience. If you only follow your own experience without due discrimination, you merely repeat samsara. The conclusion of reasoning over such a sastra would be, "I experience this because I experience this." Thus, it would not amount to anything.

Q.: Because I am keeping the entire belief structure of an individual, the world, and all the sheaths intact.

N.: Exactly so. If there is discrimination, that is, deep inquiry as to who you are, your experience reveals the causes and the destruction of suffering, and it points to something that is transcendent, which is at the core of the experience but beyond it. (silence)

Is there any further commentary on this "sastra"? (laughter)

Another Q.: I have always held worship and inquiry to be separate. I have always held worship to be, not revealing something about me or my nature, but as revealing something about something else.

N.: Something else?

Q.: Yes, as if I were not a part of it.

N.: What is the something else?

Q.: It is revealing something that is divine.

N.: The divine may be more about you than what you think of you.

Q.: Yes. Maybe, I should start at a higher place with worship.

N.: When one worships, there is, in some form or another, proportionate to the depth of the worship, the dissolution of the ego or, at least, its grossly manifested tendencies. The greater the dissolution is, the deeper the form of worship. Worship has more to do with one's Self than any thought that comes after the ego. There is great similarity in devotion and inquiry because both serve the purpose of the destruction of the ego. Both place emphasis on That. The inquiry immediately reveals That to be the only true "I." Both place emphasis on the Absolute, on the Supreme, and both relegate the ego to its proper position, which is represented in the murtis of Nataraja and Dakshinamurti as the figure beneath the foot. So, even if you think that your worship has to do with something else, that "something else" is more you than what you think you are.

The divine, extolled in the most glorious terms, has much more to do with our Self than whatever one pretends to be. Perhaps, for this reason, Sankara treated devotion in the same way as the Maharshi. In the numerous treatises that he wrote and in the numerous forms of instruction that are often depicted as being debates that he had with various people, though they may also be understood as answering all doubts rather than debates, he demolished every kind of duality, including what can be regarded as a pseudo-Vedanta, which is the stand of those who have not experientially resolved all duality, yet maintain some ideas that bear similarities to Vedanta. In tearing all of that down, like fire burning up straw, he extolled Brahman and Self-Knowledge, and he let devotion stand. Not only did he let devotion stand, he, himself, wrote numerous hymns of praise, referred to as stotras and stutis. How is it that someone who is renowned throughout the ages for being the pristine exemplar of purest Advaita, the utterly impersonal Brahman, could become so involved in preserving and extolling the virtues of devotion, inclusive of making use of the apparent name and form, mentioned in the *Saddarsanam* by the Maharshi? It must have something to do with being egoless.

Another Q.: Considering verse eight in this very nondual text, my spiritual practice of reading and sitting in meditation are forms of worship. Am I wrong? The actual inquiry is that to which the Maharshi has referred.

N.: Yes, you may interpret verse eight in that manner, but if your reading, reflection, and meditation are permeated by inquiry, where is the name and form in that? If emphasis is placed on the external aspects of reading, thinking, etc., that is still "with name and form." Because the Maharshi says that they "become means for the vision of Truth," such must be understood in light of the inherent ego-dissolution. If there is ego-dissolution, the practice is an aid to the inquiry. You must not forget the rest of the verse, which reveals that abidance as That is the true vision.

विद्या कथं भाति न चेदविद्या
विद्यां विना किं प्रविभात्यविद्या ।
द्वयं च कस्येति विचार्य मूल -
स्वरूपनिष्ठा परमार्थविद्या ॥ १० ॥

vidyā kathaṁ bhāti na ced-avidyā
vidyāṁ vinā kiṁ pravibhātyavidyā |
dvayaṁ ca kasyeti vicārya mūla-
svarūpa-niṣṭhā paramārtha-vidyā || 10 ||

10

How can knowledge shine if there is not ignorance?
Without knowledge, does ignorance shine?
And "Whose are the two?" thus. Inquiring into the source (root),
Abidance in one's own (true) nature is the Knowledge of the Supreme Truth.

N.: Beyond the range of perceptions and conceptions, and quite beyond the range of words and thoughts is the real Self, the Reality. Knowledge of the Truth is the profound abidance in the state of identity with That. In the attempt to know the Truth, the utter destruction of the false identity is of utmost importance. The false identity is the mistaken assumption that you are something other than the worldless, I-less Reality.

Are you the body? Are you the mind? Question yourself. If the "I" seems to be, inquire, "Who am I?" In this way, you should inquire into yourself.

When deeply viewed, the entire instruction, meditation, practice, and realization occur here, beyond the realm of perceptions, conceptions, words, and thoughts. The practice and realization occur in Silence. It is the "space" of Brahman, of Absolute Being. (silence)

Sri Ramana's incredibly profound words reveal this Knowledge. When, with minds turned inward, we dive deep into the meaning of his teaching, we pass beyond the expression into the Inexpressible. It is his Silence, which is the Reality. When we dive deep into the Truth that he has revealed, it is a unique dive in that the diver dissolves. It is described with the analogy of a salt doll diving into the sea. We dive deep, and we lose ourselves. In the loss of our so-called selves, we realize that which is truly the Self. It is the One without beginning or end and in which there is no division or multiplicity.

Being, itself, is the profound Knowledge, the vision of Truth. It is incomparable. Meditation upon the Maharshi's instruction is by consistent inquiry into who you are, making your vision nonobjective. Then, you find that what he declares is the singular, unopposed, extremely self-evident Absolute Truth. It is so self-evident that it becomes quite impossible to find someone who could be ignorant of this. There is not a trace of such a one in your Self.

"How can knowledge shine if there is not ignorance? Without knowledge, does ignorance shine?" They appear mutually dependent.

We may interpret the knowledge and the ignorance in different ways. The first way is to consider ignorance and knowledge as is commonly understood, which is of something objective. We know something in contrast to not knowing it, and our not knowing it is in contrast to knowing it. If we inquire for whom these two are, this objective duality is transcended. Inquiry into the root of who has the knowledge and the ignorance brings about abidance in one's True Nature, and that is the Knowledge of the Supreme Truth. The Knowledge of one's true nature is different than objective knowledge.

There is another aspect or another interpretation. We may view this verse strictly in terms of spiritual knowledge, which refers to the conception of two states. One is of knowledge, and the other is of ignorance. It is in relation to ignorance that knowledge shines. That is, we approach knowledge because we feel that we are in ignorance, and the ignorance, too, is a state that depends upon knowledge, even for it to be conceived. True Knowledge, though, lies beyond even that duality. True Knowledge is not a state. When we inquire into the root, the source of such duality, which is the source of the one that falls into duality, we arrive at that which is stateless. It does not belong to anyone, and it is not objectively experienced by any one. Rather, it is who we are.

Abidance in one's own true nature is the Knowledge of the Supreme Truth. It is not knowing anything. Consequently, there is no possibility of being ignorant of anything. It is not a knowledge of a thing. The Knowledge of Reality, which is the

Knowledge of the Truth, is abidance as one's Self. This is Knowledge of one's Self. One's Self is not a thing. Sri Ramana says, "abidance in one's own nature." Being is Knowing, the Maharshi reveals.

Do you expect to know the Self? Do you now feel that you are ignorant of the Self? These mutually contrasting states have nothing to do with the true Knowledge, which is Being as you really are. If there is ignorance, one must attain knowledge. It is in the state of knowledge, though, that "ignorance shines," for, otherwise, one would not know the ignorance. "For whom are these?" "Who am I?" That which abides without state or condition is your Self. Inherent in the Self is its own Knowledge of itself. Existence is always self-effulgent and self-knowing.

So, can you say that you do not know the Self? Can you say, "I know the Self?" Whose would be the knowledge? Whose would be ignorance? Inquire in this way, and you, yourself, turn out to be the real Knowledge. Knowledge is not possessed by anyone; nor is anyone lacking in it. You are the Knowledge. There is nothing else like this.

Here, in this verse, the Maharshi again clarifies what the nature of true Knowledge is. Ignorance appears as a state, and, from the perspective of ignorance, Knowledge is conceived of as a state. True Knowledge is transcendent of any state. It is not dual. It is quite beyond the divisions in the mind of knowing or not knowing something. Sri Bhagavan says, "How can knowledge shine if there is not ignorance?" It is within the context of ignorance that we view the Knowledge as being knowledge, and we regard knowledge as if it were Knowledge.

"Without knowledge, does ignorance shine?" The second line of the verse may be interpreted in two ways. One is the mutual dependence of the views of ignorance and so-called knowledge. Another way to interpret it is that ignorance shines by some Knowledge, for you know about the ignorance. Regardless of which way we interpret the verse, beyond the views of ignorance and knowledge lies true Knowledge. "Whose are the two?" For whom is ignorance? For whom is knowledge?

"Inquiring into the root (the source), abidance in one's own (true) nature is the Knowledge of the Supreme Truth." Because it is the Knowledge of Being and not an object, and because one cannot be separate from Being in order to know it, Knowledge of the Supreme Truth is abidance as Being. Such Knowledge is quite beyond the idea of states or conditions. Ignorance and knowledge belong to someone. Self-Knowledge belongs to itself. It does not belong to some individual.

A state of ignorance and a state of knowledge both shine by some superior Light. That Light should be traced. Something is the source, which lends its reality, as it were, to the states of ignorance and knowledge. This root, or source, should be traced. If it is traced, you find that which is self-shining and self-existing, and what you find is what you are.

It is not that the individual traverses from ignorance to another state called "knowledge." Upon inquiry, "For whom is ignorance? For whom is knowledge?" the individuality, being only a false assumption, vanishes, and the ever-present Existence, which is pure Being, remains shining for all eternity. This, your very Being, is the Supreme Knowledge. It is not perceivable or conceivable. No one attains Knowledge, and no one can be said to really lose Knowledge. Supreme Knowledge is the very nature of the Self. If you abide as the Self that you truly are, free of misidentification in any manner, that is the Supreme Knowledge.

Q.: For a long time, tracing my identity, the discrimination was from gross to subtle. Now, where the tracing seems to start is Being-Consciousness, without the intervening steps. If there is any sense of a subject, then and there, I should inquire into its nature. Before, I was looking at objects, going from gross to subtle. When there are no objects, I need to see if there is a subject.

N.: If the idea of existing as a subject is consumed in that in which there is no dyad or triad, in which there is no subject, object, and a relation between the two, the inquiry is correct. If you trace to Being-Consciousness and you are left without another identity, so that there is no one standing apart to be ignorant of it or to conceive of it, but the individuality is dissolved, or is dissolving, the meditation is on the right track.

Another Q.: Is that which transcends duality non-conceptual and so should be experienced?

N.: It should be experienced, but it is experienced as one's own nature. So, Sri Ramana says that abidance as That is the Supreme Knowledge. Such Knowledge cannot be learned, but it is realized conclusively. In some Vedanta texts, it is said that, because of ignorance prevailing, there is a need of knowledge. Knowledge, then, clears the muddy waters of ignorance, and, it, itself, is done away with or disappears. That which remains is pure Consciousness. Abidance as pure Consciousness, with no other identity is the real Knowledge. Rather than think in terms of a duality of ignorance and knowledge, with one being the remedy for the other, why not go straight to the inquiry, "For whom are these two?" In the Supreme Knowledge, you simply are That. Then, there is nothing to pick up and nothing to discard.

Q.: So, I should bypass the duality.

N.: The emphasis is on the nonobjective approach. Ignorance is constituted of misidentification, the objective outlook, or the worldly vision. If we approach Knowledge as if it were within the same context as the ignorance, we do not get the supreme benefit. If we make our vision nonobjective, inquiring, "For whom is this?" and thus keep the focus entirely on the non-objective, we find that which never was ignorant and is in no need of another kind of knowledge, but which is innately the pure, real Knowledge.

बोद्धारमात्मानमजानतो यो
बोधः स किं स्यात्परमार्थबोधः ।
बोधस्य बोध्यस्य च संश्रयं स्वं
विजानतस्तद्द्वितयं विनश्येत् ॥ ११ ॥

boddhāram-ātmānam-ajānato yo
bodhaḥ sa kiṁ syāt-paramārtha-bodhaḥ |
bodhasya bodhyasya ca saṁśrayaṁ svaṁ
vijānatas-tad-dvitayaṁ vinaśyet || 11 ||

11

Can that knowledge that does not know the one who knows oneself (the Self)
Be Knowledge of the Supreme Truth?
(or: Can that knowledge which is of one who does not know the Self ((oneself)))
(or: Can that knowledge that does not know the Self, the one who knows,)
Of knowing and of knowledge (or: the to bė known), the support, oneself,
The one who knows shall destroy the two.

N.: A variety of interpretations of the first line may be considered correct. The emphasis of each of them differs slightly, yet the essence of all the interpretations is the same: You must know the knower of all knowledge. That knowledge which knows the knower, your own Self, is alone true Knowledge.

In the last line, which are "the two"? It refers to knowing and knowledge, which is the knowledge to be known or the objective portion. There appears to be knowing and the known. The support of them is the knower, one's Self. If you know That, the other two are destroyed, and only the Knower remains, which is oneself.

Trace the known to the knowing, the knowing to the knower, and the knower to the true Self. This applies not only toward the so-called knowledge of objects, but it is also applicable to the knowledge that is regarded as spiritual knowledge. In true, profound, spiritual Knowledge, which is Self-Knowledge, there is no independent thing called "the known," even if you consider the known to be the "Knowledge" that you are trying to obtain. If you think that you want to know the Self-Knowledge, Self-Knowledge is being treated as the "thing to be known." Knowing is your relation to it. The knower is the one for whom these are. The knower is the support of these and is quite without these. Knowledge of the knower is not a thing to be known, is not a knowledge to be known, not a principle of relation of knowing, and not an activity of the mind, but is, rather, Knowledge of the one for whom these appear. This is real Knowledge. If we know outer things, spiritual matters, and even teachings of Vedanta but do not know ourselves, which is the abidance in a state of identity with That, as That, Brahman, the Maharshi asks, "How could that be true Knowledge?" If we know about Brahman, but we are not in the perpetual experience of being Brahman, can that be true Knowledge?

"Can that knowledge that does not know the Self, the one who knows, be Knowledge of the Supreme Truth?" Even if one has the idea that he knows all about the Self, he has to truly know himself. Within the duality, or pseudo-division, of the Self and oneself, there still lies delusion. Let everything be swallowed up in the Consciousness, which is your Self, and this Consciousness, abiding singularly, without division, naturally self-luminous, is the Knowledge. Knowledge of the Truth, then, has nothing objective in it. It has none of the relations or functions of the mind that one may associate with knowledge. It does not, therefore, have forgetfulness and remembrance, which are holding in mind and losing in mind. It does not become more or less. It does not have unsteadiness or wobbling or any other such thing.

"Can that knowledge that does not know the one who knows the Self be Knowledge of the Supreme Truth?" Can knowledge that belongs to the ego be Knowledge of the Supreme Truth? The Self alone can know the Self.

"Can that knowledge, which is of one who does not know the Self, be Knowledge of the Supreme Truth?" Only one who knows the Self has the Knowledge of the Supreme Truth. Any other kind of knowledge, from worldly to scriptural, cannot be the Supreme Knowledge. Self-Knowledge is Supreme Knowledge.

"Can that knowledge that does not know the Self, the one who knows, be Knowledge of the Supreme Truth?" The non-objective Knowledge of the one who knows is Knowledge of the Supreme Truth, the Truth's knowledge of itself, for the Knowledge belongs to none other. It cannot belong to the ego. A dualistic view of ignorance and knowledge can belong to the ego. Inquire into its nature. Whose is it? Sri Ramana explains that the Supreme Knowledge is Knowledge of the one who knows. In that Knowledge, differentiation is nonexistent.

"Of knowing and of knowledge" signifies of knowing and the "to be known," which is the thing to be known. "The support is oneself," the one that knows that support. That is the one who knows oneself, the one who knows the knowing one, the One that alone knows.

"The two shall destroy." Which two shall be destroyed? Knowing and knowledge shall be destroyed. What remains? What remains is only the Knowledge that is solely pure Being. It is not knowing in the sense of being the relation between a subject and an object. It is not "I" knowing "this," the "to be known," as an object of knowledge. Self-Knowledge is nonobjective. Self-Knowledge is inconceivable. Self-Knowledge is Knowledge of the Self, by the Self. The division between subject and object should be abandoned, and the tendency to objectify should be relinquished.

This Knowledge is Sat-darshanam, the revelation of Reality. Unless you know the one who knows, what do you really know? Unless you know yourself, whether you conceive of "I" or "this," or of ignorance or knowledge, what do you really know? Without the Knowledge of the Self, knowledge so-called is merely conjecture, dreaming, silliness, or delusion. One's Self is that which ought to be known, but the Self is not a small, particularized thing.

If you know the nature of the Self, you are what you know, and there is nothing else to be known. In the knowledge of the perceivable and the conceivable, there is always something more to be known. Fortunately, one often forgets something that was previously known, so there is enough space to continue knowing some more. (laughter) Aside from that, there is always something more to be known, but in the Knowledge of Existence, which is not of the multiplicity of appearances, nothing else remains existent to be known. Self-Knowledge is final knowledge, and, in the spiritual sense, Supreme Knowledge. Sri Bhagavan expounds on the nature of Knowledge and reveals this Knowledge in his Silence.

Q.: The language points to That. When I say, "Who knows?" I am saying that the subject is the only thing that "Who?" relates to, and the subject can never be an object. As such, it can never be anything but infinite.

N.: Exactly so. Everything else is completely conjecture and wild fantasy.

Q.: That word, "Who?" takes me right to the subject.

N.: The beauty of the inquiry is that it cuts right to the core. Any other motion in the mind deals with what is not really there. Such is based only upon a false supposition and cannot be true Knowledge. True Knowledge is a very simple thing. Pointed out by "Who?", it is so simple that it is silent. Most of spiritual instruction, therefore, is for the purpose of sweeping away the extraneous complexities of the imagining mind.

Another Q.: All pairs of apparent opposites, such as victory or defeat, gain or loss, war and peace, pleasure or pain, are swallowed up in the Knowledge of one's Self.

N.: In the Knowledge of one's Self, there is just the undivided Existence. Last night, we were reading from a text composed by Sankara. In it, he states that you are all the opposites and that you have no opposite. If it is night, you, yourself, are the night; if it is day, you, yourself, are the day.

So, destroy the object, which is the known, and destroy the knowing. Abide only as the Knower. Relinquish the idea that there is something to be known and a knowledge to be attained. Know the Knower.

Another Q.: Sankara declares "Abide in the state of grand Silence." This term, "grand Silence," struck me. Similarly, Ribhu says, "Be steeped in serenity." I can experience this deep peace and Silence, what these mean, much more clearly now. It is more experiential, and the words are powerfully meaningful now.

N.: The deeper the inquiry, the vaster the view. "Within" is not something small.

"Within" is infinite. It is a vast, grand Silence. All of the turmoil in life is only the turmoil in one's own mind. Inquiry cuts at the root of the mind and puts an end to the very causes of the turmoil. Where the causes are eradicated, there is this vast serenity. Steeping yourself in That, you look back at the previous turmoil and see that it was but a dream. It is like someone comfortably sleeping on her bed dreaming that she is drowning somewhere and flailing, but all is peace the entire time.

Q.: The state of clarity is now, but it seems that to remain in that state requires more inquiry. My mind is lulled and not destroyed. It is sure to come back.

N.: Yes. It may come back, but it will not necessarily come back as before. It may be missing some parts, because, whenever one has deep spiritual experience, it leaves an indelible mark on her. Something has changed, and she never quite returns to the same limitation. She knows something better, and she cannot actually forget it. Since you know that it will recur, and you also know in what manner the turbulence will recur, you can, from the vantage point of higher truth, begin to examine it. You meet it to address it, rather than waiting for it to catch you.

Sometimes, Siva is depicted with a bow and arrow and described as a hunter. He is described in many ways, of course, but one of the descriptions is that he is a hunter. For what does he hunt? He hunts and, shooting a single arrow, destroys it. You should be a hunter in your mind. Do not hunt for animals, of course, for they are innocent. You should be a hunter in your own mind. You know that there is delusion lurking in the woods of your mind in the form of various vasanas. Go hunting for them with the strength of meditation. Look from this vantage point. You will find that the vasanas tend to run away from you then. With this approach, they do not run toward you; they flee from you. You can hunt for them because you know how to destroy them by the Maharshi's inquiry. If, meeting an obstacle or tendency, you inquire, what was turbulence turns into great serenity, or grand Silence. Therefore, you need not have any fear of encountering the tendencies, if you fearlessly approach them with an intense inquisitiveness to find out what is at the root and to destroy them. You will find that the vast majority of them simply run away from you, and the rest of the tendencies that seem to remain will be easily dealt with. They burn up in the inquiry. You pull out their very roots. You will find that all the tendencies, without exception, are based upon misidentification, which consists in taking yourself to be an ego, to be a particular kind of person, and, usually, to be a body. The more aggravating ones are those in which you mix up your happiness, as well.

The thoughts of ignorance have no more power than that which is lent to them by you. Withdraw that power in light of the Knowledge of Truth. Inquire. The inquiry is the single arrow of Siva. That one arrow had the power to destroy three cities in one shot, with laughter, as well, from Siva. One arrow destroyed three cities. If one arrow destroyed three cities, or three states of mind, it can definitely destroy your tendencies. By inquiry, you have the boon of that arrow; you must use it. Is it clear what to do?

Q.: Yes.

निद्रा न विद्या ग्रहणं न विद्या
गृह्णाति किञ्चिन्न यथार्थबोधे ।
निद्रापदार्थग्रहणेतरा स्यात्
चिदेव विद्या विलसन्त्यशून्या ॥ १२ ॥

nidrā na vidyā grahaṇaṁ na vidyā
gṛhṇāti kiñcin-na yathārtha-bodhe |
nidrā-padārtha-grahaṇetarā syāt
cid-eva vidyā vilasantyaśūnyā || 12 ||

12

Sleep is not knowledge. Perceiving (sensing, seizing, grasping, taking into the mind) is not knowledge.
One does not grasp (seize, perceive) anything in true Knowledge.
Different from the categories of sleep and perceiving is
Consciousness alone (indeed); Knowledge shines forth [and is] not a void.

N.: Knowledge is beyond the states of grasping and sleeping. The grasping states, which involve taking into the mind, are waking and dreaming. Deep sleep is obvious.

Within the context of meditation, a blank mind is sleep. The perceiving of things, taking them into the mind or focusing on the senses, is grasping. Seizing upon objects in the mind is grasping. A blank without objects is sleep. Neither one is true Knowledge. True Knowledge lies beyond the states of mind. It lies beyond the appearance and disappearance of things in the mind. One does not grasp or seize anything in true Knowledge, for, in true Knowledge, there is no object. There is not even a blank "object," as there is in sleep.

"Different from the categories of sleep and perceiving is Consciousness alone." Examine your own experience. When you think, "There is something," this is grasping or seizing with the mind. It is commonly known to all. When you think of nothing, this is like sleep. This also is commonly known to all. Between the two states or conditions, the mind oscillates. That which shines so that both states appear is of the nature of neither. It is the unmoving Consciousness. It is not sleep, yet there is no grasping. There is no object in it.

Sleep is not Knowledge. Perceiving, grasping, or taking into the mind is not Knowledge. In the waking and dreaming states, there is this seizing upon the knowledge of objects, the taking into the mind, or grasping, with the mind alighting on one object after another. In sleep, there is the absence of objects. In waking and dreaming, there is the presence of thoughts. In deep sleep, there is the absence of thoughts. The absence of thoughts and the absence of objects, which is a state of sleep, is not Knowledge. It is merely a mental state in which certain activities are inactive.

Perceiving, or grasping with the mind, is not Knowledge. "One does not grasp anything in true Knowledge," and one does not conceive of anything in true Knowledge. True Knowledge is beyond the perceivable and the conceivable. Perhaps because there is a greater tendency for the aspirant to misidentify with what appears in the waking state, Sri Ramana has emphasized, by stating it twice, that one does not grasp anything in True Knowledge. Grasping is not the Knowledge, and sleep is not Knowledge. Grasping and not grasping, thinking and not thinking, conceiving of something and not conceiving, and having perception and having no perception are mental modes. These are modes of states of mind. True Knowledge is different from the categories of sleep and perceiving. What is it that neither grasps nor sleeps? What is different from these categories? The Maharshi states it clearly. Consciousness, alone, is different from all these categories. Consciousness does not sleep. Consciousness does not grasp, conceive, or perceive.

Within you, as the core of your Existence, lies this Consciousness. It is not awake when waking occurs. It is not dreaming when dreaming occurs. It is not sleeping when sleeping occurs. It is utterly unaffected by the presence or absence of thoughts and their imaginary, corresponding objects. The Self just is, as Consciousness, alone.

Everything else in one's experience falls within the domain of the manifested, the grasping, the perceiving, and the unmanifested, sleep-like states. Consciousness does not alternate and does not change with such states. It cannot be defined by any of the content or even the absence of content that occurs in those states. It just shines. The Consciousness is the Knowledge. So, Sri Ramana says, "Knowledge shines forth." How does it shine forth? In Truth, it is always shining, as the inexhaustible, never-diminishing Light of pure Consciousness, but it is realized conclusively when you abandon the misidentification with whatever appears in the previously-mentioned states.

What you are is never in any of the three states of waking, dreaming, or sleeping. What you are cannot be described as perceivable, imperceptible, and so forth and so on. What you are is pure Consciousness. Abidance as That is Knowledge. Knowing yourself only as pure Consciousness, having abandoned misidentification with anything else, Knowledge shines forth. There is the realized Knowledge.

Sri Bhagavan says that it is "not a void." When all that can be negated is negated, what remains is very real, and it is no mere emptiness. When everything vanishes in the Realization of the

Truth, the Truth, which is the perfect fullness, is shining, space-like, yet more solid than any object could ever be. You are not a thing that can be grasped, and you are not "nothing" either. You are something entirely real. Nothing can compare with That. It is the infinite, undifferentiated Consciousness. We should know ourselves as That, and, thus, Truth is revealed.

Q.: If there is some grasping or seizing in the mind, it seems to me that there is dualism involved in that conceiving. The dualism occurs if my identity, reality, or happiness is falsely superimposed upon an object or activity. Then, there is the fear that the object is going to be taken away from me, and I must grasp it and lay claim to it, in order to not lose it. There seems to be quite an underlying dynamic involved in this.

N.: It is not benign.

Q.: It is not benign. It is not a simple thought that passes by. There is some significance given to the idea.

N.: Though what you say is very much the case, in the text, the Maharshi is instructing us to look at the very basis. One may be accustomed to seeing the mind, supposedly awake, grasping or perceiving things. To the wise, such is nothing more than dreaming or hallucinating. If the object part is removed, and if there is nothing for the attention to alight on, the person is prone to go to sleep or to assume that there is just a blank, or nothing.

Q.: Those become a tamasic or rajasic state of mind.

N.: A person who is unacquainted with meditation may be accustomed to consider being awake and being alive as the perceiving of his senses. If the perceiving is removed, even by his own volition, he falls asleep. If only he comes to know about tracing Consciousness, he will neither be agitated in mind nor fall asleep. He will neither chase after the senses, or conjure up such in his mind, nor will his mind become a blank and enter a sleep state. Consciousness is something else. The Maharshi says, "Different from the categories of sleep and perceiving is Consciousness alone," that is, all by itself, and "Knowledge shines forth and is not a void." It is neither something, as appears in the waking and dreaming states, nor a void, or nothing, such as appears in the deep sleep state. It is neither an object nor simple nonexistence, but the perfect fullness of Consciousness, which is ever shining. This is knowledge of the very basis. If our minds do not hold either perceiving or sleep, what is left of our minds? Consciousness shines forth, without a trace of the mind. It is the ever-existent One, the solid Reality. Therefore, he says that it is not a void.

Another Q.: The one-pointed meditation engaged in being mindful of the surroundings and what is sensed, in which I am trained, is grasping, too. So, that is not Consciousness?

N.: Yes. It may have its benefits for some particular aspects of spirituality, but in the meditation of the depths of absolute Truth, in the final, highest Knowledge or Wisdom, that is simply grasping at objects, the state of seizing upon objects, paying attention to the sense perceptions, and taking things into the mind. Such involves the attempt to focus more on those things or sensations rather than experience the dissipation of the mental attention. It is one side of a duality. When that mode comes to an end, one enters a sleep, a blank, or a void. The Consciousness that we are, though, lies quite beyond the taking into the mind and the blank, or void, of the mind. Therefore, he says that it "shines forth."

Q.: So, all the fear comes from the grasping. All that I practiced elsewhere previously needs to be thrown out, too. All other practices need to be thrown out.

N.: One need not throw them out, for they may serve some purpose for some one at some time. All we have to do for ourselves is to focus on taking the direct path, which is the Knowledge of Consciousness. We can focus on the True Knowledge that Sri Ramana expounds. As for your practices, what is helpful stays with you, and what is not helpful falls off by itself. You need not worry yourself over what to cast off. In the end, you abide in Knowledge, as the Knowledge, itself, shining in your own Light. This rests on nothing else for its support. We may say that is the one who has completely cast off all else, which is the meaning of "Avadhuta."

Q.: My idea of perfect peace has always been associated with being in the middle of a forest, but that is just another form of the grasping.

N.: It is another image in the mind, but what it reminds you of is something that is not in the mind and not in the forest. The forest will pass away, and the mind will also pass away. The shining Consciousness does not pass away.

Q.: In my youth, there was such a longing for a connection with something beyond. It took form as various addictions that used to be of such urgency. That urgency needs to be honored.

N.: The urge was right, yet the manner in which you were trying to fulfill it was mistaken. The urgency, which is the intense, unquenchable desire to be in a state of serenity, profound happiness, and grand Silence, was completely right, but it cannot be fulfilled by outer sensory things, in bodily ways, or in worldly conditions. It cannot be fulfilled by grasping anything in the mind. It is fulfilled only by knowing yourself. You were frantically searching for your Self. It was an intuition of your real nature, of your real state, but overlaid with the mistaken idea that you had become something else. The moment you thought that you had become something else, it became urgent to return to your Self, but how would it be possible to find your Self by looking at that which is not your Self?

When the conception of objects ceases, there is not nothing left. When the conception of objects ceases, and when the conception of nothing also ceases, the self-luminous Consciousness remains, which is neither something nor nothing. It is stateless. It does not enter into any state that grasps or seizes. It does not take anything into itself. It is One. It is limitless. It does not sleep. It does not wake. It just is. It is perpetual, uncaused Light. (silence)

Inquire so that you identify yourself as the Light of Consciousness. Identify as the Light of Consciousness, and not as one who takes in, one who sleeps, one who perceives, or any kind of mind whatsoever. The same One, who neither perceives nor sleeps, possesses neither the category of ignorance nor knowledge, but is the Supreme Knowledge. Remain steady in this. Steadiness comes by the cessation of misidentification. (silence)

Another Q.: Whereas Consciousness is full, I have often regarded the void as peace of mind or as a quiet mind. Is this true?

N.: What actually is this void?

Q.: Shining.

N.: If it is shining, it is not a void. It may be devoid of the thoughts that otherwise would cause problems, but something exists, shining, and is the support of the peace. Dive deep into that. If you want to call it a "void," that is all right, but it is a very substantial void. It is entirely real. In the verse, the Maharshi says that it is "asunya," not a void, to show that it is not nothingness. The Reality is. The conception of nonexistence is like sleep. The conception of things existing is "taking in, perceiving, and grasping." The Reality, immovable and solid, infinite and space-like, is our real Being. It always shines. When ignorance is removed, it shines forth clearly in Knowledge. Sri Ramana says that it is "not a void," because it is not nonexistence. It is not things, and there is not a thing in it, he emphasizes. There is no world in it, no body in it, and no mind in it, but it is not nothingness. You are not a thing, and you are not nothing. Just that "you," by itself, is your peace.

Q.: (about using outer experiences and states of mind to promote deeper inner knowledge)

N.: If they did not prompt that, they would be merely more passing experiences. Knowledge deals with who you are. If one looks toward phenomena, including mental phenomena, for the phenomena to do something to him, to bring about some occurrence or event, one is looking for some transformation of the "self." What comes to him will also go. Knowledge deals with the Reality of what exists, that is, with who you are.

Another Q.: With true discrimination, there is no desire to look elsewhere or for a state, because it is clearly seen that the Self is utterly nondependent. If there is lack of clarity, which is a lack of discrimination between what is real and what is not, one looks in all the wrong ways and directions for the eternal Self.

N.: One who is engaged in real Knowledge is like someone who possesses the world's most precious, priceless diamond. He is simply not interested in the various mundane pebbles. It is like someone who is awake. He is no longer interested in a dream, however peculiar the dream might be. From the position of Knowledge, all those events, states of mind, sensations, etc., are very trivial and small. They are of no real consequence, for they are of no substance.

Q.: All of them are just a hallucination.

N.: Reality is much more fascinating and far more expansive. Abidance as the silent witness of all states of mind of all beings is more fascinating than making your thoughts slow down or stop. Abidance in and as the one Existence in which there never is a mind is far more fascinating than imagining a mind, creating various states within that mind, and tasting them one at a time.

Another Q.: I have heard you use this phase, "fascination of the Self," a number of times. It is not my experience that the screen of Consciousness, devoid of images, gross or subtle, is fascinating. I do not experience fascination with an empty screen.

N.: You have had a great number of interests. At any one time, you are usually interested in something. What have you been looking for the entire time?

Q.: The Self.

N.: With that very simple recognition, all of the interest, which is all the fascination that was doled out to myriad different sensations, mental interests, etc., is condensed into one point. That one point is your Being. It is that with which you have actually been fascinated the entire time, since the Self is the source of happiness. All the fascination that was placed on things that you had thought might provide you with happiness is on that one point. The Self is the Reality. All the fascination that was applied to your thinking and that appeared in your thinking as, "this is so," "that is so," "this is the case," "this is so," "this is so about such and such," is on that one point. How many times have you thought in such a manner, in this lifetime alone? How much does a man yearn to know who he is, his own real identity, which is the greatest mystery? All of that interest is on this one point.

Q.: I am understanding that the focus is to be inward on the Self, where Being, Knowing, and Bliss are one and the same. Being devoid of mind, devoid of images, though, leaves an empty screen in which there seems to be little or no fascination. The screen without images would soon result in an empty theater.

N.: The analogy of the screen and the images is to show that which is stable, unchanging, unmanifested, unformed, invariable, detached, and so forth and so on. The analogy, given by the Maharshi, of the screen in the cinema show is not meant to demonstrate all of the explanations of all aspects of the spiritual teaching. You may say that you imagine staring at a blank movie screen would not be particularly interesting, but the analogy was never intended for the purpose of expressing what is entertaining to you. Perhaps, if you have had enough of seeing a number of bad movies, the blank screen does become interesting and a relief from those bad movies, (laughter) but the analogy was never intended for such extrapolation.

Q.: The word, "fascination," does not seem to be indicative of my experience. There is the peace, the happiness, the bliss of the Self, deep satisfaction, and tranquility of the Self, but I have not experienced what is indicated by the world, "fascination."

N.: You have, but you do not recognize it. It is your own gravitation toward knowing the Self.

Q.: I feel that as the desire to know and abide as the Self.

N.: That is the fascination, and the actual fascination becomes not less, but stronger for the finding. Hence, in the description of his so-called "death experience," or Self-Realization, the Maharshi says that, from that moment onward, the Self focused on itself with a powerful fascination.

When we obtain something in the world that was previously fascinating, it is always less than what it seemed that it was going to be, and so fascination is followed by boredom. In the spiritual quest for the Self, it is just the opposite.

You have yearned for what is real. You have yearned for happiness, and you have been fascinated, or interested, to find these. Knowing your source, you become very fascinated with the source. Then, abiding as the source, you adhere to your Self with what can be described as a very powerful fascination. So, one who knows himself is never bored with his perpetual meditation. Does this make sense to you now?

Q.: Yes.

Another Q.: When one reaches the state of mind with no thoughts and he inquires, "For whom is that no-thought state?" it shows the inquiry is outside of the domain of thought.

N.: That is right.

Q.: The inquiry is mixed with thoughts about it and some impression of thought. Does that make the inquiry false?

N.: It is better to say that you have the real inquiry, but that you also carry thoughts about the inquiry as auxiliary accoutrements. They are ornamentation and are not the real substance. The inquiry can go on without those thoughts, and it can go on fine with those thoughts. Whether you have thoughts about inquiry or not is inconsequential. The actual Knowledge that reveals the Self is much deeper than thought.

Q.: That I can't contemplate. Knowledge is present throughout, before a thought comes and after a thought goes. Is it at that depth that the inquiry occurs?

N.: The inquiry does not depend on the thoughts.

Q.: Thoughts cover it up.

N.: Seemingly, if you misidentify with them or take them to be real, but, if not, they are nothing. They do not matter. The Knowledge and the inquiry occur transcendent of thought. The inquiry and the Knowledge are always possible, regardless of the state of the body, living or dead, and regardless of any state or mode of mind. In addition, if one has spiritual experience, the inquiry will never obstruct the experience but only make it deeper. So much is this so, that if someone is in samadhi and the inquiry is continuing, it will only make the samadhi deeper and will not break the samadhi.

Q.: The inquiry is not an interruption?

N.: It only deepens it, using the very quintessence of the samadhi to do so.

Q.: If that questioning occurs outside of thought, will it bring the Knowledge? It must be the Knowledge that knows the thoughts.

N.: The very same Consciousness, which knows the thoughts always, is the source and the goal of the Knowledge.

Another Q.: The question takes me outside of thought, because I can go no further. It takes me to the source. It appears in thought as a question, but where it ends takes me out of thought.

N.: That which prompts the question, "Who am I?" apparently expressed in thought, to commence in you is already beyond thought. The inquiry does not start in thought. The beginning, the middle, and the end of the inquiry are completely beyond thought.

Q.: Is that so because there is nobody that can inquire, and there is nobody that can "get it"? It's illusion?

N.: No. Inquiry shows you that there is nobody there. Practice it, and illusion stops.

Another Q.: In my meditation this afternoon, I felt drowsy at times. At one point, I was able to inquire, "For whom is this drowsiness?" There was a very energetic experience after that. It picked up the level of consciousness. Reflecting on that, I see that my practice and meditation involve spiritual thoughts revolving in my mind, as opposed to actually inquiring. When I inquire, is the inquiry in reference to that from which I wish to disidentify? For example, there is the perception in the body. I inquire, "For whom is this perception in the body?" "Me." "Who am I?" That seems to be a direct inquiry in regard to some experience.

N.: Yes. By such inquiry, you should have the revelatory experience within you that you are not the body. You should know your identity as being beyond the body, so that the sensations of the body are no longer binding or troublesome. Whether the sensations and the body come or stop, such does not make a difference. If you need to attend to something bodily, such as aches, pains, and emergencies, you still are not the body. Not being the body, you are not the doer. You are not the limbs that move or get up and walk or whatever. Aim for the Knowledge that your identity is quite free from the body, its attributes, and its activities. This is not opposed to spiritual thought. Spiritual thought does not get in the way of inquiry. To fill your mind with spiritual thought is good. I do not think anyone could possibly object to that. Imagine blaming someone for thinking spiritual thoughts! It would be absurd. Only, the inquiry, the Knowledge, is so much beyond thought. What those thoughts paint pictures of, so to speak, the Knowledge shows you as it is.

Q.: If, when inquiring, there were not a sensation of the body, and I were to inquire to disidentify with the body anyway, would that be on the mind level? I would still be thinking about that, so would the inquiry be only on the mental level?

N.: It could be, but the inquiry should be much deeper. The inquiry should be a deeper Knowledge that you are not the body, whether it is attended by the thought, "I am not the body," or not. It should be a deeper knowing and not merely holding the phrase, "I am not the body," in the mind. Dive deep into the meaning, and come to identify with what the significance of "bodiless Being" is.

Q.: Yes. Thank you.

Another Q.: In last night's reading, there was mention of the hand gesture of cin-mudra being like the radiance of the sun. I had never heard that previously.

N.: Sankara refers to the gesture of placing the forefinger to the thumb as an example of how ignorance is erased by Knowledge. It is not a statement about the significance of cin-mudra. The example is that of using the cin-mudra to represent the sun and then saying, "This is the measure of the sun," when obviously the sun is much larger. This is an example of taking sense perception to be valid, which is invalidated by a better knowledge. In the particular case, he was citing the knowledge presented by the sruti-s, that is, the Vedas. It overrides sensory knowledge in the same way, the very same text says, that the knowledge that the sun is several hundreds of thousands of miles in diameter overrides one's sensory data of the sun seeming to be only the size of the circle formed by the thumb and forefinger. The sun is obviously not that small size. He did not focus on the symbol of it. He used it as an example of why we should discount sensory impressions on the basis of higher Knowledge.

Another Q.: Within duality, there is grasping and release of that grasping, but the wrong identity remains unchanged. If there is release from that grasping of an object, without questioning the identity, no good comes of it.

N.: It is just like falling asleep. When the mind falls asleep, you release the hold on all the objects, but there is no Self-Realization forthcoming. One can sleep any number of times, and still Light does not dawn.

Q.: Even a meditation practice that concerns itself with not thinking of objects would be some kind of mental state?

N.: It would fall short. A meditation practice based on grasping an object, such as concentration on a particular object, could not yield Self-Realization, because it would not be revelatory of the pure Consciousness beyond the grasping or perceiving. Likewise, a meditation practice that aimed only at placement of all the perception in abeyance would not result in Self-Realization. It would just be an alternative state of the mind, because if would not reveal the nature of pure Consciousness.

Q.: This is important because he mentions this twice.

N.: He mentions the grasping twice. First, he says sleep is not Knowledge, so any sleep-like state should be discarded as unrelated to the Knowledge. Although, sometimes, sleep is pointed out to the aspirant to show that he exists even with the absence of objects, a sleep state is not the aim. It is just instrumental in instruction.

Then, Sri Bhagavan says that grasping is not Knowledge, because one is more accustomed to grasping, including the attempt to grasp the Knowledge as if it were something perceivable or conceivable, as some object to be experienced. He emphasizes, "One does not grasp, or perceive, anything in true Knowledge," because there is no perceiver, perceiving, and perceived. There is just pure Consciousness.

Q.: Grasping, again, is also a matter of the false identity left unchallenged.

N.: Exactly so. Therefore, one who knows himself is not surprised or dismayed, if everything appears or if everything disappears, be it for the senses or for the activities of the mind. Such is utterly insignificant. The Consciousness that you are is indifferent to the appearance or disappearance of anything.

Q.: What about effort? The effort is still valuable, isn't it?

N.: Yes. Spiritual effort is always worthwhile, but the effort bears its highest fruit when one inquires, "Whose effort?" When the attempt to know the Self turns in on the one who attempts to know and his nature is revealed, the highest good results. Spiritual effort in any form is never a waste of time. In the eighth verse, Bhagavan said, in the context of the inclusion of all kinds of spiritual practices, "Let them be spiritual practices for the darshanam of Truth, worship of the Supreme with name and form." He then declares that the direct path, though, is to know one's Self, one's own nature.

Q.: Since the worship is for that formless one and because the right intention is there?

N.: Because there is the intention for something greater than the ego, because there is the aim of that which is divine and transcendental, and because of the Knowledge-essence, even if only vaguely discerned, it is always beneficial.

Q.: The more cognizant of the formlessness it is, the more powerful it is. This is so, even if the practice still had outward aspects?

N.: Yes.

Q.: The mind is dissolving, in a certain sense, because one knows in his heart it is deeper.

N.: The more the Knowledge-essence is emphasized, the more keenly aware one is of it, the more powerful and deeper the spiritual experience is.

Q.: No matter what the expression is.

N.: Yes.

Another Q.: Without knowing who I really am, it is almost as if not existing. The first thing I ever heard that Ramana said was, "You exist." I don't think I actually knew that before, or it was so veiled that I did not even pay attention to the fact that I actually exist.

N.: You overlooked that which is most fundamental and conceived of other things, but you did not really doubt your existence. You did know it at a depth that is beyond conceptual knowing. It may not be within the scope of mental attention, but you knew it in a deeper way. The Maharshi's teaching makes use of this deeper knowledge. It would be superficial to say that he has brought your mental attention to bear on it, because mental attention is a transient thing.

Q.: It would never know the Knowledge.

N.: That is not the inquiry.

Q.: No.

N.: The inquiry into pure Consciousness, the one who knows about the movements of mental attention, cannot be within the context of mental attention. Mental attention is only within the sheaths. The Knowledge of the Self lies beyond the sheaths. You exist, and it can be said that the one who does not know his existence does not exist.

सत्यश्चिदात्मा विविधाकृतिश्चित्
सिध्येत्पृथक्सत्यचितो न भिन्ना ।
भूषाविकाराः किमु सन्ति सत्यं
विना सुवर्णं पृथगत्र लोके ॥ १३ ॥

satyaś-cid-ātmā vividhākṛtiś-cit
sidhyet-pṛthak-satya-cito na bhinnā |
bhūṣā-vikārāḥ kim-u santi satyaṁ
vinā suvarṇaṁ pṛthag-atra loke || 13 ||

13

The Truth is the Consciousness-Self. Various (manifold) forms of Consciousness
Are not established (accomplished) apart (different). True Consciousness is not divided.
(lit., The Truth is the Consciousness-Self. It is various ((manifold)) forms of Consciousness that are established [as] apart ((different)) [yet] true Consciousness is not divided.
(or: The Truth is the Consciousness-Self. Various ((manifold)) forms of Consciousness are not established as apart [or] divided [from] the true Consciousness.)
Can the change (transformation, modification) of ornaments exist truly
Without the gold, separately (apart), here in this world?

N.: "Here in this world" indicates that this is an example. It is not to be taken past what is exemplified by it. The analogy is that the ornaments of gold are nothing but gold. Someone who sees the substance sees just gold. A person who looks superficially sees the ornaments and seems almost oblivious of the gold. If the person can be brought to see the gold, the ornaments will be insignificant and will be seen to be not actually existent at all apart from the gold. There is nothing of the ornament apart from the gold. Not an atom of the ornament is apart from the gold. What is present is only gold that is perceived or conceived as the ornament. In the same way, everything is of the nature of Consciousness. It appears as if manifold. The manifold, or many forms of Consciousness, are really just one undivided Consciousness. "The true Consciousness is not divided." Therefore, the forms are only apparent and are unreal.

The true Consciousness is not divided, and all the forms that Consciousness seems to take are, after all, just Consciousness. Just as the ornaments are never apart from the gold, so the mind and the world, which are the ornaments of Consciousness, are never apart from Consciousness. There is not even the least bit of existence to them apart from that of which they are made.

Consciousness does not become transformed into something other than what it is. It remains as Consciousness, just as gold remains as gold, no matter in what shape it apparently is. It does not actually undergo any kind of transmutation. Consciousness does not undergo change at any time, whether during the time of thinking the world exists or during the time of knowing the world is not, and during the time the mind seems to be active or when the mind is entirely inactive and has disappeared. Always, everywhere, there is just this Consciousness, which is undivided. We should perceive in this way; we should understand all things in this way.

"Can the transformation, change, or modification of ornaments exist truly without the gold?" Do ornaments have any separate existence apart from the gold of which they are made? They are ornaments in name and form only, but in substance, they are just gold, and there is nothing to them but gold. It is not really true that one sees an ornament. One sees the gold, and, then, with the use of name and form, conceives of an ornament, but the only thing really there is the gold. Gold, in its own substance, has no particular form. In the same way, Consciousness is the only substance, the only reality. It is of the nature of Being and Bliss. Thus, Sat-Chit-Ananda. Here, Sri Ramana calls it "Cid-atma," the Consciousness-Self.

"The Truth is the Consciousness-Self." The various forms of Consciousness, which is the manifold Consciousness, including all the states of mind, all conceiving, all perceiving, all experiencing, and all things, wherever they may be, are only Consciousness. They are not established apart from or different from the Consciousness. If we regard the names and forms of things as real, as if existent, such is like seeing the ornaments, such as a ring, a bracelet, etc., but saying that one does not see the gold. The truth of the matter is that one sees only the gold. The bracelet and the ring are in name only and are in relation to a form of the gold. Similarly, manifestation, or multiplicity of any form in one's experience, is entirely composed of pure Consciousness.

Consciousness is the only actual substance. You never deal with anything else. There is no perceivable object, and there is no conceivable object. There is just Consciousness. These things are not divided from Consciousness. Nothing in your experience, from gross to subtle, stands on its own and exists separately. All of it is utterly dependent upon pure Consciousness, just as the ring is entirely dependent on the gold of which it is made. The ring depends upon the gold so utterly and is pervaded by the gold so utterly that the gold is the only thing actually there. Similarly, Consciousness is the only thing actually present in all the great multiplicity of experience, whether it is in the perceivable or conceivable, ignorance or knowledge, or in any state, such as in waking or sleeping. All is pure Consciousness. Nothing is established apart from or different from Consciousness.

Sri Bhagavan then states, "Satya-cito na bhinna," "True Consciousness is not divided." Everything is only Consciousness, but Consciousness does not become divided into everything. Everything is spoken of as "everything" when undue emphasis is given to name and form, to the conceived and the perceived. If you truly see what exists, you recognize that only Consciousness is present. Nothing else has ever been experienced by anyone, but Consciousness, itself, is not divided into anything or anyone. All "this" is only That; That has not become "this" at all.

Everything is only Consciousness, but Consciousness is utterly indivisible and has not become anything "other." Loosely, it is said that there are modifications of gold, but, actually, only the ornament is the so-called modification, and the gold just remains as gold. Consciousness just remains as Consciousness. The ring can be melted and made into a bracelet; the bracelet can be melted and made into a ring. Birth follows death, and death follows birth. Endless changes of names and forms appear, but Consciousness undergoes no transformation and no change, and it is the actual, and only, Reality present.

You are not an ornament. Your nature is pure Consciousness. That which is real is not the transitory, superficial appearance. That which is real is pure Consciousness, and, when we dive deep to know the Consciousness as it is, it is realized to be forever undivided and undifferentiated. Nothing has happened.

Q.: This is a very powerful image. I visualize the gold ornament and then imagine the ornament saying, "I would like to experience gold. I must experience gold. Where is the gold?" Then, another ornament comes along and says, "You are gold!" I can't help but see the humor of it. (laughter)

N.: (smiling and to all) It seems that he has talking ornaments. (laughter) It would be ridiculous for the ornament to say that it does not see the gold and that somewhere else there must be gold, for the gold is all in all, apart from which there is no ornament. So it is with the "I" and "the mind." They are all only Consciousness and nothing apart.

In this verse, the Maharshi has given a two-fold spiritual instruction. One is that everything is of the nature of Consciousness and does not exist apart. The other is that Consciousness is not divided, just as an ornament is an ornament in name only and is truly just gold. The mind is in name only, and there is really just Consciousness. There is an "I" in name only, and really there is just the Self. We can prove it to ourselves easily by inquiring deeply and determining what actually is the nature of one's own mind, or what is the nature of "I"? "Who am I?" Hold the ornament, and you have gold. Trace inwardly the "I," and you find the Self. Trace inwardly the mind, and you find the undivided Consciousness, and nothing but that.

Another Q.: I did not see the two-fold aspect of the teaching imparted.

N.: The verse first says, "The Truth is the Consciousness-Self." That is the plain uncreated Reality. Then, Sri Ramana speaks of various forms of Consciousness, which refers to anything created at any time, from subtle thought down to the forms of the universe. All of that is the "form of Consciousness." If something is created, it is only Consciousness that is the creator, the creating, and the created. They are not established as apart or as different from the true Consciousness, which is uncreated. So, the whole creation is not apart from, or different from, the Uncreated. Then, the Maharshi says, "True Consciousness is not divided," which reveals the indivisible, nondual, uncreated view.

Q.: So, even though it is objective, all aspects of the so-called object are just Consciousness?

N.: Just Consciousness. No matter their number, any ornaments made of gold are just gold. Perhaps, the analogy would become clearer for you if you think of one large piece of gold with various designs etched in bas-relief. The substrate is just gold, and the substance is just gold. They are not apart from each other. They are just gold. From the gold's perspective, there is no form whatsoever.

Another Q.: There is no such thing as an ornament. What is an ornament? It is just gold.

N.: For this reason, in *Ribhu Gita,* and also in the text we were reading last night, experience is said to have a five-fold aspect: sat-chit-ananda, Being-Consciousness-Bliss, and nama-rupa, name and form. Name and form are characterized as being purely illusory, and the first three are Reality. By inquiry, you eliminate the name and form and know what actually exists.

Q.: If you try to remove the gold, there is no ornament left.

N.: Not even its talking or the talking ornaments. (laughter)

Q.: You cannot, however, remove the gold.

N.: It is impossible to remove that which the gold represents. If we extend the analogy, you can melt and remake the ornaments again and again; hence, the great myriad of experiences and the multiplicity of bodies or lives, life after life. Just as there is only gold the entire time, so there is only Existence the entire time and not a multiplicity of experiences, lives, beings, etc. If we think of the manifold, it is only Consciousness. If we see the true Consciousness as it is, it is utterly undivided. If we think that there are ornaments, we should know that they are only gold. If we see the gold as it is, what ornaments would we be speaking about?

Another Q.: This meditation seems to start on the objects as Consciousness, but, in the depth of meditation, objects disappear because Consciousness becomes, not the background, but the foreground.

N.: That is right. The belief in the reality of objects disappears entirely, because Consciousness is the Truth. "The Truth is the Consciousness-Self. Various forms of Consciousness are not established apart. True Consciousness is not divided." The rest is the analogy. Consciousness, which is the Self, is the Truth; all this is only Consciousness; Consciousness is not divided.

We should not interpret such statements to mean that the objects actually exist or that differentiation actually exists. The purpose of the instruction is to consume the objective outlook and reveal that Consciousness alone is. The analogy elucidates that there is just gold and no actual ornaments and does not imply that the gold changes and is fashioned into these various ornaments.

Q.: It is a strong meditation on how everything is just Consciousness. The outward mind is drawn back to the Self by the meditation that all is Consciousness.

N.: Once your mind is drawn back to the Self, it is no longer outward. The imagination of differentiation ceases. It is only by overlooking the nature of pure Consciousness that one can think in terms of differences. When we trace the differences to the Consciousness that knows them, the Consciousness being alone real, we find that the Consciousness is not differentiated at all. There is, then, no "you," no experiencing, and no thing experienced. There is just Consciousness. We have not renamed those three parts of the triad and said that, ultimately, this is only Consciousness. That might be a step in the right direction, but it is not the finality. The Maharshi indicates that the truth is that Consciousness, which is the Self, is alone the Reality and does not exist as anything other than itself. So, have you ever seen anything? One who knows that he has never seen anything has the right Vision—Sat-Darshanam.

Q.: It is very clear. It is not a mental state at all.

N.: Spiritual instruction and spiritual practice should totally uproot the prevailing preconception, or mistaken orientation, and reveal that which is eternal, but which was not known before. It should not correspond to the preconception. If we merely add the name, "consciousness," or the idea of "consciousness," to the belief that objects actually exist, what have we actually accomplished? One may sound as if wise by saying that all this is only Consciousness, but if he still believes that there is all "this," that is the same view as he had previously. Only new terminology has been added. So, the instruction must always be something deeper, which always involves Self-Knowledge and an uprooting of the previously-held conception.

The previous conception was that objects exist. In verse after verse, Bhagavan has shown that they have no independent existence, they do not illumine themselves, and they are not real. Therefore, we abandon the objective outlook entirely. Then, we can truly say, "Consciousness alone is. Consciousness alone is all this," without there actually ever being any "this." The words may sound similar, but the meaning is completely different.

Q.: In my own mind, the way that I discriminate is to see that one is living Truth and the other is just the mental mumbo-jumbo of the same old concept. (laughter)

N.: The same principle can be applied to all aspects of the instruction. If we say, "The Self within me," and realize our identity with the Self, that is illuminative Truth. If we retain the idea of individuality and view that self as distinct from other selves, determined by bodies, what have we really gained, except that a high sounding term of Vedanta has been added to the previous conception of being a personal, embodied entity? The instruction of the Maharshi and other scriptural texts must always be approached, not by trying to fit the instruction into one's preconception, but by abandoning that very preconception, or by abandoning the previous orientation. Then, the instruction becomes clear. We do not bring the instruction down to the level of one's limited experience. Rather, we expand our experience until it matches the instruction. This is true with every aspect of the teaching. This makes the difference between mere grasping, or taking into the mind, and actual Realization.

Another Q.: A few days ago, an e-mail announcement at work arrived that stated that a funeral was to be held for a co-worker this Sunday. It was a total shock to me. I felt shaken for a while, but I did not question that reaction or say to myself that this is not correct. I did not judge it; nor did I question my reaction. It was fine to react. Is that going in the right direction?

N.: At some point, you will want to advance beyond the surface duality of you should not feel some thing and it is fine to feel something. One can endlessly oscillate between those two views regarding emotions, and no permanent, spiritual gain will be acquired thereby. If, for a time, someone thinks that she will let her emotions play as they have before, after a while, such is felt to be terribly samsaric. Then, there is an attempt to control the emotions. Because it is done without true Knowledge or inquiry, it amounts mostly to mental suppression, which is superficial and temporary. After being suppressed for a while, one announces her great spiritual release in enabling, or allowing, herself to feel these emotions again, but, really, there is no deep wisdom coming from either side of the dualism, is there? The approach is still only on the surface. One side is like that of holding a cork just below the surface, while the other side is taking one's finger off the cork, so that the cork is popping out even above the surface. Get beyond that entirely, and dive more deeply into yourself.

To excuse ignorance by thinking that it is a "form of Consciousness" is delusive. Though ignorance is not other than the sole-existent Consciousness, Consciousness does not become ignorant. Abidance as this Consciousness is true Knowledge and liberation from ignorance. It is in abidance in the Self, without the least trace of the possibility of ignorance, that the Maharshi speaks of forms of Consciousness being only Consciousness.

Find out the significance of life and death. Determine what it is that is born and dies, and what it is that is not born and does not die. Come to the certain Knowledge of your Self. Then, you will not be plagued or limited by such feelings, emotions, etc. You will not be generating them out of ignorance; nor will you be suppressing them. The question of judging or not is a very superficial view that leaves the personal identity of the ego very much intact.

Q.: I have been trying to take an approach of not judging my actions. Is this not the way to get some peace?

N.: Judging oneself over no wrong done, and thinking, "Oh! I have done terrible things. I have fallen. I am judgment-worthy," or, if you prefer the more classical expression, "I am a sinner," does not really bring about much advancement toward peace. Of course, on the other hand, doing some wrong action without a self-critical approach to the examination of oneself does not do much for advancement, either. The answer is far simpler. Go deeply and directly inside to know your Self.

I am reminded of an incident that occurred a good number of years ago at Tiruvanamalai. I had gone to the place in which Sri V. Ganesan was staying, for he knew me and I knew him. He invited me, and so I went to visit him. When I arrived, there were some people there having a satsang. I did not intend to say anything. I was just quietly sitting there to offer my respects.

A woman, who appeared to be from Europe, was explaining how she was trying to deal with all the judgments she apparently felt for herself. This was not judgment from other people but from herself. She did not seem to be concerned about her judgments of other people. Sri Ganesan compassionately encouraged her to get over this self-judgment. Then, he asked me to say something, though, at that time, I preferred to simply remain silent. He kindly insisted that I please say something along these lines. So, I turned to her and said, "Why do you not just stop doing whatever it is that is so judgment-worthy? If you feel that badly about whatever you are doing, just stop doing it." Of course, that answer was immensely unpopular with her. (laughter) The answer was simple. It really was not silly. It was the simple recognition that she had the freedom to direct her life in wisdom as she wanted. It was superficial of her to think that she compulsively wanted to do some things, drawn by fear and desire, but did not want to judge herself over it. The cloying or ruination of one's conscience is not helpful or beneficial.

If you become upset concerning someone having passed away, turn that upset state of mind inward, and use it as a goad to your practice. It is a motivating factor that prompts you, then and there, to inquire. What is it that dies? What is it that does not? The idea of being personally calm at a given moment in time is completely meaningless. You need to find the real peace and the conclusive Realization of the deathless Truth.

Q.: If I had been firmly established in the knowing that there is nothing but Awareness, would there have been a reaction so that I would appear calm?

N.: If there is only Awareness, whose would be the reaction? If there is only Awareness, about what are you speaking? You are mixing up the personal and the impersonal. Dissolve the personal. Worrying about how the personal appears to others or to an imaginary reporter in oneself, as calm or otherwise, is quite meaningless.

Q.: It is. It is. I do not know why I am asking this.

N.: Because you need an answer. The answer comes by inquiry into the deathless nature of your own Self. Use death to help your inquiry. When faced with death, does it really make a difference whether you are judging yourself or not, or whether you are calm or not? What matters is whether or not you know the Truth of your Being, which is immortal. Abidance as That is what is important. Abidance in That, as That, removes all suffering. So, as the *Gita* says, "Neither for the living nor for the dead do the wise grieve." Dive deep into impersonal Truth. The personal is only an illusion.

तद्युष्मदोरस्मदि संप्रतिष्ठा
तस्मिन् विनष्टेऽस्मदि मूलबोधात् ।
तद्युष्मदस्मन्मतिवर्जितैका
स्थितिर्ज्वलन्ती सहजात्मनः स्यात् ॥ १४ ॥

tad-yuṣmador-asmadi sampratiṣṭhā
tasmin vinaṣṭe'smadi mūla-bodhāt |
tad-yuṣmad-asman-mati-varjitaikā
sthitir-jvalantī sahajātmanaḥ syāt || 14 ||

14

"That" and "you" have "us" for a firm basis.
Upon the destruction of that "us" from (by means of) the knowledge of the root (source),
Without the "that," "you," and "us" notion, the One
State (Abidance, Stand) shines, the innate Self shall be.

N.: "That" and "you" are regarded as third and second persons in grammar. Our experience of everything "other," whether we address such directly as "you," or as something apparently removed from us as "it," has the "I" for its firm basis. The plural, "us," should be taken as an expression of "I," as is done in certain languages. We can also interpret this as not proving a multiplicity of selves, but indicative of the knowledge that, as long as we assume that there are "you" and "it," the selves, the "I's," will seem as if multiple; hence, "us." The destruction of that "us," which, in the singular first person, is the destruction of the sense of "I," is by Knowledge of the root, the inquiry, "Who am I?" Where does "I" spring? From where does this conception of being an individual spring? If we so inquire, we are left without the "it," "you," and "us." There is no indirect object, no direct object, and no "I"-subject. What remains? That which remains is something that is absolutely One, not divided into subject and object, not a multiplicity, not divided in itself, and not divided from anything else. That is the abidance, the state, and the stand that you have, and that shines as Knowledge. It is not a light that is perceived through the mind or senses. By "light" is meant Consciousness. It shines without a subject and object.

Sri Bhagavan concludes by declaring that "the innate Self shall be." For whom shall it be? For the one who inquires to know who he is, eliminating all sense of "I," "you," and "it." For that one, the innate state of the Self shines. Without such inquiry into the "I," the notion that something else exists will continue. That is illusion. Only by a profound Knowledge of the root of the "I," in which the individuality vanishes once and for all and in which only pure Existence-Consciousness remains, is one's natural, or innate, state realized. This innate state of the Self, which is without beginning or end, without gain or loss, the Maharshi proclaimed to be Sahaja Samadhi.

All of that which is objective has the subject as the basis. The Maharshi speaks of the destruction of that first person subject-basis. It is a destruction that comes about by Knowledge of its source, or of its root. Then, there is no longer a "that," a "you," an "us," an object or a subject.

If you search for that which is regarded as the subject, the object is consumed and the subject dissolves. That which remains is absolutely One and not "I," "you," "she," "he," or "it." That is the real state. To know yourself as in that state and as the state is abidance. That shines as the result of such inquiry into the subject. In reality, it shines always, but, in your experience, you realize it by examining the subject, which is the basis for all that is objective. Thus, you eliminate both the object and the subject, and all differentiation, and remain in, that is, abide as, the One that shines, which is pure Consciousness.

Sri Bhagavan further declares, "The innate Self shall be." That which you realize, by virtue of such inquiry, is not newly acquired. It is innate. That which is innate has no coming or going and no beginning or end. The innate is never apart from you. It is not distinct from you, even in the least degree, so that you could lose it at one time and acquire it at another. The innate is not something that becomes impure and, later, is purified, but rather is as it is. The innate undergoes no kind of transformation. That which is innate is not produced by anything bodily, not produced by anything in a sensory fashion, not produced mentally, or anything of the intellect, and not produced by any other means. What is innate is that which exists. That the Self is innate means this is your very nature, which is the real nature of "I."

The usage of "us," the first person plural, may also be attributable to two other reasons. The first is a concession to the spirit of including the aspirant, or reader of the text, so that he understands that this spiritual instruction refers to his own very nature. The second could be that, since Ganapati Muni wrote the Sanskrit version, in order to show great reverence, he may have placed it in the first person plural and employed such as if it were in the words of the Maharshi.

Q.: One of the manifestations of the "I" is projection. Would a fruitful inquiry be the question, "Who projects?" as opposed to looking at what the fascinating object is.

N.: What do you mean by "projection"?

Q.: When the mind goes outward to a form, an activity, or a desire.

N.: Is the belief that form exists also a projection?

Q.: Yes.

N.: We can say that, when you project your own happiness on some inert object, the result is of the form of desire. The projection disappears in the course of inquiry, because you enter the very source of happiness. One becomes free of the concepts of desire.

In Vedanta, projection has another meaning, as well. Once one's own nature is apparently veiled by the root delusion, "I," there is then the projection of "you," "it," and "other." This appears as the form of thoughts and the world. Everything other than "I" is a projection. Ignorance is said to be characterized by two aspects and is described in a two-fold manner: veiling and projection. Veiling is the not seeing of Reality. Projection is the imagining of the unreal. Once you have imagined the unreal, you can personally project all kinds of desires upon it, as well. It is the same mechanism of delusion at work, but by the time the delusion is to that extent, you are occupied with a very small corner of this universe.

Q.: What is required, then, is to direct the mind inward toward the source of happiness.

N.: If you return to the source of happiness, your mind is directed inward, and the attachments to outward things dissolve. Diving inward, fascinated by the happiness, you continue your inquiry into the very source of this root-notion of "I." What happens? The projection is un-projected. The "he", the "she," and the "it," the "world," and "you" vanish. They vanish in proportion to the "I" vanishing. With the utter dissolution of the "I," the projection is over, and the veil is no more. The veil is cut asunder.

Q.: If one takes the unreal to be real, and if one questions if this is truly real by asking, "Does this really last forever?" would that be one way of cutting asunder the false assumption?

N.: Discerning whether or not it lasts forever is one way to discriminate what is real. The significance of knowing something to be unreal and knowing that which is real, though, is even more expansive than the observation of that which is transitory. We may still take something to be real, though we recognize that it is transient. It may be regarded as being temporarily real. When the wise sages, saints, and scriptures proclaim something is unreal, such means it does not really exist; thus, the analogy of the silver in the shell called the mother-of-pearl. There is no silver there. When it is said that the silver is unreal, that does not mean that the silver will not last or that it is rapidly decaying silver. There is no silver there. There is the sea shell; there is no silver. Likewise is it with the analogy of the rope and the snake. The snake is not there. It is not that the snake is temporarily there. The snake is not there at all, and something else entirely is there. When it is said that the manifold forms are not real, or that the "I," the "you," and the "it," are not real, this does not merely mean that they are temporary. They are, indeed, temporary, but they are actually an illusion, as well. That which is illusory is not really existent. Something else is existent. We call it the Self, or Brahman.

Another Q.: When the second and third persons arise, that is an instant pointing to the fact that the unreal "I," that unreal character, has already made his appearance. That is a clear sign that that assumed "I" needs to be immediately investigated.

N.: Exactly so. If we follow the Maharshi's instruction here, what actually exists, if the "I," "you," "it," "us," "them," etc., are not there? In Sanskrit, one should cover the singular, dual, and plural in all three persons. They usually reside in a chart, and I have seen them there, myself. (laughter) In our experience, what is actually there? In the grammar book, it is easy to see that the paper is there, and the print has been superimposed upon it. All of the "I," the "you," the "she," and the "it" are one sheet of paper. Only the appearance of ink makes one think that there are a variety of meanings or different things here. In your experience, what corresponds to the sheet of paper?

Q.: Not any of the printed stuff, ever.

N.: Not any of those objective things. In your own inquiry, ensure the dissolution of the notion of "I," and, with it, the utter dissolution of "something other," whether that is considered to be immediately present or remotely present. The entire idea of "something else" and of an "I" that experiences it, whether such be you and another person, you and another object, you and an event or occurrence, or you and anything whatsoever, is false and should be abandoned. Neither you nor a thing exists as such. Something else exists that is vast, serene, undivided, without differentiation, and utterly without form. That is the perfect fullness. It shines as Being-Consciousness. To realize it conclusively, inquire into the first person, "I," and go to the root of that one, since your experience of the others depends on that one. If you get to the root of him, which can be by Knowledge alone, there is no multiplicity, no veiling, no projection of multiplicity, and nothing other, but just one Self.

भूतं भविष्यच्च भवत्स्वकाले
तद्वर्तमानस्य विहाय तत्त्वम् ।
हास्या न किं स्याद्गतभाविचर्चा
विनैकसंख्यां गणनेव लोके ॥ १५ ॥

bhūtaṁ bhaviṣyac-ca bhavat-svakāle
tad-vartamānasya vihāya tattvam |
hāsyā na kiṁ syād-gata-bhāvi-carcā
vinaika-saṅkhyāṁ gaṇaneva loke || 15 ||

15

The past (the having been, the gone) and the future (the to become) are the present (being) in [their] own time.
Relinquishing the Truth of what is presently existing (the present),
Will it not be laughable, repeatedly thinking over (discussion) [what is] gone [and] will be,
Like counting without the number one, in the world?

N.: "In the world," indicates that this is an example. We cannot count without the number one, which is the very unit of which all other numbers are composed. It is the starting place. All the other numbers are just so many ones combined. Likewise is it if we ignore the basic existence and consider what will be and what has been.

If we regard this verse as a statement about time, it serves some purpose. Obviously, thinking of, or discussing, the past and the future without relation to the present, or, without dealing with what the present life is, thinking of the far past and past lives or the far future and future lives, would be laughably absurd. It would be missing the most important ingredient.

If we interpret this verse in terms of what is existent, what has been and what will be have, as their common denominator, the present Existence. It is within the present Existence that there is knowledge of the past or future existence.

"Relinquishing the Truth of what is presently existing," is the key to a profound comprehension of what Sri Ramana reveals in this verse. What is it that is presently existing? What is it that is like the number one in his analogy? To go on repeatedly thinking about the past and the future, and it does not make any difference how near or remote the past or future is, and to be thinking, "I was," or "I will be," without knowing the fundamental "I am"—would it not be absurd? Repeatedly thinking about what is gone and what will be would be like counting without the number one and would be missing something so important.

If we would interpret the verse as referring to dealing with time, the next verse would not follow very well. Muruganar has wisely arranged the Maharshi's verses, and Ganapati Muni has translated them into Sanskrit. The composition of the verses is supremely wise, and the arrangement of them is quite particular. Some aspects of the preceding verses would be ignored and the next verse would not cogently follow if one would think that this verse is about time, such as being about the present moment, in contrast to past moments and future moments. Something deeper is being indicated. It must pertain to our own Existence. If one thinks that he is in the present moment and simply divests his mind of expectations of the future and memories of the past, he will still have the duality of "I" and "this" and everything else Sri Bhagavan just negated. There will still be the ego-notion, and there will still be the misidentification with the sheaths. There will still be the idea of "I am the body." There will still be the mistaking of the names and forms of the world to be existent. So, the "one" to which Sri Ramana refers must be something other than the present moment and must be, rather, what is presently existing.

So, there are two ways of understanding this verse. The first is the ostensible meaning, and the second is a deeper, indicated, more profound meaning. The first is that the past and the future are present in their own time. What one experiences is the present and never actually the past or the future. Even memories of the past and anticipations of the future occur in the present moment, which is the well-known "now" moment. When one relinquishes the now-moment, which is a shift of that to which one is paying attention, the mind can wander to memories and to anticipations and is filled with the clutter of thought. Consequently, taking that into account, if the aspirant keeps the attention on that which is present, he eliminates much of the clutter of thought, and, to that extent, he has an advantage. If one takes that approach, though, it is limited in scope for several reasons.

Upon deeper examination, that which is referred to as "being in the now moment" is a corruption of the usage of "Being" into meaning mental attention, and the "now moment" actually pertains, not to the abstract moment of time, but to the present set of circumstances that are perceived through the senses. This is something contained entirely within the conjuring of the five sheaths. Consider the similarity to the experience in a dream. In a dream, the "now moment," or the present moment, is no more real than the past moments or the future moments of the dream. Similarly, that which is "here" in the dream is no more real than that which is "there" in the dream, no matter which direction the "there" might be—in front, behind, to the sides, upward or downward.

Moreover, this sacred text deals with Sat-darshanam, the revelation of Truth. Whatever might be the temporary benefits of shifting the mental attention to the present time or the present circumstances, it would not offer Liberation, because it would still be in accord with the same misidentification with the body and the same objective orientation that one is trying to abandon. The purpose of spiritual instruction is the undoing of the present preconception—no pun intended on "present." If our interpretation of the instruction is at the same level as the preconception, no great benefit is gained. Rather, we should lose the preconception, so that our experience merges with the significance of the higher instruction. Therefore, there must be a deeper way of approaching the verse.

This verse appears in the middle of the text, and the text is not written in an ascending or descending order. It is Sat-darshanam, the revelation of Truth, from beginning to end. All of it is at the highest, indeed, the supreme, level. So, why is this verse placed here, if the next verse utterly negates time entirely? There must be another way of understanding the text.

The word for "the past" means "the having been" or "the gone." The word for "the future" means the "to become," and the word for "the present" is "the present being." So, we may read the verse in this way: "The having been, or the gone, and the to become are the present being in their own time. Relinquishing the Truth of what is presently existing, will it not be laughable, repeatedly thinking over what is gone and what will be, like counting without the number one in the world?"

The Maharshi has given the analogy of counting without the number one. The number one is the basis from which all other numbers proceed, and it could very well be said that all other numbers are nothing more than collections of the same one appearing many times over. In the first verse, the word "eka," one, is mentioned, and, in verse fourteen, Sri Ramana proclaims it to be the innate Self. Counting without the number one is analogous to leaving off the Knowledge of your Existence and trying to determine what was or will be. An example of this is thinking that you came from the Absolute as an origin, which is what was. Another example of this is an assumption that you will be realized in the future, that you will reach or merge with Brahman in the future, which is the supposition of what will be in the future. What is it that is presently and, therefore, always existent?

Because this is Sat-darshanam, the Maharshi's emphasis must be upon the nonobjective Existence. If it were just upon the moment, it would merely be paying attention to time, which is not Reality. If one attempts to only pay attention to the present moment, the best one can hope for is the clearing away of certain thoughts, while certain other thoughts remain, and the misidentifications remain intact. However, if we take this deeper approach and focus upon what is it that is actually existing, which is what we always are, always were, and always will be, the verse makes much more sense. We are not to worship time; we are to worship the Self.

If one takes an approach of giving mental attention to the present moment, he may gain the experience of a sense of continuity of the present moment, of the now going on and on. This borrows the ever sameness and continuity of the Self and mixes such with time, so that there is the superimposition of time upon the Self. Or one may gain the experience that each moment is different than the one before it and the one after it. This borrows from the ever-shining, ever-sparkling, ever-fresh nature of the Self and mixes such with time, so that time is superimposed upon the Self.

If we approach the spiritual instruction bestowed in this verse with the understanding that the "having been" and the "to become" are "the present Being, in their own time," what is the present Being? "Relinquishing the Truth of what is presently existing": what is it that is presently existing? Certainly, it cannot be the "world," which he has utterly negated. Certainly, it cannot be anything sensed, which he has also utterly negated. Certainly, it cannot be the mind, or anything of the dyads and triads, all of which have been totally swept aside by the Maharshi in his previous instruction.

What is presently existing? It is that very same innate Self, shining by itself, alone. Therefore, rather than consider where you have been, as if the Absolute were an origin, or consider where you will be, as if the Absolute were a goal to attain, you should know your present Existence, which reveals that the Absolute is you, and is as it is, always. Ignoring that Existence and attempting to determine, "Where have I come from, where will I wind up, and where will I be?" is like trying to count without the number one. It is laughable. It is missing what exists for what does not actually exist at all. Now and always, start and end in your own Existence, for therein lies the Truth.

It is evident that many writers, speakers, seekers, and teachers may prefer the initial, ostensible explanation, yet, if you seek Liberation, this other explanation is more pertinent to you.

As is the case with any form of concentration, focusing mental attention on the present time can yield a reduction of the quantity of thoughts. This result is inevitably transient. If the thoughts in abeyance are of a defining, confining character, their subsidence brings a corresponding, temporary unveiling of the natural joy of the Self. For eternal Bliss, thought-transcendent Knowledge is necessary. This Knowledge is of the Self, timeless, and nonobjective.

The instruction in this verse also prompts a greater intensity in spiritual practice. The past is gone and irrecoverable. If precious time was lost in illusion, determine that now you will earnestly practice. The future is not guaranteed. There is no purpose served in delaying intense spiritual practice when the opportunity to engage in such is now. If this is understood, there is little point in repetition of regret or anxious anticipation, which would be wasteful of the present opportunity to realize the ever-existent Self.

In the present Existence is found the eternal Existence. Even in this moment, one finds forever. That which is the Reality now is the Reality always.

If emphasis is placed upon the term "svakale," which means "in own time," we may also approach understanding the verse in this manner. All that is known of the past and future is in the present, which is the present knowledge, just as the present, itself, exists only in the knowledge of it. They are now known in the present, and they are the present when experienced. If the objective portion of the experience or knowledge of "now" is negated, the ever-existent Being-Consciousness remains. Just as this is so with then and now, so it is with there and here. There is known only from here. If the objective portion is negated, inclusive of the misidentification with the body, what is it that is immediately here, which is nonobjective and interior to the senses and the mind? Thus, invariably the inquiry leads to the subject, "I." Inquiry into the nature of the "I" is direct, and these other considerations, such as here and now, may be regarded as a circuitous path to the same final inquiry.

Q.: This completely removes the time factor from the equation. Even if one were to refer to a past or future, it can happen only outside of time, which is the timeless. There is no past. There is no future. There is just this, and any of "that," is this.

N.: "This" is not a present moment, too.

Q.: It is not in time. It is outside of time. It eliminates time.

N.: As you perceive, the verse by the Maharshi, while using the elements of time, has nothing to do with time, which is why the next verse, which is about timelessness, follows. It pertains to the fundamental One that presently exists, of which everything is composed, forgetting which, past, present, and future are conceived. If one would reduce the conceptions in his mind to the ones considered present, how would Liberation be forthcoming? If, though, we ask ourselves, "For whom is the past? For whom is the future? For whom is the present moment?", we pass beyond all three times and find That which is presently existing, which is the one Substance in every experience, yet which is transcendent of every name and form of every experience. After all, this is Self-Knowledge, not knowledge of "it," and a present time would be as much an "it," as anything else. Knowledge of what presently exists, though, leads you to your own nature.

Another Q.: So long as there is any contrivance of the mind, such as of time in the past or the future or present, and I ignore my own essence, it is not Liberation.

N.: The Maharshi has placed emphasis upon Existence. In ignorance, one may conceive of the existence as that which he once was and to which he needs to return, to gain yoga, or to attain union with what he once was, or one may conceive that he is not the Self now but will realize it later. Bhagavan advises one to examine the present Existence. Know the present Existence. The emphasis is not on a moment in time. Most people already have familiarity with experience in the present, in contrast with experience in the past and the future, unless one contemplates Vasistha, in which case that theory does not hold. (laughter)

Q.: To start with the concept that I was the Absolute is to start from ignorance.

N.: Or, it is ignorance mixed with knowledge. It is the knowledge that the Absolute exists and is your starting place, but the belief is that you are somehow, at the present time, separated from it. So, why not find out the Truth of the present existence? Then, you will know what you have been and what you will be. The aspirant may feel that later he will be a jnani and will realize the Truth, but, now, he is practicing. It is knowledge mixed with ignorance. It is good intention to practice. It is knowledge inasmuch as one knows that this is the goal, but what is being regarded as the goal that can be attained in the future is actually the very nature, the innate nature, of the Self and is presently existent. To ignore that which we always are and go in search of something else is laughable. This is not laughter with scorn, but laughter because it is downright silly. Why overlook that which, in truth, we are, and what we always are, and assume it to be objective and removed from us, whether in space, in time, or by any other imagined chasm?

Another Q.: By the Grace of Ramana I have seen that, when I was thinking of a task to be accomplished, it brings in the idea of a future. Then, I would have the idea that the completion of the task would bring happiness associated with the accomplishment.

N.: Happiness is identical with Existence, so what you expect in the future actually presently exists. Why forsake that which presently exists and push it ahead, so to speak, in time, thinking that you will catch up to it later?

Another Q.: Would you say that, owing to superimposition and veiling, one has the feeling of not abiding as Being? I remember that, in *Talks with Sri Ramana Maharshi*, some visitors said, in effect, "Well, that is all very good for you, but I do not feel it." If one does not feel it at this moment, it is because one veils it and makes an object out of it and starts looking for it in the past or future. Is that what happens?

N.: That is as good of an explanation as any. Any explanation of illusion must necessarily be as illusory as the illusion, itself. If, from such an explanation, you are prompted to inquire into the nature of the one who is veiled, the one who is bringing about this veiling, or the one who says that he does not feel it, the "I," that will resolve everything nicely, and any illusion will dissolve.

क्व भाति दिक्कालकथा विनाऽस्मान्
दिक्काललीलेह वपुर्वयं चेत् ।
न क्वापि भामो न कदापि भामो
वयं तु सर्वत्र सदा च भामः ॥ १६ ॥

kva bhāti dik-kāla-kathā vinā'smān
dik-kāla-līleha vapur-vayaṁ cet |
na kvāpi bhāmo na kadāpi bhāmo
vayaṁ tu sarvatra sadā ca bhāmaḥ || 16 ||

16

Where shines (appears) talk of space (direction) and time without us?
The play of space and time, here, is if we are the body.
Nowhere we shine (appear), at no time we shine (appear),
But we everywhere and always shine.

N.: "Here" and "there," "now" and "then," are for "me." There is someone for whom all such experience is. This is so concerning not only what plays out in time and space but time and space as factors of experience. They are for someone. By rough analogy, we could say that time and space are woven like a cloth. The world is painted like a picture on that cloth. Neither the cloth nor the pictures are the viewer. The one who sees them is not in the picture and is not in the cloth.

"Where shines (appears) talk of space and time without us? The play of space and time, here, is if we are the body." The play here signifies the experience in the world. If we are not bodies, what is space? If we are not bodies, what is time? "Nowhere we appear, and at no time we appear." We are not in space. We are not in time. We are the Self, which is of the nature of Being-Consciousness-Bliss. This is spaceless and timeless. Bodies and objects appear in time and space and are determined by them. Are you the body? If you are not the body, you are not here, and you are never elsewhere. If you were the body, you would be in time, and thus the concepts that you once were, you now are, and you will be sometime else are conceived. Are you the body? If you are not the body, there has been no birth, there will be no cessation, and there is no between time. If you are the body, there is the world in which there is this weaving of time and space. If you are not the body, what is the universe? If you are not the body, is there anything outside you? Time and space are the merest appearances within you, but you are not in them. What is in you becomes absorbed in you or is of the same nature. Your nature is Being-Consciousness. When is time? Where is space?

"Nowhere we appear, at no time we appear, but we, everywhere and always shine." It is Being-Consciousness, alone, that shines. There is nowhere where it is not. There is no time when it is not. You are always That. You are not the body. Understand your bodiless nature fully. There is no moment in which you are, be such past, present, or future. You have no personal life in the past or one spreading out in the future or one with which to be preoccupied in the present moment. You are not the body. If you are not the body, the very senses used to perceive some signs of time and space are not yours, and the experience they provide does not pertain to you.

Always you are. What could disturb your peace? Always you shine. What darkness could come over you? You have existed always. You have been shining always. You will exist always, and you will shine always. Time does not measure you, and it does not diminish you. You are not the body, so you are called "the Infinite," and "the Eternal." In truth, you are timeless and spaceless. You are not big and not small. Those conceptions do not apply. You are not long and not brief. Those conceptions do not apply. You are not only That which presently exists; you are That which alone exists, ever.

This verse clearly follows what was referred to as a more profound meaning of the previous verse. If you were to adhere to the ostensible meaning of the previous verse, it would seem as if the Maharshi is contradicting himself, but there are no contradictions in his seamless teaching.

"Where shines" can mean "where appears." "Talk of space and time without us": "Talk" indicates the perception or conception. You are not in time. Time does not create you. You are not in space, and you are not encompassed by space. Space does not create you. Time and space are conceived by you. With the rise of the mind, time and space appear. With the dissolution of the mind, time and space disappear.

Space is conceived in relation to a body, which becomes the locus, the point of experience, in illusion due to superimposition. Time, likewise, is conjured up in the mind, requiring two or more thoughts in order to even appear. The time becomes the distance, as it were, between the two thoughts.

"Where shines (appears) talk of space and time without us?" However conceived, or supposedly experienced, time and space depend on us. We do not depend on time and space. Whatever is in time is not us, and whatever is in space is not us. That means that the body and mind are not us. The play of space and time, here, is if we are the body. If we are the body, there is reality to here and now and to there and then. These are dependent upon the "I am the body" conception, but are you the body? This is the basic inquiry: Are you the body?

If you know with experiential Knowledge the truth that your nature is bodiless, you find that so much confusion is absent for you. So much confusion is built up on the "I am the body" conception, including confusion regarding your bondage or your liberation. Without the "I am the body" notion, there is tremendous clarity, and the Truth has a simplicity that is Self-evident.

"Nowhere we appear, at no time do we appear." Bodies appear and, consequently, disappear. A body appears in time; a body appears in space. You, though, do not appear. You do not appear in space, and you do not appear in time. You remain unformed, unborn, timeless, and spaceless. The timeless is also eternal; the spaceless is also infinite.

Sri Bhagavan says, "but we everywhere and always shine." The nature of your Consciousness is unembodied. Your very Consciousness is everywhere and at all times. Wherever and whenever anything shines, it is you that shine, and that is your own Consciousness. You never appear, yet everywhere you are. You never manifest, yet at all times you are. If there is manifestation, you are all of that. You shine and appear as all that. Yet, in truth, you remain forever unmanifested, as the Timeless and the Spaceless. For such a one, how could there be limitation?

If you are timeless, what is birth? What is death? If you are spaceless, you have no location. What is the meaning of "here" and "there?" To know your Self in this manner, all that is required is to inquire deeply into your innate Being, your own natural Existence, which is the Self, and, in the course of doing so, to abandon any misconception that associates the body as a definition of your Self.

Another Q.: I am considering a possible stumbling block.

N.: Are you considering stumbling or planning on an obstacle? (laughter)

Q.: Sri Ramana says that the sage is the body and other people are the body, but, for the sage, the body and everything else are names. Thinking of that, I think that there is a loophole if people want to say that they are the body.

N.: But the instruction is for those who are desirous of Liberation and not for those who are hoping for a loophole. (laughter) For those who are loopy, any amount of loopholes can be imagined. (laughter) If your point is that, throughout all time, there are those who can manage, by some way or other, by hook or by crook, to misinterpret and distort the most well-intentioned instruction, you may be correct, (laughter) but for those who are desirous for Liberation, it really is of no interest. Such imagination would merely show what a funny animal a human can be.

Another Q.: As I am listening, meditating while you are speaking, I realize that there still is misidentification. When I inquire as to who has misidentification with the body and who is the one who somehow thinks there is misidentification left, it starts to fade. It is hard to keep the idea that there may be somebody who has some misidentification with the body.

N.: Is the one who supposedly has it a body?

Q.: I don't think he is anything.

N.: If the one who might become misidentified is not the body, how much more so not the body is the real Self? If even the jiva is not the body, certainly Siva is not the body, and this can be understood even before resolving the jiva.

Q.: It is very hard to think I can be a body. I can think it, but that does not make it so. The more that I try to make it so, the more obvious it becomes that it is not going to happen.

N.: You cannot truly become the body. Bodilessness is the natural state and not something we become. Knowledge simply reveals it. It does not transform you from a body into a bodiless state. The Knowledge just reveals the fact. The vast Vision revealed here by the Maharshi, shining everywhere at all times, yet appearing nowhere and at no time, is self-evident for the bodiless.

Q.: What you just said points out a mistake in my approach, and that is, "If I am the body, how do I get out of being the body?" Similar to what was commented upon about time, it is an approach of some kind of mental contraption that I am attempting to use to get out of the contraption that I have made. I can't get there, because I am trying to make up something that isn't real, saying that this something is real, and then thinking that, somehow, I am going to get out of this "real" place to some place that is more real.

N.: You do not change places. You just find out how unreal your former imagination is. You un-realize all that you were previously realizing.

Q.: So, it is really self-un-realization. (laughter)

N.: Yes. The Maharshi has indicated that. All we have to do is unrealize what we have regarded as real. Speaking of realization is only a formality. If you are never the body, and if that which presently and always exists is bodiless Being, space and time are not measurements of you, and whatever appears in time and space cannot be your definition. Nowhere you shine; everywhere you shine. At no time do you shine; at all times you shine.

Q.: Stating "at no time" and "all time" does not mean that time is real, does it?

N.: He said, "Where shines, or appears, talk of space and time without us? The play of space and time, here, is if we are the body. Nowhere we shine, or appear, at no time we shine, or appear, but we everywhere and always shine."

Another Q.: Is that a new translation of Bhagavan's words? I do not recall it in those words.

N.: What do you recall the verse as saying?

Q.: I am just wondering whether you are clarifying things, as we go along, from the printed edition.

N.: This is printed.

Q.: I meant previously printed.

N.: It is fairly literal. Kva bhati, where shines, in the third person singular, dik, direction or space, kala, time, katha, talk, vina, without, asman, us. I do not know if a more literal translation is possible. That is the first line of this verse. Do you have questions about the other lines?

Q.: I wonder, if I look at the previous printed edition, whether or not I will find those exact words.

N.: It depends upon at which printed edition you look. There are numerous excellent translations of the text.

Q.: But do they discuss shine in that way?

N.: Does someone have another edition here now? As what are they translating bhati, bhamo, and bhamah?

Another Q.: Here is the translation from the Tamil version.

N.: In this translation from the Tamil version, one can see the word "exist" instead of "shine." Someone who is fluent in Tamil must look into the scholastic details of this. This translation is from the Sanskrit. Naturally, I would assume that Ganapati knew what he was doing when he translated it into Sanskrit, especially since Ramana's hand was also on the text, overseeing the Sanskrit translation and going over it in fine detail.

Both terms are fine and will do. If you want to exist, rather than shine, continue existing. If you like shining, rather than existing, continue shining. They amount to the same. If you want to both shine and exist, as Consciousness-Being, here, you can feel free to do so. (laughter)

Another Q.: All misidentification is in the mind. The misidentification with the body is only thought of in the mind.

N.: Yes, the misidentification with the body does not occur for the body. It is inert and quite innocent. So, in spiritual practice, we do not do anything to the body, for it has not caused any problem.

Q.: It is weird that we think that we are something objective, such as the body.

N.: Yes, that is weird. (laughter) I agree. Obviously, our nature is Consciousness, and we always exist and, also, always shine. (laughter) This is known even by those who say that they only exist. (laughter)

Another Q.: We could have Shine-ites and Exist-ites. (laughter)

N.: Two different sects? (laughter)

Previous Q.: So, the mind lays claim to the body as being itself. Then, there is the idea that the body is who I am, even though it is just a rotting thing.

N.: Yes, if the mind sees it as that, it quickly renounces it. The mind can be regarded as the illusory connection. The Maharshi says so in another verse. It is the illusory connection between the Reality of pure Consciousness and the inert body. It borrows the reality and identity from Being, or Consciousness, and ties it together with the form of the body, and this appears as the mind, or the individual being. This is the misidentification. The odd thing about the misidentification is, if we examine it, it disappears before us. We find that there is no mind or particularized being. There is no such connection. Breaking this illusory knot is simply a matter of inquiry. The more we inquire, the less of a knot there is.

Q.: If I have an ego, I have time. Is that right?

N.: Certainly, when there are thoughts appended to the ego, there is the notion of time. Generally, two thoughts are required to conceive of time.

Q.: Thoughts appear in multiplicity and in groups, inclusive of the ideas of being the body and the mind.

N.: Even if an entire herd of thoughts go wandering by, inquiry reveals that none of them are you. You are that which always exists and shines. You are always Consciousness. You are always Existence. You are never the conceived. You are never caught up in the conceiving. You are never the individualized conceiver. The triad is not for you.

Q.: Yes, this seems to be what the verse is about. Anything that is not space-like is not I, who have no form or shape.

N.: As the Maharshi instructs, simply by realizing that we are not the body, the All-pervading and the Ever-present, the Timeless and the Spaceless, is revealed as our own nature.

Considering yourself as a body is an attempt to squish the Eternal into a brief moment of time, called a lifetime, and to reduce the Infinite to a very small speck. It is just not true; nor is it really possible. That which is supposedly experienced from the "I am the body" position is like a short dream.

Q.: Yes, it is like a dream. Even, in illusion, it is momentary and does not last.

N.: Yes. First, there is the assumption of the individual. The individuality cannot stand alone, so it takes a form. That form is a body. From within the embodied position, time and space, even on a vast scale, are dreamed. Then, the illusion continues, and some small point in that vast scale of time and space is picked as our place and as our time. Then, we call that little speck, "us," and think that we are bound. Unravel it.

Q.: Attending satsang unravels it. It is questioned, and there is meditation upon the true nature. The illusion already has holes in it, and more holes are made in it. There is something deeper than the illusion.

N.: Go on inquiring, until you find that illusion is only holes and that it has no substance. Reality, which is deeper than the illusion, remains self-revealed.

देहात्मभावे ज्ञजडौ समाना -
वेकस्य देहे हृदि दीप्त आत्मा ।
आक्रम्य देहं च जगच्च पूर्णः
परस्य मेयं तनुमात्रमात्मा ॥ १७ ॥

dehātma-bhāve jña-jaḍau samānā-
v-ekasya dehe hṛdi dīpta ātmā |
ākramya dehaṁ ca jagac-ca pūrṇaḥ
parasya meyaṁ tanu-mātram-ātmā || 17 ||

17

In the body being the Self, the wise (the knower) and the ignorant (the unintelligent) are alike (the same).
(or: In the state of the body-self, the wise and the ignorant are the same).
For the one, in the body, in the heart, the Self illumines,
Including (encompassing, spreading over) the body and the universe, the Perfect Fullness.
For the other, the Self is discernible as only the body (the Self is only the measure of the body).

N.: There are two ways of interpreting the first line. In the body being the Self, with the idea or knowledge that the body is the Self, the wise and the ignorant are alike. Or, we can say, in the state of the body-self, meaning the state of the body, with its physical experience, its matter, and such, the wise and the ignorant are the same. Why does the Maharshi begin the line this way? He does so to eliminate any possible doubt that Self-Realization has anything to do with a bodily state or condition. Self-Realization is not a transformation of the body from one form into another form. Self-Realization does not rearrange the chemistry of the body, and it is not an anatomical change. The body and the bodily experience of the wise and the ignorant are the same, in terms of its pleasures, pains, itches, and other sensations. There is no particular difference, other than the differences that are found among all kinds of bodies. It is not that the realized have some sort of different kind of body or a different condition of the body, and one should not expect them to have different sensations or not to have sensations, as if they had an anesthetized body. Nothing of the sort should be the idea.

"For the one" means for the wise. "In the body, in the Heart, the Self illumines," signifies that, in the core of one's Being, and even in the body, it is the Self that provides the illumination. It is not that the Self is bound inside the body. Rather, within the body and the body's experience, what provides the illumination? The same Self that is in the Heart, that is, in the core of one's Being. It includes the body. It encompasses the body. It spreads over the body, and not just the body, but the entire universe. It is the Perfect Fullness. Even in the midst of the body, there is the bodiless Perfect Fullness. The Perfect Fullness cannot be a bodily state. It is purely a spiritual one, and that is the state of the real Self.

"For the other" means for the ignorant, the one who is not intelligently discerning what his nature is, "the Self is discernible only as the measure of the body." Such a one thinks of the body as himself, the bodily sensations as the proof of existence, and he determines everything about his identity by the measure, or the limitations, of the body. So, in relation to what the body does, he thinks, "I do." The body is born, and he thinks, "I am born." When the body perishes, he thinks, "I perish." Usually, after the perishing is over, he is not thinking that any more, for the time being, until it is time to think, "I am born again." This, the Maharshi declares, is the difference between them. The difference is in that which is regarded as the reality and the identity, or what is regarded as the Self. It is not a bodily difference, but a difference in knowledge, from misidentification to the true recognition of the all-encompassing, all-illumining Consciousness. Just as there is nothing mental about Self-inquiry and Self-Knowledge, so there is nothing sensory or physical about it.

Both the wise and the ignorant may say, "I," in reference to the body. Both may regard the Self as the body, but there is a distinction: "For the one, in the body, in the Heart, the Self illumines." In the previous verse, Sri Bhagavan said that the Self shines nowhere, but it shines everywhere. It also shines in the body, in the Heart, that is, the core of one's Being. This Self is all-illuminating, including, encompassing, and spreading over the body and the entire universe. The Perfect Fullness is the Self.

Everything is only in and of That, without exception and with no difference.

"For the other" means for the person who unintelligently engages in ignorance. For such a person, the Self is discernable only as the measure of the body, and the person thinks that what happens to the body happens to him and that the characteristics of the body are his characteristics. Such is the misidentification with the body. The one who knows the Truth knows that all, the body included, are only the Self, yet the Self is infinite and eternal.

A question was asked earlier about pains in the body. It is your identity that is the focus for freedom. Before knowing you are not the body and after, the pains of the body may be the same pains, and just so may it be with aches and itches. With clear Knowledge of the Self, there is no suffering due to the pains and such.

Q.: Do the ideas that I am a husband and I am son also stem from misidentification with the body?

N.: The entire personality, or personal identity, is squarely based on the cornerstone of the "I am the body" notion. Without that notion, you cannot be any of those characters.

Q.: So, this applies to all relationships?

N.: You know that you relate to another person only from the perspective of being the body. If not, there is blissful love and identity in Truth, but there is no relating. The wise will understand this.

अज्ञस्य विज्ञस्य च विश्वमस्ति
पूर्वस्य दृश्यं जगदेव सत्यम् ।
परस्य दृश्याश्रयभूतमेकं
सत्यं प्रपूर्णं प्रविभात्यरूपम् ॥ १८ ॥

ajñasya vijñasya ca viśvam-asti
pūrvasya dṛśyaṁ jagad-eva satyam ।

parasya dṛśyāśraya-bhūtam-ekaṁ
satyaṁ prapūrṇaṁ pravibhātyarūpam || 18 ||

18

For the ignorant and for the wise, the universe is (exists).
For the former, the seen universe, indeed (alone), is the real (the true).
For the other, the seen the resting place has become; the One,
The Real (the Truth), the completely Full, shines as formless.
(or: For the other, the One that has become the resting place of the seen,
The Real, the completely Full, the Formless, shines.)

N.: The slight variance in the verse in the last line depends on whether we consider the presentation of Knowledge as a description of that which has become all this or as a description of that into which all this dissolves. The essence is the same. It is the formless Reality, which is the perfect Fullness.

"For the ignorant and for the wise, the universe exists." In light of the previous instruction by Sri Ramana, what is meant by this declaration? "For the former," that is, for those who are ignorant of the Self, "the seen universe," which is the objective world, "indeed, is real" and "that, alone," is seen to be "true." The objective portion of one's experience is regarded as the reality, even though it is not actually the Reality at all.

"For the other, the seen the resting place has become" signifies that the seen has been absorbed in its substrate, which is naturally the nature of the Seer. "The One" refers to the indivisible Existence, and to "the Real" which is the Truth. It is the "completely Full," because its nature is Bliss, as well as Consciousness and Being. This shines formlessly. All of this creation is but the Uncreated. This entire universe is absorbed in, and abides as, only the Formless.

"For the other" means for the wise. "The One that has become the resting place of the seen'" means that the one

Existence, the one Reality, became the substrate upon which all the seen is displayed. That very One, which is the Real, which is the completely Full, and which is the Formless, shines. If the substrate is formless, such tells you something about what is upon it. What is real, perceived or misperceived as the universe, is actually the formless Existence, which is perfectly full, utterly One, and indivisible. It never becomes other than what it is.

Just as in the preceding verse, it is the Self that is the emphasis. The Self has never actually become embodied. It is unborn. So, verse seventeen deals with the Self, in terms of it being the Unborn, and verse eighteen deals with the nature of no-creation. The Maharshi is very thorough, though his verses are extremely pithy. The Unborn removes any false impression of identity; the Uncreated removes any false impression about what is real. The Knowledge of identity, Self-Knowledge, is the Knowledge of Reality, Sat-Darshanam, the vision of the Real, the vision of the True. The verses are arranged by Muruganar in this order because, if we are thoroughly disidentified from the body, the comprehension of what the universe is, or how there is actually only this perfectly full Existence and no universe as such, naturally follows. From clarity of Knowledge of one's identity, comes the Knowledge of Reality.

Both the ignorant and the wise regard all "this," the universe, as existing. In a state of ignorance, one thinks that the world is real as it is and that the seen objects are what is. This is the corollary of thinking that the body is what I am. Thus, the vision, or experience, of existence, is limited to the appearance of the body and the world. For the wise, however, it is different. "The One that has become the resting place of the seen" refers to the substratum, which is the abode of the seen. "The seen" is every objective thing. Where does everything that is objective exist? In what "space" does all "this" occur? In what "space" do even space and time occur? In what "abode" is all "this"?

First, you see that the seen rests upon a substratum or is encompassed in some space-like Existence. Then, you see the substratum, or Existence, as alone being the Reality. So, the Maharshi declares, "For the other, the One that has become the resting place of the seen, the Real, the completely Full, the Formless, shines." All the form of this universe is really only the formless Existence. The form of this universe appears only in this formless Existence. This Existence, being formless, is without differentiation. Therefore, where you may think that you perceive form, there is really only the Formless. Precisely where you think that you experience the universe, there is actually only the infinite, unformed Existence. This is the Vision of Truth.

Q.: You say, "the Unborn" and "the Uncreated."

N.: Yes. The point of these verses is not that the body is really existent or the universe is really existent. Sri Ramana begins by saying that they exist, or that they are the Self, for the wise and for the ignorant, but then he explains that, for the wise, the emphasis is on the Existence, or Being, and not on the form at all.

Q.: The Unborn and the Uncreated seem similar.

N.: It is the same Self, but, in the Maharshi's spiritual instruction, he explains it in terms of the body and the universe to reveal identity and reality. In both verses, however, the conclusion is that this one indivisible Existence, or the Self, alone is what is.

Q.: If one is unborn and one is uncreated, it seems that it would be hard to create something from what is unborn.

N.: It would be impossible. So, for those who have the realization of the Unborn, the realization of No-creation is identical with it. This truth is explained in two passages, one following the other, which is well arranged by Muruganar. Perhaps, you can see the reason for the order of the arrangement. The verses deal with one topic. Only if one thought he were dealing with separate topics would there be confusion, but that would be a division between jiva and jagat, which, Sri Ramana said, are parts of a triad that appears as a triad only so long as the ego is taken to be real. Jiva is the individual life, and jagat is the universe.

Q.: It seems that this point is extremely important. If this is not realized, even if ignorance dissolves, it can re-form somehow. If the unreal ignorance is not thoroughly and clearly seen as such, it appears to persist or form again.

N.: Why plan for that possibility? (laughter) Rather than anticipate that ignorance will not be entirely destroyed, be thorough in the Knowledge of who you are, in which there is no possibility of ignorance, no you, and no world, which is just perfect Fullness, and which is of the nature of Being-Consciousness. That is what you are; That is all that there is.

On the level of phenomena, your body will be as before; likewise the universe. It is not that the realized have different bodily sensations; nor do they experience different objects in the world. They see, at all times, the Existence of the Self, which, alone, is actually there.

Q.: That is a big difference.

N.: It is the difference between the unreal and the Real, darkness and Light, death and immortality, suffering and ultimate Bliss. Sri Bhagavan treats this as very matter of fact because it is the Reality.

Another Q.: Would you read the verse one more time, Nome? Now that you have explained the verse, I am curious to hear the verse again from a deeper understanding.

N.: (reads the English translation of the verse again) The verse follows a certain order of inquiry, or depth of experience. In wisdom, you see that only One is the substratum, the all-encompassing basis for all that appears as if with form. For the entire universe, it is the resting place. Not only is it the resting place, but it is the Reality.

First, there is the substrate and that which rests upon it. Then, the substrate is the Real, which means that whatever rests upon it has been absorbed in it or has been negated as unreal. Finally, it is the completely Full, because its nature is Being-Consciousness-Bliss. Being completely full, there is no room for anything else in addition to the Formless. That which was apparently created has been returned, through Knowledge only, to its innate, uncreated state. That shines as formless.

Q.: As aspirants clarify their nature, what was just imparted becomes a fact for them.

N.: You may start from the position of thinking the universe to be real, but, when you realize that something else is real upon which it rests, this is the dawn of wisdom. Then, having seen it as the resting place, the place where the entire universe is, outside of which there is nothing, you discover that that is actually the Reality. It is not part of the reality, as if there were a substrate and a surface part of reality. It is the Real. Not only is it the Real, but it is completely full. It is perfect. Therein lies your Bliss. It is utterly formless. With no birth and no creation, it shines, and this is called "Enlightenment."

Q.: Everything is returned to the right place, which is the source. There is no longer any externalization, whether it is of happiness or reality.

N.: There is no external projection. As described in these two verses, both the ignorant and the wise regard the body as the Self, and both regard the universe as real. What, though, is meant by "real" and what is meant by the "Self" is understood differently. One views the self as measured by the body, and one views the Self as being the body and everything else and infinite and eternal. One views the world as if that alone were real, and what is formless as if nonexistent. The other sees the Reality as formless, and knows that this entire universe is only That.

Q.: That's a big difference!

Another Q.: It seems as though all of these errors of ignorance rest on some kind of basic, imagined motivation to objectify. I have been thinking a lot about the nature of the nonobjective. Since it is difficult to make an object out of the nonobjective, this seems to be a form of meditation that, on the one hand should be fruitful, yet, in the meantime, seems difficult.

N.: Where is the difficulty?

Q.: I am trying to objectify what cannot be objectified, and the attempt falls apart.

N.: That which can never be made into an object is you, yourself. You are the closest thing to yourself. You are so close that there is no distance. How could it be difficult to meditate on your own nature?

Q.: If I am looking for it to be something that I can perceive objectively as a form by the senses.

N.: That would not be your Self. We are told by Sri Bhagavan that we should meditate upon the Self by means of inquiry to find the nature of the Self and not to form ideas about it or to search with the eyes and ears for it.

Q.: It seems that anything else, other than the meditation on this particular tendency to objectify, is a bypath.

N.: What motivates the tendency?

Q.: The tendency to what?

N.: The one you just described: the tendency to objectify.

Q.: The search for happiness.

N.: Why are you searching for happiness?

Q.: I hear that it is because it is the intuition that it is who I am.

N.: Do you know that?

Q.: I know it, and I don't know it.

N.: Hmm. This sounds like the *Kena Upanishad.* (laughter) You are either incredibly deep, or you have really missed the boat. (laughter)

Q.: My attempts to cease to objectify, to cease having even the desire to objectify, assume that to objectify can provide any form of happiness. I am trying to look there.

N.: Are you trying to obtain your happiness through such objectification?

Q.: I am trying to see that happiness is not objectifiable.

N.: Why do you want to see that?

Q.: Because I intuit that the real "I" is what I am looking for.

N.: Is that happiness?

Q.: On the basis of those I trust, it is full.

N.: But what are you looking for? Yes, it has been said that it is completely full, but why are you looking?

Q.: Why am I looking?

N.: Yes. There must be a reason for your searching.

Q.: Discontent with the way reality feels.

N.: Without, at the moment, delving into what you regard as real, examine the way it feels. You are unhappy with it, which means that you must know that you are meant to be happy.

Q.: Yes.

N.: So, happiness must be what is right for you and what is natural for you.

Q.: That is true. Perhaps, I just made a foolish mistake and listened to the wrong people, but I don't think this is the case.

N.: Even if all of them were mistaken, you would still be unhappy with your unhappiness, wouldn't you? Your search for happiness did not start when some spiritual talk that you may have heard or some spiritual book that you may have read decades ago said that the search for happiness should be turned inward or something similar. You were already searching, were you not? So, no one actually informed you of this. The search for happiness is self-generated. You generate the search yourself. Why do you do so?

Q.: The assumption is that I am supposed to be happy.

N.: You cannot get away from that assumption, can you?

Q.: No.

N.: You really cannot turn off the search for happiness. You can only turn it in different directions, but you cannot turn it off. You can satisfy it, but you cannot turn it off. Now, how are you going to satisfy it?

Q.: I could give up looking for happiness as something objective, whether it is subtle or gross.

N.: Will that help you find it within?

Q.: Sri Bhagavan says that, if one stops looking for happiness in the unreal, he returns to Reality, which is there all along.

N.: So, the Reality, which is simultaneously happiness, presently exists. It is there all along and is within you. It is your very nature, and if you relinquish the imagination, or the ignorance, that causes you to look elsewhere for what is actually you, what is truly your own, this detachment, or wisdom, will yield the desired result.

Q.: It is not complicated. Why should I complicate it so?

N.: Why do you not first find the happiness, and, later, you can deal with the question of why you complicate it?

Q.: I occasionally ask myself, why, after pursuing these descriptions of Nonduality for so long, I do not have samadhi experiences, for example, which would be very motivating.

N.: If you expect samadhi to come over you as if it were from outside, that would be the same objectifying tendency, would it not? If you turn within, in search of the Bliss of your own Being, giving up the objective outlook, which is giving up the misidentification with the body and other objects, your own nature will shine as perpetual samadhi.

Q.: So, it is simply a matter of giving up misconceptions and misidentifications. That is all there is to it.

N.: If the illusion is dispensed with, the Reality shines, because it exists.

Q.: Those thoughts about samadhi are definitely objectifying tendencies.

N.: You will be very happy to know that, in samadhi, those thoughts do not exist (laughter).

Q.: Yes.

N.: Why do you not have some samadhi right now? (laughter)

(Silence)

N.: For the Sat-darshanam, or the seeing of Reality, the revelation of Truth, the Maharshi has instructed us, again and again, in the best course to take, which is abidance as the egoless Self. With abidance as the egoless Self, all questions are answered, all doubts are resolved, and all differences are dissolved. All confusion and perplexity, all ignorance and all bondage, stem from this ego-conception. According to the attributes ascribed to the ego, such as being the body, the perplexities manifest. All that is needed for the blissful revelation of the Truth, for Truth to know itself, for being in the Knowledge of Being, is abandonment of the ego-notion. Abandonment of the ego-notion also means relinquishment of its attendant definitions. If the ego-notion is abandoned, the Self knows itself by its own Light. The very idea that you are something other than the Self is to be questioned, inquired into, and, thereby, destroyed. This brings the highest good. Let us dive into the Maharshi's instructions.

विधेः प्रयत्नस्य च कोऽपि वाद -
स्तयोर्द्वयोर्मूलमजानतां स्यात् ।
विधेः प्रयत्नस्य च मूलवस्तु
सञ्जानतां नैव विधिर्न यत्नः ॥ १९ ॥

vidheḥ prayatnasya ca ko'pi vāda-
s-tayor-dvayor-mūlam-ajānatāṁ syāt |
vidheḥ prayatnasya ca mūla-vastu
sañjānatāṁ naiva vidhir-na yatnaḥ || 19 ||

19

The talk (controversy) of fate and of effort (striving) shall be for
Them who do not know the root of these two.
For those who know well the root thing of fate and effort,
There are not, indeed, fate or one's own activity (free will).

N.: There are multiple understandings conveyed in this one verse. To start with, it is natural for a person to contemplate whether the directions of the events and experiences that pour through life are due to one's own effort or because they were meant to happen that way. If we consider them as meant to happen that way, we regard that as fate or divine dispensation, and, if we think it is all of our own doing, we say that it is our own free will or our own activity.

Some explanations combine these, such as the expedient teaching given in the earlier parts of *Yoga Vasistha*, in which it is said that the fate that seems to be unbreakable is one's own doing from the past. One's own will in the past manufactures the fate, which then seems unbreakable, at least in terms of prarabdha karma, which pertains to the events of this life.

The Maharshi points out that there is a root for these two views, upon which both views depend. Natarajan has interpreted this root as the individual: someone to have fate, someone to have his own effort or free will, and someone for whom occur the experiences that one is trying to explain. If there is not the individual, there are no experiences occurring to anyone, and what is there to explain?

The basis of the root of the individual is Existence, which is the one Substrate, or Root, of all. The Existence does not come about due to one's own efforts. Existence is not determined by fate, as if it were in a procession of events. It is not an event. It is of a nature that is beyond such considerations.

Sri Ramana says, "For those who know well the root thing of fate and effort," that is, who know well that the individual does not exist and that there is only the timeless, real Being. For that which is timeless and not individualized, there can be no fate or its opposite. Therefore, Sri Bhagavan declares, "There are not, indeed, fate or one's own activity." We think of our "own activity," as long as we have the conception of "I," and that "I" is coupled with the instruments of the mind and the body. If you are not the body, can you have your own activity? If you are not the body, through what experiences are you going, or what is occurring to you?

The same principles elucidated in this verse apply to one's own spiritual practice. We can consider whether accomplishment in one's spiritual practice is due to one's own effort, one's own activity, or if it is destined to be so and divinely ordained? The Maharshi says that the consideration of either possibility is only so long as the root is not known. If the view is that it is divinely ordained to succeed or to fail, for whom is it ordained?

If the view is that it is one's own effort, how can one's own effort be applied to the Realization of Being, which is completely without the ego, the mind, and the body?

Regardless of which side we would choose, if we would not examine the root, the view would be incorrect and unclear. If we were to think that real Being, which is the real Self, is within the domain of the ego's decision and that the ego has the power to be in the state of the Self or to be otherwise, conceiving the idea of "my mind, my ego, determines my Existence," such would be foolish. It would be due to lack of inquiry. If, on the other hand, we were to think that "the realization of my Being is divinely ordained, or according to fate, so I have no say in this," such would be a view of Realization as an external event. This view would leave the ego solidly intact. The idea of, "If you are destined to realize, you do, and, if you are not so destined, you will not," is ridiculous. It shows no understanding of Realization and no understanding of the nonexistence of the ego.

The Maharshi says that we should "know well the root." If we know the root of any duality, including this one, the duality vanishes. Dualism is always a product of ignorance, an obscuration of what the real Existence is. The verse says, "mula vastu," "the root thing." "Thing" is a vague term. It can signify the ego, or it can mean the Real Thing.

At the root of every duality is the ego, the "I"-notion. At the root of the duality of what happens to "me," is, obviously, that "me." If there is no such entity, who would be destined for what, and how could there be "one's own activity"? Activity of whom? Being, the Self, ever is. It is not created by self-effort. It is not a result of fate. It is not a result of a combination of these, such as the fate produced by one's own self-effort. The Self is pure Existence, and, we cannot say that the Knowledge of it is by fate or by one's own activity. Knowledge is not an activity and is not a result of an activity.

Whether you are considering the direction of your spiritual practice or you are considering the totality of all the events that supposedly make up a lifetime, it is best to be free of both views. In various scriptures, for purposes of instruction, both views are employed. In the Maharshi's instruction to the

Mother, Azhagammal (Alagammal), at Pavazhakunru Temple (Pavalakunru), he says, "The Creator, remaining everywhere, makes each one play his role in life according to the unfolding of the divine law. That which is not destined will not happen despite every effort. What is destined is bound to happen. This is certain. Therefore, the best course is to remain silent." (translation of A. R. Natarajan). The same response to her appears in the biographies of Sri Ramana as, "The Ordainer controls the fate of souls in accordance with their prarabdha karma. Whatever is destined not to happen will not happen, try as you may. Whatever is destined to happen will happen, do what you may to prevent it. This is certain. The best course, therefore, is to remain silent." How does this instruction correlate to the present verse? How is any perceived disparity reconciled? Consider the final line: "The best course, therefore, is to remain silent." Silence is egoless, "I"-less.

Effort was recommended by the Maharshi when he said that one should strive to inquire. *Yoga Vasistha* lays emphasis on self-effort and proclaims that effort will bring good results. The *Gita* also describes such. Other texts declare that everything is by divine command. For what purpose are these spiritual instructions? The purpose is to pull the ego out of the picture. Why is there the recommendation of self-effort? It is because every effort should be made to dissolve the ego-notion and to get to the root. Is getting to the root our fate? Are we destined to do so? Or, do we need to put in our own effort to do so? We should think in neither manner, and we should simply know ourselves, which is the goal of all those other expedient teachings. Self-Knowledge is the goal. If we know ourselves, we are egoless. We are not an entity. For that which is not an entity, there are neither events nor a procession of events, neither experiences nor any need to explain them. By analogy, the rope exists, there is no snake, no life or wriggling of the snake, and no explanation needed as to whether the snake's wriggling happens by its own effort or because it is made to do so.

Observing one's experience, generally, one is led to draw one conclusion or another: that all things and all experiences unfold by divine ordainment or that experiences are shaped by one's own will power, or effort. If we think that we shape them by our own effort, of course, there are the efforts of others, as well. The collection of all the efforts of all the jivas is then considered to make up the presently appearing experiences or circumstances. How all those efforts become coordinated must involve some divine intelligence.

Some say that what is called divinely ordained "fate" is only the karma, one's own doing, from the past, whether such is apprehended now or not. Karma is the cause. The cause being seen now or not, the effect is obvious to the experiencer. The divine ordainment of God is simply the bestowal of the fruits of karma at the appropriate time that is best for all the jivas.

Examine your own experience. Can you say that your experience is created by your own efforts, or can you say that your experience is in a much greater stream of a greater power that ordains everything? If there is a power that ordains, it ordains everything, including one's own efforts.

The potential difficulty for the aspirant arises in that, if he feels everything happens by destiny, he will not make efforts for his own Self-Realization. So, he may stagnate, saying, "What can I do?" To such aspirants, wise sages and the scriptures advise self-effort. Such scriptures state that the appearance of divine fate is nothing more that the effect of one's own previous efforts, even if one is not aware of such.

Of course, if one relies on one's own will power and effort, it does not take long to be humbled and to realize that what occurs, that which he experiences, and, indeed, this whole universe unfolds on a much greater scale than one's own personal effort.

The Maharshi reveals that both views are only so long as we do not know the root of these two. His instruction is addressed to those who seek Liberation through the highest Knowledge of the Self. The advice is addressed to those who are ardent in their inquiry to know the Truth of the Self, and who, in the course of this inquiry, ponder what the cause of all experience is. What is all this? What is its nature? Why is it the way that it appears? Sri Bhagavan says that one needs to know the root.

Sri Ramana says, "mula," which means "root," or "source." That the root is God may be one interpretation. If the root is God, all of one's efforts, without exception and even to the smallest degree, are determined by that same God that is said to be in charge of fate or destiny. If we seek to know the answer in terms of what power is at work, we say that the source, or the root, is God. If we accept that there is God, this God must be omnipotent, and, if God is all-powerful, there is no scope for another's power.

Even if one does not accept that there is God, such is also within God's power, and the denial of such power is merely further proof of the very same power. If everything occurs only by the power of that one God, nothing is outside it. There is no room for that which is imagined to be personal or for the ego. No scope for the ego remains. That view in which the ego is entirely cut out is in accord with Truth. Thus, the source Reality of fate and of one's own effort is only one.

If one contemplates the two viewpoints and asks if this is fate or due to his own efforts and what is the reason for either, he could address the root, or the source, considering it to be the individuality, the jiva, who can be involved in either as the one whom destiny has affected or the one whose own efforts are being reaped in the form of karma. If we examine the root, we find it missing. In the ego's nonexistence, how can we speak of fate? How can we speak of free will, or one's own activity? Whose would it be? In this way, also, there is no scope for the ego.

"Those who know well the root thing of fate and effort," know that God is all, in all, at all times, and so there is no ego; or they are only the Self, and there is no ego to be involved in any of this.

"For those who know well the root thing of fate and effort, there are not, indeed, fate or one's own activity (free will)." In light of this, consider what becomes of "your life"? It vanishes. If neither a "you" nor "your life" are any longer imagined, where is suffering? Where is bondage? Where is limitation? Would anyone who understands the significance of this verse ever again have the doubt, "Oh! Why is this happening to me?" The "me" is excluded, and the doubt is set at rest.

Q.: When I inquire deeply, the experience becomes space-like and peaceful. There is also a wave of bliss, but it seems to come to someone. Someone seems to experience the bliss, which makes me question if that is really Bliss or if that is just a nice state of mind. After the experience is not a bad state, for it is still very peaceful. Later, there is a very intense experience of bliss. There is nobody left to experience it, at some point, but there still is somebody who knows about it.

N.: As "he" forms again, does the wave of bliss recede?

Q.: Yes, and he is left saying, "That was great!"

N.: When he starts to report on it, does the bliss increase or decrease?

Q.: It decreases. Then, there is this idea of what happened.

N.: And when it becomes a memory, does the bliss increase or decrease?

Q.: The answer is obvious now. It is like the question, "Who is buried in General Grant's tomb?" (laughter)

N.: The formation of an ego apparently brings the experience to a conclusion. It is not Bliss that comes and goes. It is the "I"-notion that comes and goes. Now, you think of Bliss as the wave and you, as an ego or experiencer, as the solid shore. It might be better to think that the Bliss is the shore and that there are mere "I"-waves rising and falling. When you form the notion of the individual, the Bliss seems to diminish. It becomes obscured. It does not really go away, but it becomes obscured in your experience. When you then set the Bliss as an object in relation to that "I" and report on it to yourself in your mind, the Bliss substantially reduces. That is, further limitations are imposed upon it.

First, the notion of "I" arises. Then, the experience is relegated to the objective sphere, even though Bliss is really the subject, who is of the nature of Consciousness. The Bliss, of the nature of Consciousness, which is your own Being, is relegated to the position of being objective. Once it becomes objective, it falls to the past and becomes a memory. The only further stage of obscuration would be forgetfulness. "I," an "object," "memory," and "forgetfulness" are layers of limitation. In forgetfulness, multiplicity is projected in illusion, and one wonders whether that experience really happened or not, with doubts of whether it was real or just imagined, even though, in the experience, there was no imagining at all. In the deep experience, one's own activity, or one's own effort, has dissolved.

Q.: The experience is unmistakable. There is no questioning or wondering occurring at that point.

N.: One kind of questioning would actually deepen the bliss: "Who am I?" because it would dissolve the remaining seed of the individual who later attempts to stand apart from the experience to look at it. That questioning, which is of a nature of continuous Knowledge, precludes the rising of the "I"-notion. Consequently, it precludes the objectifying of the experience. So, experiential Knowledge would be timelessly present and would not be relegated to the past. Since Bliss would be identical with your own Being, by virtue of Self-Knowledge due to inquiry, you could not forget it, any more than you could forget your own Existence.

Q.: I can see the point in the evolution of this wave. As soon as it starts to appear like a wave, that should be the first indication that there is somebody surfing it or experiencing it.

N.: One can tell that this is Santa Cruz. (laughter) [ed.: Surfing is a popular water sport in Santa Cruz.]

Q.: It is like being caught up in a wave, riding it for a while, and, then, the wave peters out, and I swim back out and look for another wave.

N.: Maybe you should take up snorkeling and remain submerged. (laughter)

Q.: Continuous bliss. No waves. It looks like a wave as soon as there is an idea that there is somebody in Bliss.

N.: Yes, but you need not time the inquiry for the wave. (laughter)

Q.: I sense that is when the objectification must start. There is some idea that bliss is occurring, because it must be occurring for someone.

N. When there is the notion of "I," Bliss will be seen as an occurrence, rather than the abiding Being. It will be considered as an event that occurs, rather than That which exists. It will be considered as something objective that happens to you, rather than actually being your Being. In the scope of considering delusion, it is the "I" that is rising, and not the Bliss. When Sankara speaks of "waves of Bliss" in some of his stotrams, he is referring to the utter inundation of Bliss upon Bliss in one's experience. He does not mean that it is something that comes and goes.

Q.: That was my misinterpretation.

N.: Bliss does not come and go; the ego-"I" comes and goes.

Q.: Yes. I have this notion of an individual that is being "blissed." I am mistaking that for Bliss, itself.

N.: Bliss, itself, is of the nature of Being. The Maharshi says that if it comes and goes, that is not actually Bliss or Ananda. That which comes and goes is not what the scriptures refer to as "Bliss." The very same scriptures, such as the Upanishad-s, and the Maharshi's own instruction, point out that all happiness is really of one kind. So, how do we reconcile the two statements? Happiness, in whatever way it appears, is of one kind, and, if it comes and goes, that is not the real Bliss. What is meant by "Bliss" is steady and identical with Being. If it comes and goes, the experience of the limitations superimposed upon the Bliss is not real. The bliss, or the happiness, you experience is of the real essence. It is the limitations that are false. The inquiry should not stop until there is no coming and going of Bliss. Bliss is identical with Being and Consciousness. When you think that bliss is receding or disappearing, it means that misidentification is occurring. It is the equivalent of saying that your Being is diminishing, or that your Consciousness is going elsewhere, but Consciousness does not go elsewhere, and Being does not cease to exist. Being does not increase and diminish. Sat-Chit-Ananda, Being-Consciousness-Bliss, is declared, again and again, to be Brahman. It is not that two-thirds of Brahman remain, and one-third of the Self is lopped off and lost on the beach somewhere. (laughter)

Wherever there is Being and whenever there is Consciousness, there is Bliss. As Being-Consciousness is everywhere at all times, so, too, is Bliss. Limitations are imagined, and the Self is thought to be an ego. Consciousness is thought to be a mind, the individual experiencer, and Bliss is thought to be either elsewhere or diminishing and increasing, as if going up and down in waves. All that is needed to deepen and establish the experience of Bliss as permanent is continuous Knowledge of your Self. For this purpose, there is inquiry. Since inquiry is not mental in character, it offers no interruption, even in the midst of the deepest experiences of Bliss. Far from interrupting, it deepens and shows the permanence of Bliss. It shows how innate Bliss is. It swallows up any remaining seeds of differentiation. So, surf's up! (laughter)

Q.: I am going to try the submerging approach and stay out of the stormy seas. (laughter)

Another Q.: With regard to prarabdha karma and will, and the instruction to his mother by Sri Ramana regarding this, it seems that the term "will" indicates two different meanings. One means to apply will and effort through inquiry for Self-Realization. The second is the conventional meaning of the word, relating to the assumed ego's presumed ability to choose and bring about outcomes.

N.: When we speak of will in spiritual practice, it is for the purpose of harnessing the desire for Liberation to pour it into right discrimination or Self-inquiry. When we speak of prarabdha, or of fate or of fruits of karma, being ordained by the Supreme Lord, it is to bring about a state of detachment in the aspirant, and, from there, the knowledge that the world is unreal. When we realize that the world is unreal and that there is no one for whom it could be, the question of prarabdha karma, fate, or divine destiny versus one's own activity or one's own effort does not make sense anymore.

Q.: There seem to be two different kinds of meditation. In one, the mind has gone outward and is worrying about something that has occurred. The meditation, then, is the recognition that all is due to prarabdha karma and is not determined by me.

The other meditation, or possibility, seems more spiritual to me in that one's intention is to realize the Truth.

N.: It is not more spiritual. It serves a different purpose. One is to bring about your own discrimination, to intensify your inquiry, to make the flame of the desire for Liberation leap high, and to remind you of the spiritual responsibility and the purpose of life. The other serves the purpose of bringing about a greater sense of surrender, certainty in detachment from the world, and to rid oneself of the "I am the doer," "I am the actor," and "I am the experiencer," conceptions. An aspirant can have both, applying the view of fate to all the outer events, while applying the self-effort to the interior meditation. Although apparently contrary explanations, the result would not be contradictory at all. This approach, also, brings about the Realization that is world-transcending, body-transcending, and ego-transcending.

Q.: As one goes deeper into one's Self, as the Maharshi instructs, these distinctions become totally irrelevant.

N.: They would have to be for some individual. Examination of the individual is getting to the root. When you examine the individual, all that you find is the real Existence. The same real Existence that is "all this," is utterly transcendent of "all this." In that view, how can we speak of "my own activity" or "this is destined to happen?"

Q.: From what I have now understood, teachings of prarabdha karma and of self-effort serve the purpose of turning the mind inward. The essence of self-effort always comes from the Reality.

N.: Certainly, the divine ordination, or fate, of everything must come from the same Reality, too. If we know the root, we annihilate the individual misconception and arrive at the Reality. The explanations are for serving a particular spiritual purpose and to bring about depth of practice. They are not only ways of coaxing the aspirant into the right state. They can be considered apt and complete descriptions, or explanations, of the experience that one is trying to comprehend, at its own level.

Q.: I do not understand.

N.: If we assume that there is a world, experiences, a lifetime, etc., the descriptions of divine fate or self-effort go a very long way, in a very complete fashion, to explain why things appear as they do. If we follow the Maharshi's deeper instruction and inquire, "For whom do they appear?" those explanations are no longer needed, because the appearance has ceased to exist. If there is appearance, those explanations are tried and true and complete. That is why you find them in the sastras. If, though, there is no appearance to begin with, who would need to bother to explain such things?

Q.: That is at a high level. These meditations can be at different levels. At the highest level, they serve a great purpose to drive one's mind inward.

N.: The Maharshi's explanation in this verse does not ridicule the purpose served by such explanations or meditations on them. This, though, is Sat-darshanam, the vision of Reality, the seeing of Truth. The seeing of Truth is naturally egoless, and, in it, the world-view, the seeing of the world, or the objective view has been completely abandoned. The purpose that the expedient teachings were meant to fulfill is already fulfilled in the egoless Realization. There is no need to explain the events in a world that was never created. There is no need to explain who has the power over the individual's life, when the individual, himself, is not there.

Another Q.: From the Maharshi's standpoint, there are not any aspirants. One must take the position of an aspirant to continue with the questioning. There is none. Who is it?

N.: Yes. The Maharshi's teaching tends to put an end to everything (laughter). The real Self remains.

Q.: I have to fight to hang on to that guy! (laughter)

N.: Yes, but Sri Ramana is endowed with this divine Brahman-weapon. It destroys everything. If you try to hold something, the holder, himself, is vaporized. (laughter)

Another Q.: When one reflects, meditates, and takes the view of which the Maharshi speaks, "God is all in all." If one's experience is not continuously God, one needs to take responsibility. I must see where I am misidentifying and what is the cause of my suffering.

N.: In spiritual practice, you may take this view that all the phenomenal things take place by God's power and the spiritual responsibility is your own effort. In this verse, the Maharshi says that you should question the individual for whom these viewpoints apply. If we truly accept that God is, as God is, there is no room for anyone or anything else. Such a state, alone, is rightly called surrender. There is no scope for the ego. Where there is no scope for the ego, there is no possibility of a personal problem, a misidentification, an attachment, etc. Or, inquire, and realize that there is no one to have such things. That which is called God is only the Self. For the Self, nothing has ever come to be. Where nothing has come to be, how could there be this talk of self-effort and fate?

Another Q.: The self-effort applies if there is a separation. Meditation is to be applied to this ego that has intervened to see that it has not really intervened and there is really a deeper power.

N.: Yes. Then, self-effort should be applied. What is the root of that self-effort's power?

Q.: The same power that enables me to notice that.

N.: Is it not rooted in the Self, which is the same as the egoless-God? Your inquiry to know your Self does not come from your own will power. It does not come from somewhere else. The very ideas of another power and your own power are not true. The very notions of separation, division, and some starting point for delusion are false. See if such things even exist.

Q.: To say to oneself that one should not apply effort would seem to be a misinterpretation of the verse.

N.: Yes, that would be a misinterpretation of the significance of saying that everything is by the power of God. If everything is by the power of God, one's own self-effort is part of that power. If room is given for the ego, the duality, which consists of the two extremes of the arrogance of ego-power and the indolence of thinking that there is nothing one can do about it, reigns in the mind. Both are delusional.

Q.: The verse says that there is no option.

N.: He has offered no option. As long as you think of fate or free will, there is an option. It is not said that you cannot use them constructively, to a certain extent, in the mind, but this is Sat-darshanam, the revelation of Reality. He has already dismissed the world, the body, and the ego in the previous verses. So, what can be involved in this fate or free will? He directs us to the source. Look at the root. There must be someone for whom these things are. What is the nature of that someone? If that someone is not a "someone" at all, but just pure, infinite Existence, or God, the division between fate and self-effort is utterly dissolved.

Q.: It goes directly to the heart.

N.: You remain and abide as the solitary Existence. All the confusion, such as the duality here being dismissed, stems from the ego-notion. It is the idea of existing as an individual entity. Once there is the notion, "I am an individual entity," the confusion of attempting to determine which part of this is God's and which part of this is "mine" arises. From there, all kinds of absurdities can proceed.

Q.: Here, Bhagavan has obliterated that very notion.

N.: Yes. He says, "For those who know well the root thing." He causes us to direct ourselves to the root, or source. Who is there? Whose life? Whose experience? What is happening to whom?

यदीशितुर्वीक्षणमीक्षितार -
मवीक्ष्य तन्मानसिकेक्षणं स्यात्।
न द्रष्टुरन्यः परमो हि तस्य
वीक्षा स्वमूले प्रविलीय निष्ठा ॥ २० ॥

yad-īśitur-vīkṣaṇam-īkṣitāra-
m-avīkṣya tan-mānasikekṣaṇaṁ syāt |
na draṣṭur-anyaḥ paramo hi tasya
vīkṣā svamūle pravilīya niṣṭhā || 20 ||

20

That seeing of the Lord [that is] the seer
Not seeing, that shall be mental seeing.
Not other than the seer is the Supreme, indeed. Of Him
The seeing is in one's own source (root) the absorption (lit., having been absorbed, dissolved) and abidance.

N.: How can there be the seeing of God without seeing one's Self? The Self is the Reality and not a part of the Reality. It is the one Reality. If we see anything else without actually seeing the Self as it is, such is just a mental image.

Sri Ramana dismisses all of the triad of the universe, the individual, and God as being based upon the ego. Showing the unreality of the world, he traces it to the "I," apparently a jiva, and, then, going to the root of that jiva, the jivahood is destroyed. The individuality is relinquished, and the pure Existence remains. That, alone, is this entire universe, and That is actually worldless.

Now, a similar approach is revealed with the experience of God. Whatever be the experience, or "seeing," of God, whether with form or apparently abstract and without form, unless there is the Knowledge of one's Self, what does one really know of God? Just as the jagat, or universe, depends on the view of the individual, likewise is the view of Iswara, the Lord, or Para, the Supreme. Even if we think of the Supreme Self, the view and experience of it are entirely dependent on the definition ascribed to the viewer, which is the apparent individual, or jiva. If the jiva loses his jiva-hood, if the individual loses his individuality, which is brought about by inquiring "Who am I?", God is seen, for, then, God is seen with God's own Eye, which is the true, clear view. If God sees God, there is no mistake.

If the individual sees God, there is room for a mistake. Due to a superimposition of limitations, people think of God in terms of human conception, rather than knowing God as God is. If we think of the Supreme, the Lord, how do we think of That? What do we think we know of That? If we think of That as a divine will that ordains all things, that is a human conception that assumes that God sees a world, that God dwells in such duality, that God has a will, and, maybe, occasionally, that will is frustrated. Then, there is a more powerful will, and so forth and so on. Those are human conceptions.

If we think of God as distinct from ourselves, perhaps even as formless but distinct from ourselves, that is a human conception based on the idea that we are distinct. Without seeing the absence of our own differentiation, we will imagine differentiation for God. If we think of God as the foundation of all, it is because we view ourselves in terms of something built upon a foundation. Likewise is it for any other conception of God. In any experience of God, the experience, expansive or constricted, is determined according to the limitations imposed upon the experiencer. Those limitations are the definitions with which one misidentifies.

So, the Maharshi declares that, without seeing the seer, it is just mental seeing. The mind is involved. If the mind is involved, that is not True Knowledge. If there is no mind existing, that is True Knowledge.

Thus, the Maharshi proclaims, "Not other than the seer is the Supreme, indeed." God is the Self. The Self is not an individual. The Self alone is the real seer, which is pure Consciousness. "Of Him the seeing," which is the seeing of God, "is in one's own source (root), the absorption and abidance." To inquire as to who you are is to gain such absorption. The false notion of individuality is effaced, and all the limitations, or definitions, connected with that individuality are similarly effaced. He says "absorption" because this is a description of what happens to one's identity. There is destruction of the unreal, and the very sense of identity, of existing, is absorbed, as Ribhu says, "In That, itself, as That, itself." When there is no possibility of an alternative state, such is steady abidance.

When do we find that there is no alternative state possible? The answer is in the same absorption. It is the same inquiry. If there is "I," there is the possibility of another state. If, in truth, there is no "I," there is no multiplicity of states. The Self is the One State that ever is. There can be no other states. If the "I" arises, there are as many states as that "I" imagines. If the "I" has never actually come to be, there are no states, and there is just the State of God, or the State of the Self. To know that beyond doubt, with the utmost certainty, in its self-evident luminosity, is the seeing of God, or the vision of Truth.

If we attempt to see God, however the Lord is conceived, without seeing the seer, who is supposed to see the Lord, this, Sri Bhagavan says, is only "mental seeing." It is a mental vision. The seer must be known, if God is to know God with God's own eye. If you want to know the Absolute, however the Absolute is conceived, it is still just mental seeing, unless you actually inquire into the nature of the seer. If you want to see the Supreme, you must make your vision nonobjective.

That which is referred to as the Absolute, God, the Lord, Brahman, Siva, the Self, the Supreme Self, and by so many other names can never be an object. If you treat it as an object, you will have a mental vision of it. According to the definition of the seer, the mental vision may have more or less form, but it is still just mental seeing, unless you see the seer.

"Not other than the Seer, is the Supreme, indeed." The Self that you are attempting to realize when you inquire is the very nature of the inquirer. Inquire into the nature of the inquirer. If you want to see God, you must see the seer. You must know the seer for who the seer really is, which is not a body, not the senses, not the prana, not the mind, not any thing whatsoever, and not even any kind of individual. The real seer is the infinite Eye of unformed, unborn Consciousness.

"The seeing is in one's own source (root) the absorption and abidance." The seer, the seen, and the seeing are identical in the Vision of God, or the Realization of the Self. There is no differentiation, such as a seer, seeing, and seen or a knower, the knowing, and the known. They appear only in the realm of imagined differentiation. If the seer is not known, but is regarded as individualized, the seen will correspond, in a mirror-like fashion, to the attributes of the seer. We see God according to the conception we have of ourselves. If we want to see God with God's own Eye, we must know ourselves with our own Consciousness.

Where there are two, there is a relation of knowing, that is, a knower that knows something known. In Nonduality, the seer and the seen are identical. So, what composes the seeing? What is the knowing in Self-Knowledge? It is only Being. It is not thinking, remembering, or knowing in the commonly understood manner. In the real Vision of God, God is only Being, the one who sees is only Being, and the seeing, or the knowing, is only Being.

Another Q.: My question relates to the reference to the mental imagery of God. Is that indicative of anything that is not the Absolute?

N.: The interpretation just offered of the present verse is that anything other than absolute Consciousness is a mental image. It may also be interpreted as pertaining to visions of Deities, of God, in one form or another. Such forms may be distinct, as the form in which God or the Gods are represented, or more abstract, as light, space, Om, and such. All of them are still within the context of the mind. I have interpreted the verse to mean that any conception of God is not the same as God being God, which is God seeing God. Since your own Being is what God is, there being no God but That, and no Self but That, Being as the Self, abiding as That, absorption in the Knowledge of That, is the seeing of God. That is God seeing God.

Q.: Mental imagery of God is short of Self-Realization.

N.: Yes. It is still just an image in the mind.

Another Q.: What was meant in the *Ribhu Gita* recitation in which it is said, "without a trace of sankalpa"?

N.: "Sankalpa" means a fixed idea or a concept. It can also mean volition, but the Maharshi has already resolved that notion in the previous verse, so we need not deal with that particular definition now. Ribhu advises you to remain free of even the least trace of any kind of sankalpa, any concept, or any fixed idea. In doing so, you abide in That, itself, as That, itself. If the seer abandons every notion of himself, all that remains of him is That. He abides in That, as That.

The Maharshi says, "The seeing is in one's own Source." The realizing is in one's own source the absorption and the abidance. What is absorbed? The individual—the "I"—is absorbed, and, with him, all that is objective—the "this"—is absorbed. No trace remains of them. What remains is the abidance, which is Being, just as it is. No one abides. It is not meant that there is an individual who abides as or in something else. Once one conceives along those lines, he will wonder, "How do we do this abiding?" Abidance indicates identity; Being is the Knowledge.

Q.: You said, "Truth is never what is thought of." That is the same thing as what is said now.

N.: Then, what is it? (silence)

Another Q.: Each one of these verses is just so beautiful and perfect to hear. As I follow his instruction, it always returns to the same place. If I follow what he says, it takes me directly to that spot, and I can just be my Self again.

N.: There is nothing more direct and pithy, and nothing more sublime, than what the Maharshi has bestowed. He has revealed the Truth in the most exquisite, terse, yet fully explanatory, manner. He has done so even in perfect Silence and is still doing so. Within that great Silence, these words appear to reveal the same silent Truth, and that is Grace upon Grace.

Q.: It is so holy; it is the holiest of the holy and the love of loves. It is so full.

N.: To be absorbed in that which he has given in his instruction is the holiest of the holy. It is the highest form of worship and replete with Bliss. It is the Supreme Yoga. It is the one Knowledge, which is the Supreme Knowledge. It is this alone that need be realized. If this is accomplished, everything is accomplished.

आत्मानमीक्षेत परं प्रपश्ये -
दित्यागमोक्तेः सुलभो न भावः ।
नात्मैव दृश्यो यदि का कथेशो
स्वयं तदन्नीभवनं तदीक्षा ॥ २१ ॥

ātmānam-īkṣeta paraṁ prapaśye-
d-ityāgamokteḥ sulabho na bhāvaḥ |
nātmaiva dṛśyo yadi kā katheśe
svayaṁ tad-annī-bhavanaṁ tad-īkṣā || 21 ||

21

See the Self, see the Supreme;
Thus, the Agama (the scripture's) declaration. This is not an easy bhava (state, meditation, contemplation).
If the Self is not, indeed, the seen, how can there be talk of the Lord? (how to seek the Lord?)
Oneself becoming His food is that seeing (is seeing Him).

N.: The instruction everywhere, in all nondualistic texts, is: "See the Self, see the Supreme." Each phrase may be taken individually, so the instruction may be understood as, "See God, search for God; see the Self, search for the Self," or the phrases may be understood together as, "If you see the Self, you see the Supreme," or, "If you have seen the Supreme, you have seen your Self." The Maharshi says that this is the declaration of the scriptures, but that it is not an easy state or contemplation. What is the significance of this? It is explained with, "If the Self is not, indeed, the seen, how can there be talk of the Lord, or how can one seek the Lord?" The instruction is difficult only in this manner. You are instructed, "See the Self," but the Self is not an object. So, how are you going to see the Self? Unless you see the Self, you do not see the Supreme. So, how can those scriptures tell you, "See the Self, see the Supreme," knowing full well that you cannot see the Self? This verse says that it "is not easy." The proclamation of the scriptures is not a trick commandment. Sri Bhagavan elaborates, "If the Self is not, indeed, the seen, how can there be talk of the Lord, or how one can seek the Lord?"

The Maharshi comes to the rescue: "Oneself becoming His food is that seeing (seeing Him.)" If you want to see the Absolute, you must be swallowed up, consumed by it, and thoroughly digested.

"See the Self; see the Supreme." These are the injunctions or commandments of the scriptures. This instruction is given in no uncertain terms. It is sublime instruction and ought to be followed. Sri Ramana says, "Thus, the scripture's declaration."

"This is not an easy bhava." "Bhava" has many meanings, and, in this case, it means a state, a meditation, or a contemplation. "See the Self, see the Supreme," may seem to be a contemplation that is not easy or a rather steep meditation and may appear to be not an easy state. As always, though, the Maharshi is there for the rescue.

"If the Self is not, indeed, the seen, how can there be talk of (how to seek) the Lord?" If the Lord, or God, is not an object, how does one seek God? In the previous verse, Sri Bhagavan said that, if God is an object, it is just mental seeing. Seeing God cannot be that. So, when the ancient scriptures and sages say that one should seek God and see God," what is this seeing of God? How can you see something that is not objective? You cannot see God with your physical eyes, and you cannot see God with mental vision. So, how to see God? What is the seeing?

The instruction is, "See the Self, see the Supreme." As long as we treat God, or the Self, as if an object, it will seem impossible, or, at least, rather difficult, to do so. How is one to see that which is nonobjective? As long as you stand as the individual, or as a separate mind, trying to see God, when will this seeing actually occur? Whatever you see will still be objective, and this instruction to see the Self, to see God, will seem to be a very difficult bhava, indeed. There is, in truth, no difficulty in it. The way is nonobjective and consists in swallowing the seer. Bhagavan says, "How to seek the Lord? Oneself becoming His food is that seeing." To lose one's separate individuality and be consumed, without a trace, in God is the seeing of God.

You cannot know the Self as if it were an object. Once you consider the Self, or God, as an object, the seeing or the knowing seems to be some mysterious way of relation between the subject, yourself, which is unknown, and the known, which is God, the Self, or the Supreme Self. When the individuality is lost, there is nothing mysterious about the seeing, or the knowing, at all.

The individuality is lost. The separate mind is consumed. It is eaten up, with no crumbs left behind. If you would be consumed, with not a crumb left behind, with nothing to call "you" or "yours," "I" or the "mind," from what perspective would you be seeing God? Only from God's perspective. God sees God with God's own Eye. The Self knows the Self with its own innate Knowledge. It is that knowledge in which Being is the Knowledge. If you are consumed in this manner, as the Maharshi teaches, nothing remains of you to be called "a separate self." Your Knowledge of God, then, is God's Knowledge of God. There is nothing more certain or sublime than that.

This is indicated in the Agama-s, the scriptures. "Agama" refers, in a generic sense, to a number of scriptures. This Truth is what is indicated in those ancient scriptures, in which the instruction is, "See the Self, see the Supreme." Know your Self, and this is Knowledge of God.

Q.: I have this deep, devotional experience with Ramana. It comes as, "Take me. I am yours." Is that what he is referring to?

N.: Yes. When you eat some food, that food does not exist as such anymore. The matter of the vegetables that you eat becomes your own matter. The broccoli you consume loses its broccoli-hood, and it is gone. There is no broccoli left over after you are done munching and digesting. This is the imagery being employed. The individual should be consumed, utterly losing his identity. The very "particle" of the ego should be utterly absorbed and become the identity of the Absolute, so that no individuality remains at all. "Becoming food" signifies the state of complete absorption.

If you become food for Sri Ramana, you lose your ego. You lose your individuality, just as the broccoli lost its broccoli-hood.

Furthermore, you lose the misidentification with the body, just as the broccoli cannot reclaim its shape. You lose your form, and you lose your individuality. Then, all that remains of you is That, and That sees itself perfectly. God, or the Self, has no problem with the injunction to see the Self, to see the Supreme, because the Self is self-luminous. God knows God.

You cannot see the Self, because the Self is not an object. You must see the Self in order to realize the Absolute. If the individuality of the supposed seer disappears, the vision is the seer, himself, and the seer is the Self and no longer an individual.

Q.: It is just God seeing God, at that point, is it not?

N.: So, our spiritual efforts should be aimed at the dissolution of the ego, by whatever means, ensuring it becomes absorbed, and preparing the "food" in whatever way is necessary in order that it becomes consumed.

Another Q.: "By whatever means." Could you say a little more about this?

N.: It varies according to the aspirant and according to the depth of practice. Anything that brings about ego-dissolution is happy, makes peace shine, is freeing, and is beneficial. The most efficacious means is the inquiry. Knowledge lies at the core of any successful means. Even the smallest activity that is done in the name of spirituality that bears good results has a Knowledge essence. If it were otherwise, it would not spiritually work. In the Maharshi's instruction, all the emphasis is placed on Knowledge, because, whether one is practicing the inquiry or is also doing other things, those other things work for the same reason the inquiry does. The inquiry is pure Knowledge. The other things work because of their essential core.

Q.: One could infuse every task with a spiritual energy?

N.: How are you going to do that?

Q.: I do not know, because the ego is doing that, and I think that way.

N.: If you were focused on knowing your identity, which is not the ego, all of the tasks and all the experiences that would be encountered would be naturally infused with the growing wisdom inside you. Someone supposedly external to you might say of you that you are engaging in these activities in a spiritual manner and that there are some activities that are purely of spiritual, or symbolic, purposes, but you would know that it is the Knowledge-essence that is entirely responsible. You would be focused entirely on finding your real nature. For one who is diving inward, everything is spiritual.

Q.: So, even while folding clothing, I could be intent on finding "Who am I?"

N.: If you were realizing that you are not the body and never do anything, while you are folding the clothing, would it be a spiritual experience? Perhaps, someone who does not understand would think that the practice consists of folding clothing, and therefore might further consider that there are particular ways of folding the clothing, particular kinds of cloth that need to be folded, and certain times of the day during which to fold, but those who know what is really occurring would comprehend that it is the disidentification from the body—the experience of bodiless Being.

Q.: If, while doing one's daily tasks, one devoted this time to inquiry, well, even speaking of tasks is confusing.

N.: We need not limit inquiry to our tasks. If you are inwardly turned toward knowing yourself, the tasks and enjoyments, the activities necessary for everyday, worldly life and the specifically spiritual activities are, without exception, infused with the same Light of Knowledge. The Light of Knowledge and the inquiry that brings it about can go on continuously. They are not task-dependent. Inquiry does not depend upon your body moving, being still, moving quickly, or moving slowly.

Q.: It does not have to look spiritual.

N.: It does not have to look spiritual for somebody else. Spirituality is something that you carry within yourself. Even when you do something for which the intention is to look spiritual, it should look spiritual for you, and not be done to impress somebody else. If someone does something of a spiritual character or wears something that is of spiritual significance or symbolism, it should matter to her because it reminds her, or expresses to her, what she is finding within herself and reminds her of the Absolute. It should never be to impress other people.

Another Q.: "Becoming food," is indicative of surrender, but, really, it is surrender of nothing for everything.

N.: It is a good deal, is it not? (laughter) We have nothing and surrender our nothingness; in exchange, God gives everything. Who arranged for this trade? (laughter) We come up on the good side. (laughter)

Q.: Yes, by any definition, it is a good trade. It's a "no-brainer."

N.: It must be by divine arrangement. The surrender is not anything short of giving up your identity entirely.

Q.: Yes. My journey has been one of inquiry because that is more natural for me, but I see the convergence of surrendering of "me" and "mine" and inquiry into the "I" to discover its absence. Either way, one discovers the loss is of what never came to be in the first place.

N.: Either way, it is the giving up of that nonexistent ego-notion. Whether we inquire and get to the root, or we give up all and become food for Him, there is absorption of identity. Surrender is not anything less than that, just as inquiry is not just an intellectual contemplation, but something much deeper.

Another Q.: I am thinking of becoming food for Him and absorption.

N.: God is hungry and is looking for tasteless morsels. (laughter)

Q.: I try to understand and, simultaneously, see my lack of understanding of the perfection of what you are saying and the perfection of how it is said. When I contemplate that, the only way to understand it is to become food for That. It is entirely beyond anything that I can do to understand, in a form that I can understand. There is nothing to say about it.

N.: When you approach in this way, do you lose track of your previously-conceived self?

Q.: I don't become food for the Supreme, because I keep trying to objectively understand. The more I understand, the less I know.

N.: So, the food tries to get away? Is that it? (laughter)? Is it moving over on the plate, (laughter) or is the leaf-plate getting up and walking out of the door? (laughter) The Maharshi's instructions clearly indicate that it is a matter of absorption of your sense of identity. It is a relinquishment of the individuality, because the individuality is false. When you relinquish it, you are not giving up something solid, and, hence, there is absorption and steady abidance. When you listen to the instruction and follow it, give yourself over to it and put it into practice. The instruction refers to the dissolution of the separate individuality which, alone, represents some kind of obstacle, bondage, ignorance, obstruction, etc. When you inquire with your best effort, this is also becoming food. It is not different.

Q.: It is the dissolution of the "understander."

N.: Yes, the dissolution of the separate knower is the revelation of the real understanding. All of our efforts, therefore, are directed at dissolution of the false ego-individual, inclusive of whatever tendencies he seems to wrap himself in to give himself a semblance of being concrete.

Another Q.: We are having a very interesting meal today. (laughter)

N.: Stale egos are being served. (laughter)

Another Q.: Do you want that ego for here, or is it to go? (laughter)

Another Q.: When you say, "Make your vision non-objective," does that also mean to make my identity nonobjective?

N.: Yes. If nothing objective is superimposed on your identity, what remains?

Q.: For sure, nothing objective remains. It is gone completely.

N.: Does nothing pertaining to the body, senses, or conceived in any form of the mind or intellect remain?

Q.: Yes.

N.: So, what remains?

Q.: Just the good stuff is all that is left. (laughter).

N.: Shivam. Siva means "the Good."

Q.: Yes, Siva.

N.: "Good stuff," could be an American translation, perhaps. (laughter). It is true that only that which is true Bliss remains. That is the truly Good.

Every suffering is due to misidentification, which is mistaking something objective to be one's Self, which is forever nonobjective. Such misidentification manifests as an attachment to some thought or thing, to some event or circumstance, person or place or time, etc. A state of being completely detached from such depends on non-identification with the not-Self. Then, you do not hide your own Bliss from yourself.

Another Q.: There are two things of which I have been trying to get to the bottom.

N.: "I" and "this"? (laughter) It could just be one thing, "I," and that takes care of everything, as the Maharshi points out.

Q.: The first idea is that the false belief in anything objective is identical to the false belief in perceptions of any kind. The second idea is that this is a sankalpa that needs to be given up and not held or made into another objective thing.

N.: Just be very sure about the nature of the perceiver, and the perceptions will take care of themselves. Just be very sure about the nature of the one who conceives of such sankalpas and vikalpas, and they will take care of themselves.

Another Q.: That is, perhaps, true, but hold on! (laughter)

N.: In the meantime, before you inquire, you have another question?

Q.: In the meantime?

N.: Yes, in the mean time. (laughter)

Q.: Looking into the nature of perception seems useful to me, because the more one looks into it, the less there is of it. It is totally imaginary and fictitious. It is without the slightest ground, yet, I tell myself, "If that is true, it should produce the result I think it should produce," which would be a complete disbelief in objectivity of any kind. It does not seem to do that, though, and that must be why Bhagavan discourages me about it.

N.: Well, if Bhagavan discourages you about it. . .

Q.: No. I am not going to be put off here. (laughter)

N.: If he has discouraged it, why should you go on with it? You can go on examining perception "to your heart's content." If your heart does not find complete contentment, though, you will need to trace the perception to the perceiver, and know his nature. Whether you think perception occurs or you consider perception to be an illusion or you realize that there is no such thing as any kind of perception, you still must come around to the nature of the perceiver.

Q.: But one will not do that so long as he believes in something objective and as long as he continues with misidentification in the form of objectification.

N.: You have summed it up as misidentification in the form of objectification. So, the misidentifications ought to be dealt with.

Q.: And that is the perception.

N.: Whatever the perceiver's nature is, so appears the relation to the perceived object, which is the perceiving or perception. Whatever it is that appears as the perceiver appears as the perceiving and the perceived. If you can swallow the perceived in the perceiving, so that you know that there is nothing perceived, do the same thing by swallowing the perceiving in the perceiver, for there cannot be a relation between a nonexistent object and a supposed subject. Having swallowed perception and the perceived object in the perceiver, focus on and inquire into the nature of the perceiver. Knowing that, everything is complete. Then, what you have been seeking, you find already eternally present, in perfection.

Q.: It seems that any kind of perception is a sankalpa that needs to be destroyed, and how am I to do that except by seeing that there is no such thing?

N.: Trace your own nature by experiential inquiry. Gain Knowledge of who you are. You cannot be a sankalpa, a perception, or anything else. First and foremost, know your own nature. Then, we will see if you are one to which sankalpas attach themselves or if you are one that generates such things.

Q.: All of that is imagined, from top to bottom, is it not?

N.: Seek the one who imagines. That is the sure way of being done with imagination.

Another Q.: The verse states that one has a doubt and thinks that it is difficult. I am trying to confirm in my own experience what is said here.

N.: Yes. It seems as if difficult, if, being told, "See the Self, see the Lord," you attempt to do so in an objective fashion. If you, the seer, or the seeker, become food for Him and are consumed, it is not difficult at all. We could even say, "Not difficult, not difficult, it is the easiest thing there is." [ed.: this refers to the opening line of the Maharshi's "Atma Vidya"]

Q.: What is "being food"?

N.: Destruction of the individuality is "becoming food," whether that is accomplished by an inquiry that reveals its nonexistence or that is accomplished through complete surrender, in which no scope is given for that morsel, and God, alone, is acknowledged, always and at all times, as the only reality. Either way, the ego is destroyed. The "becoming food for Him" is utter absorption, so that no trace of anything that can be called "me" remains.

Q.: The same absorption will be the end result whether one inquires or surrenders.

N.: It is the same absorption, and, though God, or the Self, is not hungry at all, still He graciously swallows whatever is offered; but you must offer.

धिये प्रकाशं परमो वितीर्य
स्वयं धियोऽन्तः प्रविभाति गुप्तः ।
धियं परावर्त्य धियोन्तरेऽत्र
संयोजनान्नेश्वरदृष्टिरन्या ॥ २२ ॥

dhiye prakāśaṁ paramo vitīrya
svayaṁ dhiyo'ntaḥ pravibhāti guptaḥ |
dhiyaṁ parāvartya dhiyontare'tra
saṁyojanān-neśvara-dṛṣṭir-anyā || 22 ||

22

In the mind, the Light the Supreme grants (gives) (lit., having given),
Oneself (Himself) within the mind (or: interior to the mind), He shines hidden.
The mind is to be turned back within (interior to) the mind, here.
From the union (absorption) is the seeing (wisdom) of the Lord, not otherwise.

N.: What is called "the mind" shines by some knowing Principle. The knowing Principle is not composed of the thoughts of the mind. The Maharshi says that the Supreme grants the Light to the mind. The Supreme is of the nature of pure Consciousness. That is the illumination. Our minds actually never know anything. It is in error to say, "My mind knows about Truth," or "My mind knows anything." The mind is just inert thought, which is in sharp contrast to the Consciousness that illuminates it. Consciousness, which is the Supreme, is within the mind, in the core of it and seeming to pervade all of it. It should also be regarded as interior to the mind, since Consciousness is the subject, and the mind is the object. The verse may be interpreted in either way, as referring to Consciousness being the very core, or quintessence, of the mind, or as referring to Consciousness as being more interior, more subjective than, the mind. It is Consciousness that gives Light to the mind, and without the Light of Consciousness, the mind is nothing at all. Consciousness is the knowing Principle.

You who are inquiring and seeking to know the Truth, who is to have this Knowledge? The mind will not grasp it. There are not two knowers in one and the same person, as if the mind and Consciousness could both know. There is only one Knowing, one Illumination, and all the apparent knowing or illumination of the mind is merely borrowed or reflected.

Sri Ramana says, "He shines, hidden." Consciousness is never conceived by the mind. From the perspective of attempting to see it with the mind, Consciousness, or the Supreme, God, seems as if a mystery and something secret. Even though it pervades everywhere, it is unseen. Even though it is the very center of the mind, the mind shrugs and says that it does not see it. The Supreme, or God, is also the Self. Upon coming to know about the Self, the mind again shrugs and says that it does not experience, see, or know it. It appears hidden, because of its formlessness and its nonobjective nature. It is not really hidden or secret, but appears that way as long as one attempts to know it through the mind. If, though, we inquire, and avail ourselves of Self-Knowledge, there is nothing hidden about it at all. It is Self-evident.

In order to accomplish the change from being hidden to being self-evident, from the false so-called knowledge of the mind to the Knowledge of the Absolute by the Absolute, the Maharshi gives the direction. Ramana says, "The mind is to be turned back within the mind." The mind should dive into, or through, its very center. Or, it may be translated as, "The mind is to be turned back interior to the mind, here." The last word in the third line is "atra," meaning "here." Where is here? Of where is he speaking? "Interior to the mind." It is the timeless, spaceless "place" that is interior to, or before, the mind, and is that in which the mind has no actual existence. The mind is "to be turned back." This means that it ceases to believe in its imaginings, which are its own forms. It turns back, attempting to face That which is before it, but, when it does so, it is extinguished. It utterly loses its form.

If we consider the meaning as "within the mind," at its very core, the peripheral thoughts are discarded, and the mind dives into its own center. Its center is of the nature of pure Consciousness and not a mind at all. The result could be described as if something were to swallow itself.

What is the Light that shines so that you are aware of your own thoughts, which constitute the mind? The thoughts cannot illumine themselves. What gives light to your mind so that it appears as if it knows? It cannot be contained in thought and cannot be confined or defined by thought. It is undoubtedly present, for, without that Light, you would not be aware of even a single thought.

"Himself, or Oneself, within the mind, He shines hidden." The mind does not have a shape, so, when we say "a core" or "a center," we mean an essence rather than a particular place. At the core, or in the essence, of the mind, there God is. Or, we could interpret it as, "interior to the mind," even more subjective than the mind, is the Source of the light. The aim is to recognize the Light, the nature of which is pure Consciousness, which, although apparently hidden in the midst of thoughts, is the very light by which those thoughts are seen. The veil of thoughts is like the holding up one's hand to hide the sunlight. It is by the sunlight that one sees the hand.

"The mind is to be turned back within the mind, here." Turn the mind inward to look at its own nature. "The mind is to be turned back interior to the mind, here." If the mind is turned back to look at that which is interior to it, what happens to the mind? All know the phrase, "food for thought." In this case, thought, itself, becomes the food.

"Here" is where you are, as pure Consciousness. If the mind turns back to that which is interior to it, or if the mind turns in on itself to try to see its own essence, which is of the nature of pure Consciousness, nothing remains to be called "a mind." If the mind loses its form, can it be called a "mind"?

The Light of pure Consciousness is completely formless. Thoughts are invariably engaged in form. There is no such thing as a formless thought. There is no such thing as a formed Consciousness. What is called the mind seems to be a curious combination of the forms of thought and the formless Consciousness. Consciousness can very well exist without thought, but thought cannot exist even for a moment without Consciousness. This tells us something about what is real. Turn your mind, the very thing that seems to be engaged in thought, in on its own nature, or have it look to that which is interior to it and lights it up, and see what is there.

"From the union" of the mind with what is interior to it, which is "absorption, is the seeing of the Lord, not otherwise." When the form of the mind dissolves, Consciousness, alone, remains. Consciousness is supreme, and it shines for itself. That, alone, is the seeing of God. Anything less would be in the domain of thought, and such would only be mental vision, which Sri Ramana has already described and negated.

Where your thoughts have been transcended and where the very notion of existent thought has been absorbed, there is the seeing of your own Self, which is the seeing of Truth. If you inquire as the Maharshi advises, "For whom is the thought?" this will turn the mind inward, as described in this verse. If inquiry is practiced according to the way he has instructed, when you inquire, "For whom is this thought," the thought, inclusive of its entire objective form that it is concerned with, dissolves. What is unreal dissolves. You are left only with the most interior "I." "Who am I?" The Light of Consciousness shines of itself. It is natural Knowledge.

Q.: Is it the mind turning itself, or do I turn myself inward?

N.: Your Self cannot be turned inward or outward. So, the Maharshi says, "the mind."

Q.: But, if the mind is inert, how can it do anything?

N.: The mind, he says, is turned inward. It does not necessarily mean that the mind is an actor. The idea that the mind is doing or acting is part of the outward, or peripheral part of, the mind that is to be turned back in. To turn inward means to lose the belief in one's own conceptions. That includes the notion of an existent mind. The Self has nothing to do. Are you hypothesizing that there is another "I"?

Q.: No. Is the mind in the middle?

N.: It has no light of its own.

Q.: If it has no light of its own, what can drive it outward or inward?

N.: That is called maya, illusion, which seems to have great powers until, turning inward, it is examined, in which case, it ceases to exist. Such is the case with the mind. The Self has no outward or inward and no bound or liberated, or dark or illumined, states. So, Sri Ramana says that the mind is turned inward.

There can be no real middle between the ever-real and the never-real.

The same power drives the mind inward and outward. The duality appears only in the outward-turned mind. There is no outer in the inward. The within-ness is pure Consciousness, which is nondual and undifferentiated.

Q. As we discuss it and I try to hold this "thing," it starts to lose its form. This is just by trying to figure out where this "thing" is that imagines all this.

N.: When it looks for itself, that is the mind turning in on the mind.

Another Q.: Like a computer, the mind works with a set program. A thought comes, and there is a limited, objective appearance. Then, this computer virus comes in and breaks up the program. A plus B does not equal C anymore. It has no answer. When it has no answer, the program is shot.

N.: Obviously, you speak from experience with your computer. (laughter)

Q.: It can't find the answer. There is no more "it" to go further.

N.: All right. That is one way of looking at this. To combine your analogy with the verse composed by the Maharshi, the Self, or the Supreme, which lends its Light, is like the source of the electricity that runs the computer, regardless of the programs.

Q.: So, someone pulls the plug.

N.: Rather than view inquiry as that which scrambles the program, it is better to understand that it undoes entirely the ability to create the program. Inquiry does not scramble the mind or give the mind such a mysterious question that the mind is blown away by the riddle of it all. That might be a particular spiritual experience at one point, but the questioning of "Who am I?" eliminates the very idea that there is such a thing called "the mind." For the purpose of practice, it is said that the mind is turned inward, but what actually occurs when the mind is turned inward? Bhagavan has expressed it, "The mind is to be turned back within the mind." It does not mean that the mind is doing. The idea that the mind is active has already been taken care of in the first line, in which he says that it is the Supreme that lends its Light, which includes its power, to the mind. No doership is being ascribed to it.

Another Q.: It doesn't turn itself inward.

N.: It is not an entity to do so, but we cannot say the Self is active. The ideas that something needs to be done and that we are going from one place to another are part of the mind that is being dissolved. The answer to the question comes by experience and cannot be very well explained, except by using some temporary, expedient answer, such as, "The mind does it," "I do it," or "The Self does it." None of those answers are really accurate, in terms of the Truth, for the mind is inert and illusory, an individual "I" is only delusion, and the question of action or motion of any kind is impossible for the Self.

Sri Ramana wisely says that the mind is turned inward. It goes to That which is before itself, interior to itself, or we may say that it goes into its own core. Then, what happens? There is union. Union of what with what? That which seemed to be the mind unites with the illuminating Consciousness that was originally perceived as its core, as its background, or as the Light that illuminates it. It attains union with That. Whatever comes into union with the Absolute, though, loses its individuality, its separate identity, and any kind of differentiation whatsoever. From the Union, or Absorption, is "the seeing of the Lord," or "the Wisdom of the Lord," and not otherwise. How do you see the Supreme?

You see the Supreme only by the mind's dissolution, which is its utter absorption.

Another Q.: When the mind dissolves, are the tendencies dissolved?

N.: Because the vasana-s, the tendencies, are activities or components of the mind, all of them are destroyed. Elsewhere, the Maharshi has said that the method for Self-Realization consists primarily of the destruction of vasana-s, tendencies. In this verse, Sri Ramana does not expressly mention the tendencies. He uproots the very existence of the mind that could hold these tendencies, that could think of them, and that could think of them repetitively so that they appear. That very mind is dissolved, for it is turned back to look at its origin.

Q.: So, I do not necessarily have to address the tendencies head-on.

N.: He does not say that.

Q.: But by the mere fact of meditating or turning the mind inward, it actually dissolves the mind. That will work without addressing tendencies.

N.: He does not address that issue in this verse. He does not say, "We do not need to address the tendencies."

Q.: Oh!

N.: He simply says, "The mind is to be turned back within the mind or interior to the mind, here." When you address a tendency, what happens? What do you do? What is it that you refer to as "addressing a tendency"?

Q.: What I have done is to look at whatever is troubling me. Instead of not looking at it, I investigate what is happening in the mind. In a way, it is not being afraid to look at it that works very well to dissolve it.

N.: Observation and examination of it work better than continuing to live by it. Then, what do you do? With or without circumstances prompting you to do so, you become cognizant that you are thinking in the manner of a tendency, perhaps acting upon it or perhaps not. Now, what do you do with that?

Q.: It depends how serious it is. If it very intense, I look at it.

N.: Which means what?

Q.: It means to really look at what is troubling me and what I believe in all this trouble. I note all the aspects.

N.: And then?

Q.: It is enough to look at it and do nothing, actually.

N.: Does that eliminate the tendency permanently so there is no possibility of recurrence?

Q.: Are we actually to dissolve the contents of the mind, too?

N.: How would it be possible to dissolve the existence of the mind yet still leave the contents behind?

Q.: If we turn awareness, or the mind, inward, do we go upstream of the mind and actually dissolve the mind and its contents?

N.: Yes. It must include the dissolution of the tendencies. If, without dissolving the tendencies, you were to attempt to dissolve the mind, you might end with an intellectual insight or with a temporary experience. You would return, though, in your experience, to the state of the mind with the tendencies that were plaguing you before. This is so because your identity would still be wrapped up in them. That is why I asked you about how you "look" at tendencies. Obviously, everyone sees them, and that is how they know they experience them. So, when you said, "look at them," I wanted to know from you, what you are actually practicing. As long as your identity has not been extricated from such tendencies, they will recur, sooner or later. Such may recur after a short lapse of time or after a long lapse of time. The tendencies may recur apparently prompted by circumstances, which is really being prompted by a manner of thinking within the mind that you associate with a particular circumstance. Once one observes a tendency, whether because it is engaging one in a particular action or because she notices the veiling or the turmoil in the mind, she can observe what constitutes the tendency. This is examination of the particular thoughts. Then, she can further trace those thoughts to the definitions that are held about herself that give rise to such thinking, which, when repeated, becomes a tendency. In the case of attachments, examination of the superimposition or confusion regarding the nature of happiness should occur. Thereupon, inquire, and the tendency is destroyed, and the mind is dissolved to that extent. If the inquiry does not stop there, but continues further as an inquiry as to what it is that contained the tendency to begin with, both the tendency and the mind are utterly destroyed. Whatever is destroyed in pure Knowledge cannot possibly recur, whether after a short time or a long time, because the seed of misidentification is absent. If this is what you mean by "looking at it," it is a solid approach. If not, reconsider. Do you see that, if you would inquire as just explained, the question about the destruction of tendencies, as if such were different than the destruction of the mind, would no longer arise?

Another Q.: One has to escape the "I." Tendencies rest upon and depend upon the assumed "I"-thought. "Who am I?" does this.

N.: Yes.

Q.: That is the way to extract the false, assumed "I" and its tendencies from the true "I." Self-Knowledge then shines.

N.: The only purpose in examining the thought content that constitutes the tendency is for the usefulness in the discrimination as to "This I am not," in contrast to "This is what I am."

Q.: Self-Knowledge ends the tendency forever because the discovery of the absence of the false identity is the uncovering of the veil that seemed to hide the Self, which when unveiled, simultaneously stands Self-revealed, always free of all tendencies.

N.: That is so. If the inquiry is not actually applied thoroughly, the tendency will recur. Someone may launch into an inquiry of sorts, saying, "Who am I?" but leave the tendency utterly unexamined or excluded from the inquiry, and such provides a large misidentification of a crude nature to which to return when the meditation is over. A chasm would be thus formed between the understanding that is inclined toward the Absolute and the experience that people refer to by that strange term, "everyday life."

Another Q.: Is the key to see one's identity as divorced from the ignorance?

N.: One must be free from ignorance, from the root notion of an existent "I" or "mine" to everything streaming from the root, such as desires, fears, aversions, frustrations, and whatever attachment there may be. Unless one's inquiry is directed to the absolute nature of the Self, how will there be a final resolution of the various tendencies? Without inquiry, there may be some momentary, or even prolonged, improvement of some kind, but there won't be complete liberation from the tendency. There will be a modulation or modification of it, but not destruction of it, unless there is an inquiry that drives the mind toward the absolute nature of the Self and liberates one's identity from ignorance.

If one attempts to meditate upon the Absolute, but he does not completely apply the inquiry to everything he experiences, he will be left with dual identities of an absolute Self, in which he believes, and himself, which somehow does not quite match the Self. He will be caught within a peculiar self-created chasm, which is unnecessary, if only he just inquires thoroughly all of the time, regardless of how big or small the particular aspect of illusion appears to be. No illusion is so big that you cannot destroy it or overcome it, and no illusion is so small that you should ignore it. The illusion that you ignore is that which will poke you, so to speak, and cause suffering.

Q.: My attitude should be: why not eliminate more illusion? The more one frees himself from delusion the better.

N.: There is no such thing as too much inquiry, and you cannot remove too much illusion.

Another Q.: It does not have a limited capacity.

N.: Turned inward, your inquiry has the capacity to simultaneously destroy all kinds of delusions, from the outermost and minor to the apparently innermost and fundamental. It can destroy the ego-notion and the attachment to the body and the attachment to some particular like or dislike, all at once. There is no rule that the liberating inquiry must proceed in a particular order. You will not become overwhelmed. If you feel as if you are about to become overwhelmed by the inquiry, it is very good, because that means that you are about to shift from the mentality of identifying with the mind to being the Self.

Another Q.: In the Maharshi's teaching and in other spiritual texts, it is stated that, if one were to truly inquire and know one's Self, there would be finality. One would not return to the previous illusion. My experience in my spiritual practice is that it is an incremental movement. I couldn't even think now the way I used to think of myself five years ago. Where does it all end?

N.: What do you mean by, "Where does it all end?"

Q.: Where does the delusion end?

N.: Delusion ends where the "I" ends. The end is when there is no false assumption of individuality, no one to be deluded. The attempt to measure Knowledge in time is somewhat futile, because Knowledge transcends that which conceives of time.

Q.: The attempt to measure is a tendency, is it not?

N.: How are you going to obtain an accurate measurement?

Q.: The idea that I could measure is ignorance, is it not?

N.: Yes. One is accustomed to looking at things that have an objective character. How are you going to measure your Existence, which is the Consciousness that illuminates the measurer? You are trying to measure how quickly or to what degree you are dissolving into the Absolute. We speak of "dissolving," but we are That. It is like trying to measure the distance between where you are now and the satsang hall. You would have a difficult time measuring because you would be measuring from and to one and the same place.

Q.: You are saying that there is no distance to traverse. If I have been practicing in a way in which Self-Knowledge is being gained, what can I practice that would gain the whole Self-Knowledge or get rid of the whole ignorance?

N.: Egolessness. If the question is, then, "What will make this egolessness or attainment of Knowledge come about more quickly?" the answer is the intensification of practice, in every aspect of spiritual practice that shrinks the false sense of ego. This includes the destruction of attachment and the destruction of misidentification, the intensity of the purpose of fulfilling the desire for Liberation, the sharpening of discrimination that discerns who you are and what you are not, the equanimity that is not moved by any kind of circumstance, so that the waves or ripples in the mind subside and no longer cloud the view, the very straight-forward, interior honesty that always declares what your experience is, from the position of experience, so that you have only one way of understanding, and that is experiential Knowledge, and the humility, in which one considers the vast Absolute and stands on the threshold of dissolution into it and in the awe of that which shrinks the personal importance to the size of nothing. In short, anything that removes the ego, which is so small but which, in delusion, like the tip of your finger held in front of your eye, seems to cover the whole view.

Another Q.: I have a fear of snakes. In India, I never know when these snakes are going to come in the garden.

N.: You will want to be a Vedantin, then, because every snake mentioned in Vedanta turns out to be a rope. (laughter) Some of those snakes might be afraid of you, too. What do you advise the snakes to do, besides to stay out of the garden where you might be? (laughter)

Q.: How am I going to get rid of that fear unless I am confronted with it? Why would I have to be confronted with every situation in life?

N.: What makes you say that you must be confronted with it? There may not be snakes at hand. The time of the year may not be snake-season. (laughter) Does that mean you must live in fear until the next available snake comes around to help you out? (laughter) You need not wait until circumstances present themselves to address tendencies. What makes you afraid of the snake?

Q.: So, I begin to analyze?

N.: Are you afraid of a snake just minding his own business a hundred feet away?

Q.: I don't think so.

N.: So, of what are you actually afraid?

Q.: I have not examined what the fear really is.

N.: Are you afraid of the snake crawling on you or biting you?

Q.: (looks aghast, and then starts to laugh)

N.: I think so. (laughter) Did we just hit the snake on the head? (laughter) [editor's note: this alludes to the saying "to hit the nail on the head," meaning an accurate ascertainment, and to the illusion of a rope appearing as a snake, which is a commonly utilized example in Vedanta] Why would the snake be on you rather than just on your body?

Q.: I am recoiling at the idea. So, it is just on the body, and it is not on me. I suppose you could even love it.

N.: You become inclined toward that when you realize that the snake is not her body. The snake is not her body anymore than you are your body.

Q.: I feel better when you say "her." All of a sudden, it does not seem so scary if it is a "her." (laughter)

N.: The fear is very much dependent upon the conception of yourself as being the body, and, consequently, conceiving of the snake as her body. When her body is on or near your body, you think she is on or near you. Are you afraid that the snake might bite, as well?

Q.: The fear is just of its presence.

N.: It is sufficient to see your bodiless nature. If you were concerned with the snake biting you, which might be a valid concern, since some snakes carry poisons that will bring about the end of life in your body, you would need further meditation to bring about the realization of immortality. If, though, it is just the snakes' mere presence in the neighborhood, or the idea of the skins of their bodies' being in contact with your snakeskin, (laughter) for you can be considered as a snake with arms and legs and the snake can be considered to be a human without arms and legs, just seeing that you are not the body and that the snake is not her body will be sufficient.

Q.: I need to use discrimination.

N.: Yes, and, for that, you do not need to wait. For example, you already know that you have the fear, and you can discern very easily the ideas that constitute the fear. It did not take me long to point such out. You could have pointed it out to yourself more quickly. Once you discern the ideas, you are prompted to examine the identity that gives rise to those ideas.

Q.: They are because I think that I am the body.

N.: Yes. Once you inquire, you arrive at such a settled peace that you won't feel the need to test it. It will be certain. So, you will not have to run to the nearest snake and see if it works or not, but, if a friendly snake comes to say hello to you in the garden, it will be all right.

Another Q.: I was reflecting on the strong emotional content of my tendencies as another approach to destroy them.

N.: You will need to be more specific if you are examining this for yourself. It is fine to discuss it in generic terms, but to be free, you will need to be very specific and discriminate in the light of Absolute Knowledge.

Q.: In the Light of Absolute Knowledge, it becomes more of an impersonal nature.

N.: Yes, and what does that do to all of your flaming, raging emotions?

Q.: It shows me that they were formulated when I did not know myself.

N.: How important are they?

Q.: Not very important.

N.: Keep your eye on the goal, and perceive from there.

Q.: Keeping my eye on the goal would mean that I would be staying in my true identity.

N.: It can mean being determined to realize that which is vast, infinite, and eternal, and ultimately your real identity. With the determination to realize That, with That as your focus, knowing That is where your happiness lies, regarding That as the one thing that is really important, what will happen to all those other inflated emotions and to all those other troubles? You will find that you have far less with which to deal, and whatever remains can be dealt with very nicely through the practice of detachment and inquiry.

न वक्ति देहोऽहमिति प्रसुप्तौ
न कोपि नाभूवमिति प्रवक्ति ।
यत्रोदिते सर्वमुदेति तस्य
धियाऽहमः शोधय जन्मदेशम् ॥ २३ ॥

na vakti deho'ham-iti prasuptau
na kopi nābhūvam-iti pravakti |
yatrodite sarvam-udeti tasya
dhiyā'hamaḥ śodhaya janma-deśam || 23 ||

23

The body does not say "I," thus. In deep sleep,
No one says, "I did not exist," thus.
Upon the rise of that (which), all arise. Of that
"I," with the mind (intelligence), investigate (make clear) the birth place.

N.: The birthplace of what? Of the "I." "The body does not say 'I'." This should be evident. The Self's Existence does not derive from the body. In delusion, one can confuse himself and say, "I am the body," but it is not true. The "I"-sense does not come from the body, whether one regards the "I" as individualized or as Existence. The body is only the objective portion of the experience.

Sri Ramana says, "In deep sleep, no one says 'I did not exist.'" Deep sleep is a bodiless experience. No one ceases to exist in deep sleep. Existence continues always, with or without the body. The connection of "I" with the body, or the idea that the body determines identity, is only confusion.

Sri Ramana says, "Upon the rise of that, all arise," that is, upon the rise of the ego-notion, which connects itself with the body. "Of that 'I', with the mind (intelligence), clearly investigate the birth place." Find out where "I" springs forth. It does not come from the body. You still existed in deep sleep without the "I." At some point, it seems that the notion of "I," of individuality, springs forth and entangles itself with, defines itself by, the confining body. From where does the "I" spring forth? It does not spring forth from the body. He has already dismissed that possible misconception. You know that you exist, as in deep sleep, quite without the ego-notion. "I" still exist but not as an ego entity or as an embodied entity. From where does the entity spring forth?

"The body does not say 'I.'" The misidentification with the body does not come from the body. The body does not proclaim its own existence. Your body does not have any part of your identity. It does not say, "I." Always you exist. In deep sleep, there is the experience of no thought and of no body, yet you exist. There is no manifestation of an ego, yet you exist. There is no one to say in deep sleep, "I do not exist." The ego cannot make that declaration then, but you exist always, and the body is not that Existence. The body is an object within your experience and is not your Existence.

"Upon the rise of that," meaning upon the rise of the notion of "I," "all arise." The corollary of this is that when the "I" subsides, all subside. "All" is nothing more than "I" in various guises. What is the nature of this "I?" There is an "I" that always exists, which is utterly bodiless. There is an "I" that seems to come and go, which, though not being the body, itself, seems to connect itself to the body, borrowing the sense of reality and identity from the pure Existence. What is this "I?" Can there be two of us? Can there be an "I" that always is, and an "I" that comes and goes? "Of that 'I,'" or we may say into that "I," "with the mind," in the most intelligent fashion, investigate. "Make clear, the "janma-desam, the place of birth." Find the place where the "I" begins, the "I" upon the arising of which everything else rises.

The background Existence is without beginning or end. The body is not the cause of any difficulty or delusion, and it does not think "I." What is it that thinks, "I"? Where does it start? It cannot start in the body, for the body does not think "I." It does not start in the top, the bottom, the back, the front, the left, the right, etc. It does not start in the body. Where does the "I"-sense start? From where am "I"?

If the birth-place is the Existence of the Self, know this Existence as it is and find it to be that in which no "I" has ever been born. This is the investigation of the birth place.

Existence is perpetual, uninterrupted, unaffected by the passages of the states, and never the body. Where is the connection to the body? Where does it start? Discern for yourself the actual place where the individuality, or ego, begins. We can discuss endlessly the ego's trials, tribulations, problems, and adventures that come afterward. Can you discern where it begins? Trace out its source, or its birthplace. The real Self is unborn. Everything rises after this one thing rises. Where is the spot where this rises? By "where" is meant that you should seek this in your experience. It is not in the body.

Q.: Looking at it from the reverse perspective, could I ask to where does it go?

N.: You could do the same.

Q.: It is exactly the same "Where does that 'I' go?" for, every night, it is gone.

N.: Why did the Maharshi mention the birth place, rather than the dissolution? If we look at the dissolution, we arrive at the conclusion that there is a vast Existence beyond this "I" in which the "I" disappears, like a drop merging with the ocean. Like a small space inside a jar, when the lid is opened, the space is said to merge with the vast space. Sri Ramana says to investigate where it starts. If we know how to bring about dissolution, as the jar space into space and as a drop in the ocean, we will be in a good position to gain samadhi and similar experiences of absorption, but we will not necessarily attain perfect, continuous Realization. If we examine the starting place, "Where does 'I' begin?" and, through deep inquiry into that very root, find that there is no beginning place, then, for that which is never born, we need not be concerned about its further dissolution. It is always already dissolved. Such inquiry results in the permanence of Realization.

Q.: The "I" is already dead.

N.: Since the "I" is already dead, we need not be concerned about it dying again. Therefore, the Maharshi says that one should seek with a clear mind or intelligence, or clearly investigate, where the birthplace is. The more you dive into where the "I" begins, the less you will see of that birthplace, because it has not been born.

Another Q.: The "I" is different from any other ignorance. Here, you are pointing out investigation of the "I." Would the investigation apply to anything else?

N.: Where does the definition form to create ignorance? Where is the starting place of the definition? The starting place is the "I." Where does the "I" start? Trace inward in this way. You can use the transcendence of a false definition, or the destruction of a vasana, to spring into deeper inquiry and thus destroy the ignorance, from bottom to top, or from top to bottom.

Another Q.: Why does this "I"-thought seem so powerful? As many times as we have heard that it is just a thought and that thoughts are not real, by now, all of us ought to know that it is foolishness and no longer have this identity of being a mere thought, yet it persists.

N.: What makes you say that it is powerful? I cannot explain an experience that I do not have. (laughter)

Q.: I don't know. I have a tendency to think of myself as an individual, whether as a body or as a mind. By now, I should be past that misidentification.

N.: Who is the one who has that habit?

Q.: It is imagination.

N.: Yes, and the power of it derives from the Reality, as the Maharshi explained in verse one, in speaking of the One that appears as a variegated picture and of a Supreme Lord of immense power. That Supreme Lord of immense power is your own Being. That illusion seems as if it contains power is only a testimony to the power of Reality, so that even a drop, so to speak, of Reality can make the entire illusion seem as if real. The Reality of the Self is so powerful and so immense that a drop of it lent to a notion, which can never actually exist, can make the merely imagined seem to flourish as an individual being.

Q.: That is why you have said that the ego is the Self seen unclearly.

N.: The power behind all, including the ego, is the same Self. Knowing that the power comes from the Self and not from the ego, can you discern precisely how much power is in this ego?

Q.: There cannot be any.

N.: If we do not inquire, the ego seems as if a powerful creature with many arms and legs, capable of doing wondrous feats, and making the impossible seem possible. When we turn to look at it, asking, "Who is this fellow? Where exactly was he born? Let me investigate the matter," he starts to disappear. He loses all of his "arms and legs." His form becomes very difficult to find. His doings shrink to nothing. His power becomes nonexistent, and everyone says, "At last! We are done with this nuisance of the ego." (laughter)

Q.: It is just confusing the real "I"- am-ness with the "I"-am-thought.

N.: It is but the vaguest of assumptions, the merest imagined supposition. That one vague assumption, which is an unreal differentiation, becomes the basis for the entire samsara, with all its permutations, for however many eons it seems to last. With the dissolution of that one assumption, inclusive of all of its attendant tendencies, which are the ideas built upon it, the entire samsara vanishes without a trace. You find that there was nothing to it. This is comparable to awakening from a dream. If the doubt is, "But the dream seemed so real," the answer is, "Yes, but whose power was it?" If the doubt is, "It seemed so large," the answer is, "Yes, but whose immensity was it?" If the doubt is, "It lasted so long," the answer is, "Yes, but whose eternity was it?" When you wake up, there is not a trace of the dream.

Q.: When I am dreaming, the power in it is the Awareness. What I am seeing is myself, in any form, even if it be a dream. Nothing is real except "I."

N.: If the "I" is known for what it is, in its utter formlessness, the dream is over.

Another Q.: When I first try to seek it, there is an assumption that it is actually connected or that it has a place from which it comes. As I try to trace it back to find the place where it starts, there is a gap. In that gap, there is not actually a start. I cannot find the start of the ego-"I", and there is no start of the real Existence.

N.: That is right. The real Existence does not start and does not perish. The "I" seems to rise and fall, and, with it, everything else seems to rise and fall. Searching for this "I," it becomes nebulous. You are looking for the missing link. Though one can discuss how the ego evolves after its supposed start, there is this missing link. You must become very certain about how missing it is.

The inquiry should be pursued extremely experientially. Where in your Consciousness does "I" form, coalesce, rise up, or become born? Where is the "I?" From where does it start? Before anything else rises with it, before anything else is appended to it, where is the "I"? If you think, "I think that I am," where could that sense of "I," the assumption of individuality that is a bare nebulous supposition of "I," the assumption of existing as some kind of entity, start? Did it start? (silence) Such inquiry should be continued until the Knowledge of the egoless Self is perpetual and utterly unbroken.

देहो न जानाति सतो न जन्म
देहप्रमाणोऽन्य उदेति मध्ये ।
अहङ्कृतिग्रन्थिविबन्धसूक्ष्म -
शरीरचेतोभवजीवनामा ॥ २४ ॥

deho na jānāti sato na janma
deha-pramāṇo'nya udeti madhye |
ahaṅkṛti-granthi-vibandha-sūkṣma-
śarīra-ceto-bhava-jīva-nāmā || 24 ||

24

The body does not know. Being (Existence), is not born.
The body measured (limited to the body) another arises in the midst (between, in the middle),
Ego, knot, bondage, subtle body,
Mind, bhava (mundane existence, samsara), jiva (the individual) named.

N.: An inert body does not know. The body is not Consciousness. It is dead matter. Something seems to be between the body and Being, which is not born. "Satah," Being, or the Truth or Existence, is eternal. It has no beginning. There never was a time when it was not. There never is a time when it ceases to be. It never becomes anything, which would be a kind of birth. It is never transformed. It never gives rise to itself or to anything else. It just is as it is. Such is Being. That is your Being, your only true identity. The body is inert, so it "does not know." You are the knower and cannot be the body. The knower is Consciousness, which is identical with Being. You are Being, and you are not the body. It is an illusion when something seems to come between.

Sri Ramana says, "measured or limited to the body." This means that this other one becomes the occupant of the body, seems to fill the body, and to be sustained, in illusion, as some kind of individual being. It is something that seems to borrow the

Reality and the Consciousness of the Self and to tie these with the limitations of the body. That something is called "the ego." That something is the knot tying together the Real and the unreal. That something is bondage. If the bondage is cut, Liberation is realized to be your nature, which is egoless and has no knot. That something is called the "subtle body," in reference to a transmigrating entity that goes from birth to birth. That something between is called a "mind," while really there is just pure Consciousness. That something between is the bhava, the mundane existence or the samsara. That something between is the individual. However we name it, that something should be traced and its supposed birthplace determined, and, thus, we find that it does not exist. We should look squarely at this ego. No one has ever seen a real ego. Whoever attempts to see it finds it utterly missing, and with this truth being found, all of the ego's troubles are over.

The body has no Consciousness of its own. There is another that is the Consciousness. The body is inert. "The body does not know. Being is not born." The implication is that Being is identical with Consciousness. Being-Consciousness is the Truth of Existence. "Is not born" means that it has no form, it does not rise, it is not produced, and it does not start at any time.

Only that which is unborn is imperishable. Only that which has no beginning has no end. Anything with a beginning, or a birth, has a death, or an end. Being is not born. There never was a time when you were not. There never will be a time when you cease to be. You cannot even imagine a time when you are not. In the attempt to conceive of such, you automatically assume your own existence to be present in order to view your so-called nonexistence. There is no parting from Being, and Being is unborn. The body does not know. It is not the Consciousness. Being, which is your Existence, is not born. This means that Consciousness is not born and has no beginning or end.

"Limited to the body, measured by the body, another arises in the midst," that is, between Being, which is pure Consciousness, and the body. Something seems to come between and tie the two together, as it were, borrowing the identity and the reality of Being and the form and limitation of the body. Something seems to rise up. It is not the true "I," which is unborn and has no arising. That something is named the "ego." It is also referred to as the "knot," because it ties together, through illusion only, the Real and the unreal, the Self and the not-Self. It is called the "subtle body." It is of the form of an experiencer, but not the gross body, so it is called a subtle body, and it is this which seems to go from dream to dream, from life to life. It is not the ever-existent Self, which is without birth and without form, and it is not the physical body, which obviously perishes at death. It is called the "mind," the supposed separate knower that supposedly exists in addition to the innate Consciousness. It is that one who stands apart and thinks that it can know the Truth, but now doesn't know the Truth, wonders if it can know Consciousness, thinks that it knows the world, and generates other such ideas. It is called "bhava." "Bhava" means mundane existence and is identical in meaning with "samsara," the existence of repetitive birth, death, and illusion. It is called jiva. Jiva can mean "life," or "a life," but it also means the individual. The latter meaning is more pertinent in this case. Ego, knot, bondage, subtle body, mind, mundane existence, jiva or individual, however named, is the assumption that there is someone apart from the Self who also inhabits the body. The aim of inquiry is to destroy that assumed connection or to unravel that knot.

Q.: When I really try to find it, I find myself asking, "For what was I looking?" It is hard to remember what the thing is that I thought was there.

N.: Its seeming solidity is only supposed, and, when one inquires, one does not find anything of it. If you deeply inquire, it is not only that you do not remember what you were looking for, but you do not remember how to be an ego.

Another Q.: The ego is not even a subtle object, is it?

N.: The ego is just a case of make-believe. The Maharshi's reference to "subtle body" in the verse should be understood to pertain to that which is said to transmigrate from birth to birth, carrying with it the seeds of the tendencies for a new life. It is the same as the idea of a continuing individual entity, an ego, and continuing bondage. It does not exist. It is an imaginary knot assumed to connect the Reality of Absolute Being and the manifestation of an inert body. Something supposedly sneaks between, rises up, fills the body, as it were, and says that it is here, but it is not here.

Q.: This is a relief.

N.: Oh, yes, it is a great relief, for you recover your happiness.

Another Q.: In the verses read last night from *Ribhu Gita,* chapter 26, verse 24, there is a statement to the effect that, when the Liberation from the imagined bondage takes place, many, many jivas attain Liberation. Is that declaration similar to saying the dream characters in a nighttime dream are liberated upon awakening? Is it the same sense as, if the jiva is Siva, there are no bound jiva-s to be awakened?

N.: There are two ways of understanding "all kinds of jiva-s will gain Liberation." The primary way of understanding is that, no matter what kind of jiva it is that practices this devotion to Siva and Knowledge of the Self, when he plunges inward and realizes the Truth, he undoubtedly gains Liberation. This is so, no matter whether he appeared to be a lofty jiva or a lowly jiva. The other way of understanding is: all the perception of all jiva-s is dependent on the jivahood of oneself. When you attain Liberation from individuality for yourself, all kinds of individuals, at that moment, cease to exist, for only real Being exists everywhere, with neither a self nor others. This real Being is Siva.

Q.: That is like awakening from a dream. All the jiva-s in the dream depend upon one jiva, who is actually Siva, apart from which they are nonexistent.

N.: From that perspective, everyone is depending upon you to realize. (laughter) You have the responsibility. (laughter)

Q.: It is a tad overwhelming. (laughter)

N.: That everyone is counting on you is equivalent to everybody in the dream saying, "We are caught in this dream, because this fellow keeps dreaming of us." (laughter) We should not forget, though, those who came before us. When the Maharshi realized, all kinds of jiva-s became liberated. Therefore, since the "time" of his Realization, "you" haven't existed. (silence, then laughter)

Q.: That is true.

N.: If we realize just how true this is, it is the end of illusion.

Another Q.: You said that one loses the capacity to remember how to recreate the ego. Who is remembering how to do it when it appears?

N.: If you put that question to yourself, what is the answer?

Q.: I don't think that there is anybody doing that. Something that I think is going on that is not really going on is only in my thinking about it. If I ask, "Who is thinking about it?" I can't find the thinker. It falls in on itself.

N.: Become very experientially, thoroughly certain that there really is no individual "I," the utter absence of the ego.

Q.: It is fun to chase it and see if it is there or where it is coming from.

N.: It is fun to search out the tendencies and destroy them and to search out the misidentifications and destroy them. The joy of such aspiration is superseded only by the Bliss of Liberation, itself. Exercise your freedom to become free.

Another Q.: I have been inquiring as to where the sense of individuality arises. I think that is the knot that you are speaking of.

N.: Yes, yet I have not seen the knot. (laughter)

Q.: I have heard that no one has. I notice that there are a range of physical things that, at first glance, seem to be an arising point for me. There is the heart center, and that is how I know I exist as an individual. There is a throat cakra and a stomach cakra that have similar kinds of experiences. I notice the heart standing in Consciousness, and, from there, it is easy to see the Consciousness instead of an objective thing. The Consciousness must be in the direction of my identity, not that which is held with Consciousness.

N.: Consciousness is homogeneous. There is nothing outside of it to hold and nothing inside it to grasp. When you say, "center," "cakra," "heart," "throat," "these experiences," and such, there must be an experiencer of them. Where does that experiencer arise? What is his birthplace? Infinite, homogeneous Consciousness exists, and this, Sri Bhagavan states, is the unborn Being. The body, which is not one's identity, any object of the body, and any subtle center do not say, "I." None of them know. They are known; they do not know.

Pure Consciousness ever knows, but it has nothing to know, for it is undifferentiated. In this verse, the Maharshi alludes to something that seems to arise that is styled as "I," which is the ego, the individual, and this becomes the birthplace, as it were, for the knot that ties the Subject to the object, the Real to the unreal, the pure Consciousness to something known. Trace this, and see what is there.

Q.: I do not have clarity. I can see the Consciousness. The Consciousness does not have a beginning. By the time I see the sense of individuality appended to something, it is already there. So far, I cannot see what is between the two. I do not know whether it is a matter of more discernment or if there is nothing to see.

N.: In order to truly know if there is nothing to see or not, you must discern finely. You should inquire deeply. You see what becomes appended, from subtle objects to gross forms, from abstract thoughts to formed thoughts. It is appended to someone. That is the very one that Sri Bhagavan asks us to inquire into, because with the rise of him, all this can arise. If he subsides, all this subsides. With a keenly inward-turned mind, search for that from which this "I" comes.

There is the original, unborn Being-Consciousness. It is innately egoless, and that which is innately egoless does not bring forth an ego. It does not bring forth anything else at all. It is just One. Or, we may say that it brings forth only itself. It does not bring forth a false sense of individuality.

You negate all the various forms of the ego in the process of practice. All of the instruction regarding ego-loss, though, aims at one point, if it can be called such. It is the supposition that there is a "you" to experience, to think of, or to know "something else." See if you can find him. That means getting to the very Heart of the one who dives in and then comes out to report on it by saying, "I saw nothing," or "I saw something." That very one is to be questioned unceasingly.

The intention to dive within to find this individual is very good, but the intention will be completed only by looking at the "I" of that very one. Whether the conception is that he is there or is that he is not there, who has that conception? Who is there to realize what? You should persist in this manner so that the mind, the ego, the knot, or the subtle body, call it what you will, is utterly consumed and so that there is no scope left for him to rise again. The inquiry should be uninterrupted so that, due to continuous Knowledge, there is no space for ignorance to rise again. When you have discerned ignorance as ignorance, you do not repeat it.

रूपोद्भवो रूपततिप्रतिष्ठो
रूपाशनो धूतगृहीतरूपः ।
स्वयं विरूपः स्वविचारकाले
धावत्यहङ्कारपिशाच एषः ॥ २५ ॥

rūpodbhavo rūpa-tati-pratiṣṭho
rūpāśano dhūta-gṛhīta-rūpaḥ |
svayaṁ virūpaḥ svavicāra-kāle
dhāvatyahaṅkāra-piśāca eṣaḥ || 25 ||

25

[Its] birth (springing from) is of form, based on a mass of form.

[It is] a feeder on form, one that has given up and grasped form,

Itself formless. Upon (at the time of) inquiry into itself,
It runs [away], this ego-ghost.

N.: For an ego-notion to seem to be, there must be some belief in a form. It is "based" on form, "springs forth" from a belief in a form, and "it is a feeder on form." That is what seems to give it substance. Otherwise, it starves. It has "given up and grasped form." This false sense of identity of "I" has been associated with one form after another, letting go of one only when it grasps another. Feeding on form, as it were, to give it substance, it then goes to another form. It moves from one thought-form to another thought-form and from one body to another body. "Itself formless," is the character of the ego, Sri Ramana says. No one has ever seen the form of an ego. One sees the forms that are artificially appended to it due to delusion, but the ego, itself, is not seen. It is seen neither with the eyes nor with the mind. It is just a vague, background assumption that is parasitical, as described.

"Upon inquiry into itself," if that very "I"-sense that seems to be individualized turns inward to look at its own individual existence, its individuality "runs away." The ego is just "a ghost." This description assumes that you know that ghosts are not real. It is just a ghost, having no substance and having no life. Whenever you inquire, it runs away. If your inquiry is continuous, it runs away continuously. Such continuous inquiry becoming steady Knowledge, the egoless state is also steady, and gone is the attachment to any kind of form.

"Based on a mass of form," the ego notion cannot stand alone. Remove its trappings, and what is there?

No one has ever seen an ego at any time. One sees the forms that are its guises. Its springing forth, or its birth, has no actual birthplace, but it is of form. The subtlest form is the assumed individuality, which is so vague that it must immediately start feeding, for, otherwise, it will starve. It feeds on form. It is "based on a mass of form," which is the world of its experience. It is a "feeder on form" that "has given up form and grasped form." One form of experience follows another. All the forms pertain to the individual. The Maharshi has said that the ego is like an inch worm, going from twig to twig, leaving one twig only when it has found the next twig, grasps it, lifts up its hind legs, and brings the back legs to meet the front again. It thus sticks from twig to twig. What would happen if the twigs were removed from the inch worm? It would cease to move, and it would fall. If the forms of the various misidentifications and attachments with which the ego dresses itself are removed, what happens to the ego? This "feeder on form" is an illusory creature that goes where there is something to eat. If there is nothing put out for it to eat, it starves and runs away.

We can do more than starve it of its attachments and its definitions. Sri Ramana says, "itself, formless." To inquire, we are told to find the "I"-thought. It is to find its absence and to realize the real Existence behind it. It is not intended that we, in our minds, latch on to the word or the idea, "I." The instruction means to trace back the forms, which are the objects of experience, to this "I"-notion, which is the conception of existing as an individual. It is so nebulous, in a whirlpool of forms, surrounded by a cyclone of forms. Casting the forms aside, we inquire as to what is at the center. Like the cyclone, it is hollow. There is nothing at the center. Getting to the center, inquiring into itself, it runs away. It is an ego-ghost. It is not a real thing, and it is not actually alive. It does not know, and it does not exist. With the misidentification with the body, it gives itself a semblance of being solid. Remove the misidentification and similar attachments, and the solidity is gone. Make the attempt to so much as thoroughly look at it, and it vanishes. "It runs away," says Ramana. Trace this "I"-sense in you, and you will understand what he means.

Q.: To look at it thoroughly means to examine everything that composes it, such as attachment.

N.: The attachments are the forms upon which it feeds. They come afterward. What is at the center? To what are those forms appended? One should stop feeding it, that is, not entertain attachments and various forms of misidentifications and not entertain samskaras and tendencies. You should also discern by inquiry. Is it the individual who inquires? That could be inferred from “svavicara-kale,” upon or at the time of, inquiry into its own self. It appears as if the individual commences the inquiry, but he will not survive it. Only the real Existence, which alone knows and is unborn, will survive. So, in a very deep, profound sense, the inquiry begins and ends only by the power, by the Light, of the Self. It is born of Knowledge. In a more casual sense, we can say that the individual, whose real nature is nothing except pure Consciousness, though he does not know that, starts the inquiry. He looks at himself. He turns away from the forms upon which he has fed, looks at himself, and is gone. When he is gone, you are awake. The dream is over.

Q.: Forever? It is not a temporary disappearance?

N.: If the ego’s disappearance is temporary, he is not gone. He is just sleeping.

Another Q.: He finds Bliss.

N.: Bliss is where Being is and is the same as Consciousness. It is experienced in direct proportion to the absence of egoism. The ego feeds on various forms for the purpose of acquiring happiness, but, by feeding, it only makes suffering, which is the reverse effect of what is wished. For Bliss, the ego must dissolve. There is no such thing as a happy ego.

Another Q.: Is the illusory belief in an ego, an individual, just another form of the mind?

N.: Of what is your belief in an ego constituted?

Q.: Awareness of thoughts.

N.: If it is an awareness of thoughts, when thoughts stop, does the ego disappear?

Q.: It seems to.

N.: Then, how does it return?

Q.: I don’t know. It comes back when a thought comes back.

N.: The thought must come back for someone.

Q.: It comes back for me.

N.: Who starts thinking these thoughts? Is it that the unborn, infinite Self starts to think these thoughts, or is it somebody else?

Q.: Somebody else.

N.: That is the culprit. You need to find him. When you say that you have thoughts, that could be said to be the effect of the ego, but it is not proof of the ego's existence. Who is the "I?" What makes up the "I" who says, "I have a mind, I have my experience, I have my thoughts, I am aware, and sometimes I am unaware." Who is that? What is his nature? It cannot be the body. The body is much further down the road, so to speak.

Q.: Whoever that is, he is one step up from any thought or object, and he is aware of these.

N.: But he is lost or becomes entangled in those thoughts or objects, does he not?

Q.: Yes. He believes in them.

N.: He becomes sunk in them, mixes himself up with them, and feeds on them, but who is he? What is his real nature? Pull away the thoughts and the body and see what is left of him.

Q.: There is nothing there.

N.: You must become very sure that there is nothing there. All the wise sages and scriptures declare your nature to be the infinite Brahman, pure Being-Consciousness-Bliss, the Unborn and the Immortal, the Perfect Fullness, which never undergoes any kind of entanglement, let alone any kind of suffering. This is the Perfection. Then, there is this fellow who is rummaging around in the thoughts. Whenever he shows up, problems of some kind or another happen, and, whenever he disappears, everything is just fine. So, you must deal directly with this mischief-maker, and the best way of dealing with him directly is to inquire into his very nature. Who or what exactly is he? If you say that you cannot see him, just be thorough in your not-seeing.

Q.: He is very slippery.

N.: He seems as if he is slippery, like trying to hold a fish in your hands; it slides out. When, though, you actually inquire, he is not even slippery. The experience is more like walking straight into a mirage to find out whether there is any water in it in which to drown. There is nothing slippery about it at all.

भावेऽहमः सर्वमिदं विभाति
लयेऽहमो नैव विभाति किञ्चित्।
तस्मादहंरूपमिदं समस्तं
तन्मार्गणं सर्वजयाय मार्गः ॥ २६ ॥

bhāve'hamaḥ sarvam-idaṁ vibhāti
laye'hamo naiva vibhāti kiñcit |
tasmād-ahaṁ-rūpam-idaṁ samastaṁ
tan-mārgaṇaṁ sarva-jayāya mārgaḥ || 26 ||

26

On the becoming of the "I," all this shines (appears).
On the dissolution of the "I," not anything, indeed, shines (appears).
Therefore, of the form of "I" is this completely.
That search is the way (path) (Or: the search for That is the way) for victory over all.

N.: If "I" arises, everything arises or appears. Everything includes all duality, all the triads, the world, and the mind. If the "I" subsides, or dissolves, everything disappears. "Therefore, of the form of "I" is this completely." All of the "this," in one's experience, is just this "I" in another guise. It rises with "I", and it ceases with "I." Its apparent existence, its seeming appearance, is utterly dependent on "I." So, it is only "I" conceived as "this." One "I" is both the "I" and the "this." Therefore, laying out the path, Sri Ramana declares that the search to know the nature of the "I," "is the path for victory over all."

What is the significance of "victory"? It means Liberation, which is freedom from all bondage associated with anything whatsoever. If there is "I," there is something by which that "I" can be bound. If the "I" subsides, due to realization of the true Existence, there is no "I" and there is no "this." Where there is no "this" and no "I," who is to be bound and by what?

Whichever way you might move through the experiences that can be described as "this,' from the subtle thoughts of the mind to the forms of the world, in the end, you must come around to knowing yourself for Self-Realization, or Enlightenment, or Liberation, as we call it. That which is to be accomplished at the end should be done even at the beginning. Understand all "this" to be "I." Know the root of the "I." Know the nature of the "I." This is the formless path to realize the Formless. There is nothing objective in it, and, therefore, no possibility of any remaining bondage.

Everything experienced, of whatever kind, every kind of limitation, and every kind of object, is dependent on "I." "I" becomes, "I" arises, and everything else appears. If the "I" dissolves, nothing appears. Only Being-Consciousness-Bliss remains. The entirety of duality, the entirety of maya or samsara, is entirely dependent on the "I." So, loss of the "I" by any means is most important and most blissful.

"Of the form of 'I' is this completely." If all the "this" aspect of your experience is dependent on "I" and is never experienced apart from the "I," we know that the "this" really has no existence whatsoever. If it is an utterly dependent existence, it has no self-existence. It is just the "I" in the guise of "this." You, yourself, appear as "I," and then, as "I," you, yourself, appear as all "this." Dissolve the "this" into the "I" by knowing its nature, and dissolve the "I," by knowing its nature, into the original, unborn, uncaused Being-Consciousness-Bliss.

"Of the form of "I" is this completely." You have never experienced anything but yourself. Now, know your Self as you truly are, not as "I," and all rising and ceasing cease. "That search is the way," or "The search for that is the way." For what is the search? The search is for "I." This is the path to the vision of Reality. It is the way to attain Liberation from all of the imagined bondage. Sri Ramana proclaims that it "is the way for victory over all." It is a spiritual victory, in which bondage is permanently put to an end forever. It is victory over illusion. It is victory over birth-and-death. It is victory over all attachments.

If you want to renounce attachments, the way to be victorious in renunciation is to know the nature of the "I," to know the renouncer. "I" vanishing, all "this" vanishes, and attachment is utterly gone. If you desire victory over suffering, understand the nature of the "I," the sufferer. Searching for the nature of the "I," the sufferer, the individual, vanishes, and the "this" aspect, which is the suffering, also vanishes. The very potential to suffer vanishes. This is victory over all.

That which rises will set. If something is born, it will perish. How can you attain victory over death? In the Vedas, such victory over death is mentioned and illustrated by various stories. What is this victory over death? It is the Realization of your unborn nature. With the rise of "I," there is duality. With the rise of "I," there is birth and death. Where there is no rise of "I," where even the potential for an "I" has been eliminated, there is no cause for birth or rebirth. That is victory over death in the immortal, blissful Existence that you are.

Then, there is no maya, or illusion. "Victory over all" is a grand spiritual victory. When all is conquered, there is nothing left of the conquered. It is a unique kind of victory. Your aim is to attain happiness, and that aim has been pursued for so long. You reach the attainment of happiness by knowing the nature of the "I," for, with its individuality vanishing, its real nature as the Bliss-Consciousness, which is pure Being, remains. It is this victory to which we refer when we say, "Jaya Guru."

Q.: If there is the appearance of anything outward in the mind, I should notice the root cause of such as the ego.

N.: In your own experience, from the subtlest thought to a sensed object, does anything exist independent of the "I" that knows it?

Q.: Ultimately, the knowing part does not seem to come from what I believe in.

N.: That is true. The light, the knowing, derives from pure Consciousness, but pure Consciousness has neither an "I" nor a "this."

Q.: But once it is differentiated?

N.: Once it seems differentiated, you seem to occupy a separate identity. Then, "this" is also perceived. Sri Bhagavan points the way inward to be free of this differentiated delusion.

See that all of "this" is only "I." It rises and sets with "I," depends upon "I," and is never apart from it. It is only the "I" in the guise of "this." So, it is "I" and "I." All is just "I." Trace this "I." The known is absorbed in the knowing, the knowing is absorbed in the knower, and the knower is only pure Consciousness and not an individual at all. From here, there is no separate knowing, knower, or known.

Q.: Because Consciousness doesn't have any attribute.

N.: Consciousness has no "I," and it has no "this." The Self, or Being, is not born. In infinite Consciousness, there is no "I." The "I" has not come to be. Likewise is it with "this."

Another Q.: Is the "I" that knows a pseudo-subject? The pseudo-"I" does not know what is.

N.: It is a pseudo-subject that is composed of two parts. One part is the Reality, the identity, which is the Light of Consciousness. That is of the real Self. The other pseudo-part of it is the assumed individuality that marks it off as a knower.

Q.: Yes, because there is only one subject.

N.: If there is only one subject, and it is the infinite Reality, it is all, in all, at all times, without any change.

Q.: There is no "this," then.

N.: "This" is not.

Q.: I understand.

N.: Our bondage, our sorrow, and our difficulty, at any time, are due only to the ego-notion. Wake up from the ego-notion. This enables you to be completely transcendent of "this," whatever it may be in the world. We are not bound by anything, and there is no cause for our suffering or sorrow. Therefore, the *Gita* says, "The wise do not grieve."

सत्या स्थितिर्नाहमुदेति यत्र
तच्चोदयस्थानगवेषणेन ।

विना न नश्येद्यदि तन्न नश्येत्
स्वात्मैक्यरूपा कथमस्तु निष्ठा ॥ २७ ॥

satyā sthitir-nāham-udeti yatra
tac-codaya-sthāna-gaveṣaṇena |
vinā na naśyed-yadi tan-na naśyet
svātmaikya-rūpā katham-astu niṣṭhā || 27 ||

27

The Real State (True Abidance) is where "I" does not arise,
And that, without the fervent search (inquiry) for the place of emergence,
Is not destroyed (will not perish). If that is not destroyed (does not perish),
How may there be abidance, of the nature of Oneness of the True (own) Self?

N.: From the Maharshi's teachings and from one's interior inquiry, or direct experience, it is evident that the real state is "I"-less. That which comes with the "I" is a mere illusion. This means that every other state in which you ever seem to be immersed is not real. Your real state is the "I"-less state. Not only is this the case upon Realization, but it is the only real state for all, at all times.

Sri Bhagavan says, "Without the fervent search for that place of emergence" of that "I," the "fervent search" signifying intense inquiry, "it will not be destroyed." There is one thing that the ego cannot stand, and that is an intense, fervent inquiry into its own nature or into its source. The inquiry into its nature and the inquiry into its source amount to the same thing. If the ego is not destroyed, how may there be abidance? We cannot simultaneously realize the Self and retain the ego. Realization of the Self means that no more false states are imagined and just your real, innate state, remains. This innate state is truly ego-less.

The Maharshi describes the nature of that abidance as "the Oneness of the true Self." Oneness indicates no differentiation and no second "I." One's own Self is One only; there is never a second "I." No "I" arises. This is the real state. To realize it, all that is necessary is an intense inquiry, a "fervent search," into the very root, or source, of "I," which is into the place where it seems to rear up.

The real state, the true Self-abidance, is that in which "I" does not arise. There is no hint of duality in that state, so there is no entering it or exiting it. Abidance is not an activity. It is not something done at one time and not done at another. "Abidance" signifies that your identity is known as That, only That, always That, without exception. That is the true Abidance in which there is no assumed individuality.

The Maharshi instructs, "And that, without the fervent search for the place of emergence, is not destroyed." Unless you search for the "I," inquiring, "From where does it come?" and "What is its nature?" the imagined "I," which is the jiva, will not be destroyed.

Elsewhere, the Maharshi has said that inquiry into the Self is the one means to transcend all the duality that one is trying to get over. Every other approach includes, as a supposition, those dualities. All of them, be they activities of the mind or the body, are based on "I." How else to make the "I" perish except by seeking its nature and finding its nonexistence? Otherwise, one will go on assuming that it really is. If that assumption is not destroyed, if the "I" does not perish, how can there be abidance?

The nature of the abidance is the Oneness of the true Self. The sense of a separate identity must vanish. It vanishes by examining it to know what it is. No matter what you do in the name of spirituality, no matter how you practice, no matter what the experiences may be, in the end, for Self-Realization, you must come to the Knowledge of your Self. You must know the nature of the "I" and find the "I"-less true "I," your real Being.

The state of Self-abidance is Being, free of the assumption of individuality. If individuality is assumed, inquire directly into the assumed individuality. Unless that is done, this Self-abidance will not be your own Realization. If this inquiry into your own nature is accomplished, there is no unrealized state.

Q.: In the morning, when one wakes up, everything is just perfect. Then, there arises a kind of vague dissatisfaction. At that very moment, it would be wise to examine this and make a fervent inquiry into the nature of the one for whom there is dissatisfaction.

N.: That would be a good moment to inquire. Every single moment that comes after that moment is also a good moment. (laughter) One of the beauties of Self-inquiry is that, for it, you need not wait for an opportune moment. It can be before, during, or after any kind of experience. Inquiry does not depend on the outer experience or the state of mind. It has its beginning, its cause, and its end, or goal, in you. There is no particular time and no particular place for it.

Q.: I cannot really inquire into what is thought of or occurs during sleep at night, but I assume that there is some misidentification going on.

N.: Perhaps, but, because of what you are describing right now, it is generally advisable to inquire throughout the waking state. If you inquire throughout the waking state, the effect of your inquiry will continue in dream and in deep sleep, because what you inquire to know does not pass through the states but is actually beyond the states. It is the "space" in which those states revolve. Identifying with that "space," even while apparently in the waking state, you transcend the dream and the deep sleep states, as well.

Another Q.: Reflecting upon continuous inquiry, it seems that, when Realization occurs, all ignorance is burned up. At that point, continuous inquiry would be possible. Before that, continuous inquiry would be more difficult.

N.: If continuous inquiry is possible only upon Self-Realization, and, if, in Self-Realization, no further inquiry is needed, what are you saying? (laughter) Why is continuous inquiry not possible now?

Q.: Obscuration occurs in the mind.

N.: What prevents you from inquiring to free yourself from the obscuration and thus clarify your knowledge? What prevents you from dissolving that very mind and even realizing the mind's nonexistence, as well as the unreality of the obstruction?

Q.: I guess that there is nothing, but what if there is another obscuration lurking somewhere or left behind?

N.: The same principle applies.

Q.: It seems that, if I blow away a sheath, there is another that follows.

N.: The purpose of the instruction about the sheaths is to indicate, even now, in Reality, you are none of that.

Q.: It is said that inquiry can annihilate everything. The laser-like Consciousness burns up everything in its way.

N.: Yes, it is as sharp as a laser and as broad as space itself. It does not make a difference if there are tendencies stacked upon each other, under each other, behind each other, spread out in an array, or if a herd of them is wandering through the mind. (laughter) You must still know the real Self by Self-inquiry.

Q.: What you are saying is so, because the Truth is real, and all that other stuff is not.

N.: The Truth is real. You are the Truth. The capacity to realize the Truth is never diminished. In practical application, an inquiry into your Self is so revelatory as to the liberated nature of the Self that it may not be possible to verbally or mentally enumerate all the tendencies, thoughts, ideas, and false assumptions from which you become free simultaneously. Therefore, descriptions, be they mental or written, point in the general direction, selecting a few examples.

Q.: The essence of inquiry, then, is non-mental, because we are transcending every mental aspect. Therefore, there must be the clear recognition that everything one has ever wanted is really to be found in that inquiry.

N.: It is in the Knowledge, which is That which the inquiry reveals. It is in your Self. Everything you ever wanted is in your Being. All that you ever wanted, no matter what it was, up to the loftiest goal of Self-Realization, is your Self. All that you have wanted is just your Being.

Another Q.: The ego seems to exist. With the belief that the ego is real, any kind of form that springs forth after the ego arises is tainted with that same misconception, so that the form now is also real.

N.: Unless you unravel it. You can unravel it all at once, or you can unravel it piece by piece. If the object drops off first and the nebulous subject is still assumed, you would still be proceeding in the right direction.

Q.: The experience hinges on that one little point. That apparent separation, or apparent differentiation, falls apart as I get close to what is really real.

N.: All that is required is the light of inquiry to remove the shadow of illusion. It is not a real illusion; it is a shadow of illusion. Once the assumed differentiation is taken to be real, assumed to be an "I" that supposedly exists, there are all kinds of questions and doubts about how to be free, how to realize, or how to abide as That. Sages, such as Ribhu, say, "Abide as That, in That, as That." From the position of the individual "I," how could this be possible? In an earlier verse, the Maharshi said, "This is not an easy bhava." How are you to abide as the Self, if the "I" is supposedly differentiated? Only by inquiring, as instructed by the Maharshi, in such a way so that the "I"-sense perishes, so there is no one left to abide in such or as such. It is just a manner of speaking to say, "You abide as the Self." The "you" is the Self, the Self is the Self, and the abidance, or Knowledge, also, is just the Self. So, we could say, "Self, Self, Self," but no one would understand what we are talking about. (laughter)

If wisdom is not firm, penetrate into this "I," because the Knowledge of Being is as firm as Being, itself. Unsteadiness is a superimposition born of the ego, which rises and falls. The only thing to be done, therefore, is to inquire into this ego.

Q.: The steps in this inquiry seem to blend together. The sequence of questioning, "There is a thought. For whom is the thought? It is for me. Who am I?" is very helpful. However, the more I inquire, the less there is that much definition to it, and it becomes a single blend of such inquiries.

N.: It is a single introspective current. Steps, aspects, and stages of development are enumerated and described for purposes of spiritual instruction, so that the seeker gets a good grasp of the direction in which to head and how to meditate. The inquiry is not, though, actually divided into particular steps, any more than the current of a river is divided into particular steps or stages as it blends with the ocean. It just needs to go in the right direction, and, when it arrives at the destined goal, it has lost its individuality. The river, every drop of it, ends up completely in the ocean, but there is no river in the ocean.

Q.: That metaphor describes the experience very well. I may think that I am a river on the way, but once I get to the ocean, the experience is otherwise.

N.: It is just one vast expanse of water. There are no individual drops in the ocean.

कूपे यथा गाढजले तथान्तः
निमज्ज्य बुद्ध्या शितया नितान्तम् ।
प्राणं च वाचं च नियम्य चिन्वन्
विन्देन्निजाहङ्कृतिमूलरूपम् ॥ २८ ॥

kūpe yathā gāḍha-jale tathāntaḥ
nimajjya buddhyā śitayā nitāntam |
prāṇaṁ ca vācaṁ ca niyamya cinvan
vinden-nijāhaṅkṛti-mūla-rūpam || 28 ||

28

Just as in a well of water into [which one] has dived deeply, just so, within
One must dive (plunge) with intellect highly (extraordinarily) sharp,
Prana and speech to be controlled (lit., having controlled), inquiring (reflecting on);
One shall find the nature of the root of one's own ego.

N.: The imagery of diving into a deep well of water is self-explanatory, indicative of being one-pointed in one's task. Assume that there is no scuba gear, and there is the shortness of time involved while holding the breath. If you are diving under the water to obtain of retrieve something, you are not distracted. Your senses, your activities, and your mind are being "controlled," that is, directed for a deliberate purpose. In a similar manner, direct your life's activities, your prana, for prana is that which activates the senses, and direct your speech, which includes all relating and communicating, as well as what you say, wisely. Do not waste precious time in what is frivolous, extraneous, and futile. Reflecting deeply upon the teaching, inquiring with a very sharp mind honed by the desire to turn inward, discriminating between thought and what is real, in just such a manner, should one practice.

Inquiring in this way, "One will find the nature of the root of one's own ego." Get to the root, and it is just the Being that you always wanted, without a trace of the ego whatsoever. The Source, or the Root, is your own Existence, but, when you realize Existence, it proves not to be a launching place, or a source, for the ego at all. It is conceived as a root only so long as the ego's appearance seems to be. When, inquiring in such a manner, you discern what really exists as your own nature, the very nature of "I," it is "I"-less, that is, egoless. There is nothing in real Being to give rise to an ego. If the ego came at all, its root is the Self. If, though, we experientially trace the root within ourselves and find it, the Self, there is no possibility of an ego, and delusion is gone. If the root is not known, illusion may appear, disappear, and reappear again. If the root is known, there is no one for whom the illusion can be, and maya does not exist.

If you dive deep into water to recover something, you do not waste your time. You do not become excessively talkative under the water, and you do not thrash around engaging in other activities. You are single-minded in your purpose. You are aware of the limited time, and you keep the purpose firmly in mind. In the same way, in practice, we should dive deep and not waste our time in the frivolous activities of maya.

Sri Ramana says, "One must dive with intellect highly sharp." This refers to discrimination, discerning the Self from the not-self, the Real from the unreal. It is an extraordinarily sharp intellect that cuts itself right down the center, opening up its own thought patterns to get at the root of them. This is what is meant by a sharp mind.

"With prana and speech to be controlled" is wisely directing the activities that prana animates, which includes everything of the body, the senses, etc., and speech, which includes all forms of communicating, relating, etc. Wisely direct all of your faculties, such as the mind, prana, speech, and body, while diving inward by discrimination to discern the real Self, with that as your goal, one-pointedly inquiring. If this is the manner of approach and the orientation, so that this inquiry is not casual, nor even an insightful interest, but a matter of extremely important experience for you, knowing full well the significance of, and the opportunity you have for, Self-Realization, "One shall find the nature of the root of one's own ego," by that profound inquiry.

If an interpretation is according to yoga practices, control of speech is refraining from unnecessary talk, limiting the amount of speech or refraining from it altogether, for the beneficial effect such has on the mind, and the control of prana is for the purpose of yielding a corresponding beneficial effect on the mind. This text, though, is instruction in pure Jnana. Therefore, the emphasis is on Self-inquiry and not the introduction of different practices.

Get to the root. From one perspective, the "I" springs from nothing, for it is only an illusion. From another perspective, because it has borrowed identity and a seeming reality, it springs from a root that is Existence. Discover the falseness of the illusory "I," and get to the basic Existence, for in that lies your peace and bliss.

Q.: How to keep one's focus and intensity without wavering, always at a peak, which is necessary to dissolve the ego?

N. If you know the purpose of life and the source of happiness, the intensity is present and sustained. If you know that the purpose of this life is Liberation, or Self-Realization, and you also know that this is the only way to find happiness, because happiness is within, and within is the Self, your intensity will be sustained and will not be dissipated by other desires and vagaries of the mind.

Q.: I certainly want to know, for sure, that this is the purpose.

N.: Knowing that purpose, with that as the aim, without which life is an unreal dream, with which life and even more than this life are fulfilled, without which there is no complete contentment, with which there is a happiness that leaves no other happiness to be desired, your spiritual practice will be intense and sustained. If this is thoroughly understood, you should do everything possible to foster and to pursue the practice, availing yourself of everything that helps your practice, because this is the purpose of life, and your happiness depends upon it. Do whatever is necessary to aid your spiritual practice and detach yourself from anything else, in order to reach Liberation. Like a person under water who is holding her breath, you will be very focused.

Let us dive deep into the Maharshi's teachings.

मौनेन मज्जन्मनसा स्वमूल -
चर्चैव सत्यात्मविचारणं स्यात् ।
एषोऽहमेतन्न मम स्वरूप -
मिति प्रमा सत्यविचारणाङ्गम् ॥ २९ ॥

maunena majjan-manasā svamūla-
carcaiva satyātma-vicāraṇaṁ syāt ।
eṣo'ham-etan-na mama svarūpa-
m-iti pramā satya-vicāraṇāṅgam ।। 29 ।।

29

By silent diving by the mind [into] the true (one's own) root:
[This] inquiry (consideration), indeed, (alone) shall be true Self-inquiry.

"This I am, this is not my true (own) nature,"
Thus, [this] correct idea (understanding, knowledge) is a limb of (unessential to, secondary to, inferior to) true inquiry.

N.: In this verse, Sri Bhagavan contrasts the value of thought, even very lofty thought-driven meditation, with real inquiry. He says that the "silent diving by the mind into one's own root, or into the true root," is the inquiry. Silence is "I"-less. It is That in which the "I" disappears. There is where the inquiry occurs. Thoughts in the mind do not constitute the inquiry. The inquiry does not truly begin or end in the mind. It occurs in the domain of Silence, which is egoless Being, which is ego-dissolving Being. So, Sri Ramana says "This consideration, or this inquiry, is, indeed, alone, true Self-inquiry." It is the silent diving interior to the body, the senses, and the mind. It is not thinking about such. It is not thinking about, "This is what I am, this is not what I am, this is not my nature, and this is my nature." The inquiry is something far more profound.

The inquiry pertains to Knowledge. Knowledge, in the deep spiritual sense of Self-Knowledge, is not a thought process. It is completely transcendent of the level of thought. "This I am not; That I am; the object I am not; the Self I am," is a "correct idea, a correct understanding or knowledge," in a mental sense, but it is only a "limb," and not the core of inquiry. It is "unessential" to true inquiry, because the Knowledge that composes inquiry is thought-transcendent. It is "secondary" to thought-transcendent Knowledge. The prime thrust in your practice must be the inquiry, which is the deep diving within your own Being. Thinking about these spiritual matters or this wisdom is only secondary. The phrase may also be interpreted as meaning "is inferior to true inquiry," because no thought will bring about Self-Realization. Only the deep, silent diving within yourself, in which your identity becomes revealed as That, will yield Self-Realization.

While the inquiry is the silent, unconceived, inner opening of Knowledge, the thoughts, "This I am, this is not my own nature," are a limb of it. It is a correct idea. It is a correct understanding of the Knowledge, but it is a limb, not the thing itself. We may translate the phrase as "secondary to true inquiry." The inquiry is primary. Or, we may translate this phrase as "inferior to true inquiry," because, if we merely think along these lines, but do not actually inquire, how will that bring about final Liberation? Inquiry can go on with or without such spiritual thoughts. We can translate the phrase as, "unessential to the true inquiry." The actual inquiry is the silent diving within and the absorption of your identity, so that you remain as the Self.

All the thoughts, even the spiritual thoughts, are secondary. They may be limbs in your practice, but they are not the essential inquiry. That which is to be done is to actually inquire and know, by first hand experience, in the most interior, silent manner, your own Being.

गवेषणात्प्राप्य हृदन्तरं तत्
पतेदहन्ता परिभुग्नशीर्षा ।
अथाहमन्यत्स्फुरति प्रकृष्टं
नाहङ्कृतिस्तत्परमेव पूर्णम् ॥ ३० ॥

gaveṣaṇāt-prāpya hṛdantaraṁ tat
pated-ahantā paribhugna-śīrṣā ǀ
athāham-anyat-sphurati prakṛṣṭaṁ
nāhaṅkṛtis-tat-parameva pūrṇam ǀǀ 30 ǀǀ

30

From (by) the search is to be attained (reached) (lit., having attained, having reached), within the Heart, That.
The "I" consciousness shall fall, head bowed.
Then, another "I" shines forth, preeminent (superior).
It is not the ego. That is the Supreme alone (indeed), the Perfect Fullness.

N.: The silent diving into your own nature mentioned in the previous verse is the search alluded to in this verse. "From the search is to be attained within the Heart," means within the core of one's very Being, and "That" is Brahman, the vast Absolute. The aim of the inquiry to know oneself is nothing less than the absolute Knowledge of the Absolute, itself. It is utterly impersonal and utterly transcendent. "The "I"-consciousness shall fall," that is, the ego topples over into nonexistence, "head bowed." The imagery is that of complete ego-dissolution, complete humility in the deepest sense, and complete annihilation of egotism.

"Then, another 'I' shines forth, preeminent. It is not the ego." There is no pause between ego-dissolution and the revelation of the Self. They are simultaneous, just as the removal of the surface covering is simultaneous with the revelation of the substrate that was hidden. Ego-dissolution is revelation of the Self. Because the Self, being of the nature of Reality, is Being-Consciousness-Bliss, the ego-dissolution is always blissful, always of the nature of Knowledge, or Consciousness, and is always the revelation of what is real.

The deepest humility is the greatest glory, for where the "I" ceases, the Self shines.

"It is not the ego. That," meaning this true "I," your real identity, "is the Supreme alone, the Perfect Fullness." Your own Being is limitless and is not lacking in any respect. What this Purnam, Perfect Fullness, is can be known only by experience within yourself. Consider it deeply and you become detached from everything else. Know it first hand, and suffering becomes impossible. Where is this Perfect Fullness found? It is found only in the core of your Being, the Heart. How is it found? It "shines forth." It "flashes forth" the moment the ego-notion dissolves. The ego-notion alone is the root of all kinds of suffering and bondage. Its dissolution heralds the end of such. What is revealed is something that is perfectly full and has never been diminished. Therefore, when you know yourself as you really are, you find a happiness that cannot possibly come to an end.

Sri Ramana has urged the search for the "I," shown the discrimination, and explained the manner in which one should approach the search. Now, he describes the fruit of this search. By the search is attained "That within the Heart." Brahman is realized as the Essence of one's Being, apart from which, there is no other being.

"The "I"-consciousness shall fall." That which is the source of all illusion, which is the one who becomes caught in illusion and upon which all illusion depends, falls. "Head bowed" is indicative of ego-loss.

"Then, another "I" shines forth." There is no gap in time from the fall of the ego to the shining of the Self. When the illusion is removed, Reality, which is already present, shines. "Prakrstam" signifies "superior, preeminent." In what ways is it superior? It is not the ego; it is the real meaning of "I." The real meaning of "I" has nothing to do with ego. The real meaning of "I" has nothing to do with individuality, bondage, or delusion at all.

"Another 'I' shines forth." That is your true Existence, that which all are all of the time. It shines forth, by itself, to itself. It is not the ego; it is the Supreme, alone. Brahman knows Brahman. Just Siva is; there is no possibility of a jiva. It is the Perfect Fullness. In that Bliss, no other happiness is desired. In that Peace, there is no disturbance ever. If you know this, there is nothing left to be known. If you experience this, there is nothing else to be experienced. It is complete. The contentment of such spiritual perfection, the Perfect Fullness of the Absolute, cannot be described in words and thoughts. To know it, it is best that you immerse yourself in it.

अहङ्कृतिं यो लसति ग्रसित्वा
किं तस्य कार्यं परिशिष्टमस्ति ।
किञ्चिद्विजानाति स नात्मनोऽन्यत्
तस्य स्थितिं भावयितुं क्षमः कः ॥ ३१ ॥

ahaṅkṛtiṁ yo lasati grasitvā
kiṁ tasya kāryaṁ pariśiṣṭam-asti ।
kiñcid-vijānāti sa nātmano'nyat
tasya sthitiṁ bhāvayituṁ kṣamaḥ kaḥ ।। 31 ।।

३१

[He] who shines, having swallowed (consumed, caused to disappear) the ego,
For him, what is left remaining to be done?
He knows not anything other than the Self.
Who is able to conceive of his state?

N.: This exceedingly profound, glorious verse composed by the Maharshi succinctly describes himself, Brahman, Realization, and the means of realizing.

"He who shines" is the sage of realized Knowledge, yet such a one has consumed the ego, and all that remains of him is the Self. It is the nondual Self that shines. No individual shines. The ego has been consumed. When the ego appeared, there was something to be done. When it was seen that the something to be done was to get rid of this very ego, that was the last thing to be done. For one for whom the ego has disappeared entirely in the Knowledge of the solitary Existence of the Self, One without a second, what remains to be done?

With the Realization of the Self, everything is accomplished. With the Realization of the Self, the Perfect Fullness, which is the utmost Perfection and the final goal of all accomplishments, is found to be ever-existent. So, what remains to be done? He does not have a body. He does not have a mind. So, what remains for him to do? There is no goal for him to reach, for he, himself, is the goal. There is no happiness to attain, because he, himself, is Bliss. There is nothing for him further to know, because he is Knowledge, itself, which is pure Consciousness. So, what could possibly remain for him to do? The peace of such a one as Sri Bhagavan is entirely complete. If the ego disappears, you abide as that very same One, without the least trace of individuality and with nothing further to accomplish. The purpose of life is thus fulfilled, and even life is transcended.

Sri Bhagavan says, "He knows not anything other than the Self." If there is individuality, there is something else to know. When it is realized that there is no individual, there is no differentiation, and there is nothing else to know. If we say, "He perceives," he perceives himself only. If we do not have that idea, he is just himself, One, without a second. In either case, who is able to conceive of his state? His state is pure Being. Whatever idea may be conceived concerning it, Being is more than that.

Who can conceive of his state? Expressing devotion, we can loosely say, "He is wise. He is peaceful. He is free. He is glorious. He is illuminating." We can describe him in ever so many ways, but what really is his state? If his state is the state of Brahman, pure Being, who can conceive it, much less describe it? Just as it is impossible to have a concept of yourself, but, rather, all your concepts deal with what is not your Self, so it is impossible to really conceive of Sri Bhagavan. If you dive deep, silently, to understand him, you disappear. Then, there is the perfectly full Knowledge of who he is, of who you are, which is one and the same thing, for Being is indivisible, but nothing can be said about it, and nothing can be thought about it. The real Knowledge is, thus, silent.

"Who is able to conceive of his state?" The Self alone knows the Self. No other exists to know the Self. Should we suppose another, it cannot know the Self. Knowledge belongs to the Self alone, and it is inconceivable, as Being is inconceivable. So, Sri Ramana says, "Who is able to conceive of his state?" (silence)

Here, Sri Ramana elucidates, at once, who he is, his state, the state of Self-Realization, and the very nature of the Self.

"Having swallowed, having consumed, or caused to disappear, the ego," what shines? The Self, the eternal Existence, the One described as being unborn and imperishable, the Infinite and the Eternal, shines. "For him, what is left remaining to be done?" Having lost his ego, he is no longer "he," but only the Self. The Self has nothing to do, and, for the Self, there is nothing to be accomplished. For the individual, there is something to be done, and that something-to-be-done-impulse does not vanish until he vanishes. When he vanishes, there is nothing more to be done, whether such would be of a spiritual kind or of any other kind. Being non-ego, he is a non-actor, a non-doer, and a non-thinker. Who would do? What would be done? How could it be?

"For him, what is left remaining to be done?" The egoless state is the supreme accomplishment. It is Self-Realization, attaining which life's purpose is fulfilled. There is, then, nothing left to be accomplished. It is the Perfect Fullness and the true finality.

"He knows not anything other than the Self." For one who has realized the Self as the Reality, it alone is the Reality. There is no second reality. For one in whom the individuality, or ego, has subsided, there is no "I." If there is no "I," there is no "this." Who would know what? "He knows not anything other than the Self." If He can be said to know anything, he knows the Self as existing everywhere; not just as all-pervading, but as that which alone exists. If we do not conceive of him as knowing, but realize his nature for what it is, there is not anything other than the Self. Knowing and doing simply do not apply.

"Who is able to conceive of His state?" Can you say what Sri Bhagavan's state is? The ego-less state is Sri Bhagavan's state. What is his state? Being beyond thought, how could anyone conceive it? That state, which is the state of Sri Bhagavan, is the state of the real Self. This is the innate State. If, through Self-Knowledge, you entirely abandon the ego-notion, this state, alone, is your state. Whatever other state you ever imagined that you had vanishes into the nonexistence that it is. Can you conceive of this? Of course not, but you can realize it. All that is necessary for this Realization is the inquiry into the nature of "I" and, thereby, the realization of the perpetual egolessness of your real Being.

आह स्फुटं तत्त्वमसीति वेद -
स्तथाप्यसंप्राप्य परात्मनिष्ठाम् ।
भूयो विचारो मतिदुर्बलत्वं
तत्सर्वदा स्वात्मतया हि भाति ॥ ३२ ॥

āha sphuṭaṁ tat-tvam-asīti veda-
s-tathāpyasamprāpya parātma-niṣṭhām |
bhūyo vicāro mati-durbalatvaṁ
tat-sarvadā svātmatayā hi bhāti || 32 ||

32

Aha. The Veda has made clear (clearly opened) "That you are," thus.
So, still, abidance as the Supreme Self is not to be completely attained.
More inquiry is weakness (feebleness) of the mind (weakness of conviction).
That always, as one's own Self, indeed, shines.

N.: The first word is "Aha." In English, this may indicate an exclamation due to having found something. Here, though, the interpretation of this Sanskrit word, "aha," should be an exclamation that signifies reproof and expresses a critical attitude. In this case, such pertains to a critical discernment. A sharp discrimination is about to follow.

"Thus" signifies that the previous words, "That you are," are a quotation. Sri Ramana says, "The Veda has made clear (clearly opened)" the Knowledge of "That you are." "Tat tvam asi," the Vedas declare. "So, still, abidance as the Supreme Self is not to be completely attained." That declaration, by itself, and even contemplation in the mind about it do not necessarily bring about the Realization of the Self.

The Maharshi says, "More inquiry is weakness (feebleness) of the mind (weakness of conviction)." What is the conviction that should be present in full strength but is weak in the case upon which he comments? It is that "That always" meaning Brahman always, "as one's own Self, indeed, shines." If we think that Brahman is not our Self, the teaching, "Tat tvam asi, That you are," serves to remedy this fault. If we think that we are not the Self, the inquiry, "Who am I?" remedies that false conclusion, which is ignorance. In this exceedingly nondual verse, the Maharshi discards the contemplation, or meditation, upon "That thou art," which is the well-known mahavakya, or great saying, in

Vedanta, and he even dismisses the inquiry, "Who am I?" because we are always That.

The verse should not be interpreted as ridiculing the inquiry "Who am I?" that he has already expounded. The verse is not meant to ridicule the statement of the Vedas, "That you are," which is a statement of pure Knowledge in the form of instruction, often reiterated by Adi Sankara. Even in the Maharshi's own teaching, he has made use of the mahavakya. Indeed, it appears in one of the verses to Arunachala, the "Necklet of Nine Gems." Arunachala is realized as "That thou art."

So, what is the emphasis in this verse? He does not ridicule either meditation or inquiry, but, rather, this is a statement of keen discernment of the highest wisdom in which one's own Self is only That. Therefore, who stands in need of meditation? Who stands in need of inquiry? There is no such one. There is no such "I." That, his state, which is the state of pure Being, is not to be reached by meditation or by inquiry. It is not to be reached at all, because That alone is. There is no other or "I."

The verse may also be regarded as a critique of thought-based meditation, in contrast to transcendence. In addition, the inquiry should result in the strong conviction of the Reality, and the need to repeat the inquiry "Who am I?" is a sign of "weakness of the mind." If there were strength of mind, or sufficient introversion, the repetition would not be necessary. In light of the preceding verse, the first interpretation that there is no one but the Self ever at any time is preferable.

In the highest Truth, what is this talk of the instruction, "You are That," and meditation upon the same? What is this talk of inquiry? Even these things, which are the highest forms of spiritual instruction, are based on the need for spiritual instruction. In the Truth, which alone is, there is no such instruction, no such practice, no one bound, no one aspiring, no one practicing for Realization, and no one liberated. That is the highest Truth. This pithy verse by the Maharshi extols it.

The Vedas, specifically the Upanishads (*Chandogya Upanishad*), state the identity of the Self, you, "tvam" and Brahman, "Tat", by proclaiming that That is what you are. This is the consistent, supreme message of the Upanishads. "Still," the Maharshi points out, "abidance as the Supreme Self is not to be completely attained." Hearing it from the Veda, reading it in the Veda, studying it, remembering it, reflecting and contemplating upon it, one does not attain the steady abidance as the Supreme Self thus. In the previous verse, Bhagavan elucidated the inconceivability of such abidance. Therefore, even the finest thinking will not reach it. Even the most glorious words, though an expression of it, do not, in themselves, bring about the Realization.

"More inquiry is weakness of the mind." The word is vicarah. It can mean inquiry, as in "Atma-vicara," Self-inquiry, but it can also mean an inquiry into the meaning of the text. More studying of the text, such as the message found in the Vedas, Sri Ramana declares, will just be weakness of conviction, feebleness of mind, or lack of strength. That is not what is needed. If we interpret "vicara" as "Self-inquiry," what is needed is depth of inquiry and not more repetition. It is not that one is prohibited from repeating the inquiry, for, obviously, if the inquiry was not pursued deeply enough the first time, one should inquire again and again. What is really necessary for Self-Realization is the depth of inquiry that removes the false sense of individuality.

"That always, as one's own Self, indeed, shines." "That" means Brahman, the Absolute. As the Self, itself, it shines. Brahman is the Self. There is no other kind of Brahman. The Self is Brahman. There is no other kind of self. To truly inquire is to realize this by direct, first-hand experience, which is not knowledge through words and thoughts, but immediate Knowledge. This is the Knowledge that is identical with your own Self.

Q.: As so often has been imparted, to say, "I know, or I do not know," or to say, "The Self is obscured, or the Self is not obscured," appears to me as equally absurd statements in the deepening recognition of the very absence, or nonexistence, of that "I."

N.: They are equally absurd because the Reality ever is as it is, and there is no second "I." This utter Nonduality is, indeed, the emphasis in the teaching. This brings us to the next verse.

न वेद्म्यहं मामुत वेद्म्यहं मा -
मिति प्रवादो मनुजस्य हास्यः ।
दृग्दृश्यभेदात्किमयं द्विधात्मा
स्वात्मैकतायां हि धियां न भेदाः ॥ ३३ ॥

na vedmyahaṁ mām-uta vedmyahaṁ mā-
m-iti pravādo manujasya hāsyaḥ |
dṛg-dṛśya-bhedāt-kim-ayaṁ dvidhātmā
svātmaikatāyāṁ hi dhiyāṁ na bhedāḥ || 33 ||

33

"I know not me," or "I know me,"
Thus, expressions of man are to be laughed at.
From the difference of the seer and the seen, is this Self divided in two (twofold)?
The Oneness of oneself (the true Self), indeed, is the understanding (knowledge) [that there are] no differences.

N.: Being is forever undivided. Considering anything else, there is a "seer" and a "seen," or a "knower" and a "known." Dive deep within your own nature. Who sees what? There is no such division. Sri Ramana says that the ideas, "I know myself," and "I don't know myself," are funny, for they make no sense. When viewed from wisdom, they are just pure silliness. There is no separate "I;" nor is the Self ever an object to itself. So, how can we say, "I know," or "I don't know" in relation to the Self?

"The Oneness of oneself, indeed, is the understanding that there are no differences." What happens in spiritual practice? You do not make differences. The practice consists in the dissolution of differences. The dissolution of differences comes about by seeing that differentiation is but ignorance. It is a product of ignorance and nothing more. When ignorance is removed, there is no division in you. There is no "individual self and the absolute Self." If, in the depths of meditation, you feel that you go into the Self and come out of the Self, what actually happens? You are not going in and out. There are not two of you. The illusion of differences vanishes and then is imagined again. Seek the root of this imagination, which is the individual or "I," and you find that the "I" does not exist. The imagination by something nonexistent cannot produce a real effect.

"I know not me," or "I know me" are expressions "to be laughed at," the Maharshi says. They are absurd. Our real nature is the Self; our real nature is God. "I know myself," "I do not know myself," and similar expressions are "expressions of man," that is, a human being. You are not a human being; you are the Supreme Being. The human being does many silly things, among which are thinking in terms of "I know myself; I do not know myself." The Supreme Being, Brahman, which is the Self, has no such false notions.

"From the difference of the seer and the seen, is this Self two?" There are not two selves, a seeing self and a seen self. In Self-Realization, there is not one who realizes and the Self that is realized. Even speaking of "a Self-realized being" is a loose description mentioned for purposes of spiritual instruction. In Truth, there is no such thing as "a Self-realized being." Nor is there "an unrealized being." There is Being, which is the Self, and the Self, itself, constitutes the Realization. The Realization is not an event or an occurrence that happens to someone. The Realization is in the Knowledge that there is no such being as that someone.

"The Oneness of oneself, indeed, is the understanding that there are no differences." Every difference is rooted in the single assumption, "I." It is the first supposed difference. With that difference, there can be any number of differences. At the beginning of the text, the Maharshi spoke of the assumed distinctions between the individual, the Supreme, and the world or universe. Again, he addresses the Truth of "no difference." Here, the difference addressed is that of the realizer and that which is realized.

In the Self, there is only the Self. There is no individual outside of the Self. There is no individual inside of the Self. You attempt to realize the Self. The Self cannot be approached objectively. It is not an object. It is not the seen. You must look into the Heart of the seer. If the seer be examined, the seer is no longer a seer, but is just the infinite expanse of formless Consciousness.

This Consciousness is utterly indivisible. Its Oneness can never be fractured. Since it is absolutely One, who is it that would say, "I now know this." Or, who is it that would say, "I do not quite know this." Can you be an ignorant one? If you cannot be an ignorant one, can you be a knowing one? Do you recall the earlier verse in which the Maharshi negated both ignorance and knowledge as two different states, but spoke of true Knowledge as abidance as That?

The Self is not distinguished as a seer and a seen. There is no such division. The Realization of no-differentiation is inherent in the non-conceptual Knowledge of your own true Self. If a difference appears, ask yourself, "For whom is the difference?" Being unreal, the "you" vanishes. The idea of two states, of knowing and not knowing the Self, vanishes with the "I." This teaching by Sri Bhagavan is directed to those who are avid for Supreme Knowledge, which is Self-Realization. For this Self, there is nothing to be done, and, for this Self, there is nothing to be known; nor is there anything left unknown.

Q.: Are we to avoid the senses like a plague because they are the maya by which we appear to create separation between the ego and the Self?

N.: If by "avoid the senses," you mean to be nonattached to the senses and their objects, yes. Nonattachment is achieved by the knowledge of the source of happiness. If by "avoid the senses," you also mean not to regard the senses as that which determines reality, definitely yes. If you regard "avoid the senses" as not associating your identity, your very Being, with anything that is sensed, such as an object, or the sensing, most definitely yes. If by "avoid the senses," you mean just abstention from having the senses entertained by various pleasantries or pleasures, that depends upon the situation and the aspirant, and there is no hard and fast rule regarding such.

Q.: Anything that promotes, in the least, separation, differences, or illusion is detrimental.

N.: Yes. What promotes the illusion?

Q.: Nothing really.

N.: That is so. It is self-promoted.

Q.: Yes. By what is the belief in perception self-promoted?

N.: By that ignorant belief. The sense objects do not create the belief.

Q.: No.

N.: The belief creates the belief. The ignorance is self-generated. If ignorance is self-caused, how can it come to be? It is entirely unreal. Therefore, we have only to address ignorance, which is destroyed by real Knowledge. We do not necessarily need to rearrange the sense objects.

Q.: If I think that the ego is going to understand this, the ego is not going to understand this.

N.: Oh no, the ego never understands anything. It is a good-for-nothing. Fortunately, the ego does not truly exist. So, we are graced.

Q.: We create it through our belief in perception, don't we?

N.: You can foster the idea of an ego identity even without perception.

Q.: How?

N.: For example, if you would shut your eyes and ears and would lose the sensations in your skin so that most of your sense impressions would not occur, you could still formulate the idea that you exist as an individual experiencer of the sensory blank.

Q.: But I wouldn't have a sensory blank, because I would still be thinking about those objects.

N.: Yes. You could create the same senses in a dream world.

Q.: The belief in perception is the belief in duality, the belief in the ego.

N.: The belief in the ego brings, in its wake, the belief that there is something else to be perceived, and then a belief that the perceiving is really occurring.

Q.: Is it that way? Or, is it the other way around?

N.: You want to know the actual succession or order of something that does not exist?

Q.: Yes.

N.: Have it any way you like, but, for the purpose of Self-Realization, it is best to see that that which is objective depends upon the subject and not the other way around. Otherwise, you will attempt to eliminate the objective portion, but the subject will remain intact. If, though, you eliminate the false notion of a subject, which is the individual who appears as the perceiver or the ego, all that follows the ego, or is associated with it, such as the object, the perceiving, etc., collapses. His retinue runs away with him.

Q.: If one still believes in perception, he still believes in the ego.

N.: Yes. If someone thinks, "The world exists; the world is real," but also thinks, "But I am egoless in it," he does not truly comprehend the nature of Reality.

Q.: No differences, no differences.

N.: The differenceless state is the real state, the only real state that there is.

Q.: That is wholly contradicted by maya and the belief in perception.

N.: Yes. Maya is an inverted view. It makes the Real appear as unreal and the unreal appear as real. Where there is but one, solitary, indivisible Existence, maya brings about the imagination of multiplicity. Where there is no one perceiving anything, but just pure Consciousness, it (maya) brings about the rise of a perceiver, the perceiving, and the thing perceived.

Q.: You started from the end. I find this a difficult starting point.

N.: What do you mean?

Q.: You are assuming that one can get rid of the ego without getting rid of the belief in perception.

N.: Why would you assume that?

Q.: Because, as long one believes in the duality of anything sensed, one already believes in the separation of the ego.

N.: All right. So?

Q.: So, I can't just undo that assumption if I already assume that.

N.: Why can you not just stop assuming it by deeper Knowledge? Understand that the perception must be for someone, so it does not exist. Then, find out that there is no one for whom that perception could have been. Swallow the perceived in the perceiving, the perceiving in the perceiver, and find there is no individual known as the perceiver, but just one pure Existence.

Q.: But I have to undo the belief in perception.

N.: Yes. As long as the world is taken to be real, there will not be Self-Realization. Someone who says that he understands egolessness but still retains the idea that he perceives a world does not know what he is saying. It is impossible to relinquish the notion of the ego and still retain the idea of perception.

Q.: Perception is difference. Is it not true?

N.: Do you have perception that is without any difference?

Q.: No. But if I believe in the existence of that which does not exist, there will be perception.

N.: Yes. Such is maya. Now, when you inquire for whom is the perception or for whom is this maya or who experiences the differences, what then?

Q.: If I retain the belief in the senses, or a belief in a process of perception, I am holding onto the ego.

N.: Yes. But, then, you would not have truly inquired for whom these are. So, I am asking you what your own experience is when you actually inquire, "For whom are these?" Does perception remain?

Q.: It appears to, as maya. I can see that it is not possibly what I think it is and that it doesn't really exist. I continue to try to solve this as an exterior problem of perception, within my own mind, about Reality.

N.: Reality cannot be studied like a topic, can it? If we actually inquire, "For whom is this?" the emphasis shifts from the objective to the nonobjective, and the objective portion is swallowed up. "For whom is this?" is indicative of returning the sense of identity and reality to the center.

Q.: In other words, one sees that perception is impossible and that it never existed to begin with.

N.: If you say that you still see it as some kind of maya, the inquiry must be, "For whom is this maya? Who am I?" Maya cannot exist apart from you.

Q.: I create it.

N.: Then, you can put an end to it.

Q.: Yes. Lord be praised.

हृत्प्राप्यसद्धाम निजस्वरूपे
स्वभावसिद्धेऽनुपलभ्य निष्ठाम्।
मायाविलासः सदसत्सरूप -
विरूपनानैकमुखप्रवादाः ॥ ३४ ॥

hṛt-prāpya-sad-dhāma nija-svarūpe
svabhāva-siddhe'nupalabhya niṣṭhām |
māyā-vilāsaḥ sad-asat-sarūpa-
virūpa-nānaika-mukha-pravādāḥ || 34 ||

34

Not having attained (obtained) the abidance in the established Self (true) Existence
(or: Not having attained ((obtained)) the abidance in the accomplishment of the true ((Self)) state),
The attaining of (reaching) the Heart, the true abode, in the innate True Nature (in one's own innate nature),
A play (echo) of maya (illusion) are "real, unreal, with form,
Without form, many (separate, different), one;" [they are] proclamations of the mouth.

N.: The first two lines present the proposition of being in ignorance regarding the Self. If the Self is not realized, what then? The steady abidance in the established Self, which is "the real Existence," must be accomplished. That is "the real state." "Attaining" is "reaching the Heart," which is the core of our Being. That is the "true Abode," the one place that really is, or, we may say, the one state that really is. It is "innate," so, it is our own nature from which we can never part. We can not separate from or become different from that which is innate. Pure Existence, the Reality, is the only thing that is innate.

Without realizing That, just making "proclamations of the mouth," that is, merely talking about and intellectually thinking about, "This is real; this is unreal; this reality has form; no, it is formless; it is many; it is one; many in the one; one in the many," or cogitation over any other similar conception, making distinctions of any kind, and attempting to ascertain a state of non-distinction with the intellect and words, without actually experientially realizing this, Sri Ramana says, is "a play of maya." It is just illusion. Or, it is "the echo of maya," which is maya reverberating in the mind that is engrossed in such a discussion or in such intellectual thinking.

We must realize that which is innate, the real Existence. In the end, what does it matter what is said or is left unsaid? Or, what does it matter what you have managed to think about or not? The only thing that really matters is your abidance in full Knowledge, fully awake to the Truth of your Being. In that lies Liberation. In that lies peace and bliss. In that lies the fulfillment of the purpose of life, which is the experiential Realization of, and the steady abidance in, That, as That itself. When the Realization is present, all the statements of the scriptures, such as, "That is real," "This is unreal," "That is formless," and such, will make perfect sense to you. You will be the One who spoke them. Unless there is Realization, merely thinking about these things and coming to doctrinal conclusions, whether they are apparently dual or nondual, "with form or without form," are just "echoes of maya." By his Grace, the direct experience is so available. The Realization is so available within you.

What is necessary is the attainment of the abidance as the Self, "the true Existence, the established Self." This is solid and real. Or, instead of "established," we may translate the term as "in the accomplishment." What is necessary is the accomplishment of the abidance in and as this true Self. This is the "attaining of the Heart," and not anything less. This is "the true Abode." You do not really belong, and you do not really dwell, anywhere else.

This is the innate. That which is innate is imperishable. What is innate is unborn and will never be separate from you. The Realization of That is so important. If, not having attained this, not having realized this, we talk and think about, "This is real; that is real; this is unreal; that is unreal; this has form; no, it is the formless; it is many; it is one; it is separate; it is not separate; it is different; it is not different," and so forth and so on, all this, Sri Ramana says, is a "play of maya." The word for "play" can also mean "echo," so it is an "echo of illusion." This is all that such intellectual and verbose prattle is. Sri Ramana calls such "mukha pravadah," "proclamations of the mouth." What good does it do?

If we think and speak of form and difference, we are merely proclaiming another "echo of illusion." If, without realizing the Formless, we talk about the formless, if, without realizing the Self, we talk about the self, if we talk about the real or we say that the world is unreal, but we do not actually realize it and merely build up a collection of words and thoughts, these are more echoes of maya. Mere words, mere thoughts, and the mere learning of new names, while still retaining the same old conceptions, never liberated anyone.

What is needed? The attainment of abidance in the true Existence is necessary. This is so vitally important. Reaching the Heart, your true Abode, no longer imagining that you dwell in a body and no longer imagining that you dwell in, or roam about within, a mind, is so important. Abidance in the Innate, your True State, and to no longer think that you travel through the waking, dreaming and deep sleep states is so important.

Without this Realization, it is just a play of maya. With this Realization, and even with the one-pointed intention and sincere earnestness to realize this abidance in the Self, all that is spiritual and the discernment between the Real and the unreal, the Self and the not-Self, become supremely significant and are no longer proclamations of the mouth.

When you think and speak about spiritual matters, be sure that it is entirely experiential and completely wholehearted. What we are speaking of, what you are thinking about on your own, and what you speak among each other should be born of actual experience guided by the light of inquiry. Be certain that your aim is steadily that of Self-Realization, until your experience is consistently just this Self-Realization. Then, your words are words of Truth, and even your thoughts sparkle with the reflected light of the real interior experience, which is your real Abode.

Q.: It is covered over by that which is not. Sri Bhagavan says that, if you believe in the world, you cannot believe in the Self.

N.: Yes, but his words do not place emphasis on the supposed reality of a covering but are instruction to remove the covering, so that, even now, you abide blissfully in that immortal Knowledge of Reality.

Q.: So, how do I get there?

N.: Who am I?

Q.: How do I dissolve the belief in a world if I don't dissolve the belief in perception and come to the conclusion that perception is an impossible illusion?

N.: The belief in the perception and the belief in the world depend upon the belief in yourself. Who gives them that belief?

Q.: It is all made up.

N.: If you know at heart that it is entirely made up, it can never afflict you again, but it ceases to exist from that moment on.

Q.: The world is made up, and perception is made up. Seeing that is seeing that which remains.

N.: What does remain?

Q.: The Self. No differences in That.

N.: Well, I could say, "Stay still. Abide in the differenceless state," yet the instruction would be redundant because, if it is differenceless, there is no need to stay put. There is no one to stay put in it.

Q.: Unless I imagine there to be.

N.: Well, no, that has already been ruled out if it is differenceless.

Another Q.: What if the idea is that one is a body in the world?

N.: I am "with form," is just a "play of maya." To merely verbally reinforce, by a series of echoes, your "voice" of the same old illusion would be a waste of breath. To say that you are a body, when truly you are not, is completely unnecessary. To say that you are not a body, while still retaining the belief that you are a body, is also entirely unnecessary. The Truth is that you are the bodiless Self. You should know that and speak from there.

Q.: It is weird because the belief in a body is a temporary thing.

N.: All illusion is temporary. During the time of believing one is the body, does he actually become a body?

Q.: That is the meditation. That is really powerful. It highlights how flimsy is the belief in a body, no less so than the assertion that I am not a body. The assertions of being a body and not being a body are the same.

N.: The Knowledge of differenceless-ness, the Knowledge of bodiless-ness, is not an assertion. It is simply the plain fact. If a person asserts that he is not the body, while believing that he is the body, in order to gain a better social standing with those who are bodiless, I suppose, (laughter) it is silly because he is saying that he is not the body, while he is thinking that he is the body, even though, in truth, he not a body. Of course, the opposite, which is to say that one is a body, is completely absurd ignorance.

Q.: The first more complex assertion reflects deeper ignorance piled upon ignorance.

N.: Considering that there is no usefulness in making false statements, such as, "I am the body," when you are not, or by saying, "I am not the body," when you think you are even though you are not, we do not have to be concerned with all that, do we? If there is a sincere desire to realize the Truth and if there is the understanding that the Realization of the Truth is of the Self, that it is a matter of our own experience, for the sake of our own happiness, no one will negate his better knowledge by the denial of what he knows to be true. Of course, no one will egotistically assert it, either.

Q.: In my meditations, I find that it is good to ask, "Am I a body?" The idea that I am a body is not always in the forefront of my mind, but it is assumed.

N.: Yes. You can never be harmed by a meditation that discerns you are not a body.

Q.: I am not really located in a body, but there is a concept that I shoot in and out of the body.

N.: Even if you have the concept that you go in and out of the body, still, the "I" must be bodiless to go in and out of this form. We should know what this "I" is, in itself, and abide there. As for making statements of "this is real," "that unreal," "with form," "without form," "many and one," and so on, no one ever attained peace by mere "proclamations of the mouth." Peace is a matter of direct experience. The experience is that of pure Knowledge. It is Self-Knowledge, which is the Knowledge in which one's identity is established as, or abides as, That. Saying one thing or another is really insignificant and is just maya, or an "echo of maya."

Q.: Is this the reason for the Maharshi's silence in answer to some questions?

N.: The Maharshi's Silence is exceedingly profound. It can be interpreted in a variety of ways, even simultaneously, and, still, it is beyond that. In that Silence, there is no scope for illusion and for delusion of any kind, such as the "I am the body"-notion, and for egotism of any kind. Assertion of anything is absolutely meaningless before his Silence. Likewise is it for complaints, doubts, and dualisms of all kinds. Everything is utterly annihilated in the Silence. One thing remains, but, to know That, you become absorbed.

Another Q.: I am wondering if there are degrees of inquiry. It is much like asking if I can partially know my Self. I do not think that is possible. It seems that the inquiry does not have degrees. It is so direct that there is nothing that I could measure. There is no difference when I am actually inquiring.

N.: The inquiry consists of a very formless Knowledge, so it really does not have parts, steps, and stages. However, if, within the context of a particular span of time, the aspirant attempts to analyze the progress of his practice, and if he is engaged in inquiry, he can say that the inquiry becomes deeper and deeper, or he might say that the superimposed illusions become thinner and thinner. If the inquiry is continuous, it is no longer wrongly associated with any kind of mental activity, however astute. Once it is entirely off the mental level, and thus continuous, it would be very difficult to describe it in steps, stages, or degrees. The attempt to measure it would necessarily bring in an examination of, or inquiry into, the nature of the measurer.

Another Q.: Yes. I would have to find some entity that experiences the Self in a way that is less than direct. I would have to be an individual that supposedly is somehow a filter.

N.: Yes. Or, a mind that is outside it that could analyze or report on it that would not be engaged in the inquiry at the moment of its reporting. However, for the purposes of the practice and instruction, we can loosely say, when a certain depth of experience is there, "Inquire more deeply," and thus proceed to remove some other misidentification. When you inquire, what actually is occurring, and how are you going to measure that?

Q.: When I am inquiring, there actually is no one who is concerned about the depth anymore or how to measure it. That is just not there anymore.

N.: The quintessence of the inquirer is the depth. The inquiry is always into the nature of the inquirer.

Q.: Yes. There is simply no one else involved. It is absolutely singular.

N.: In an infinite ocean that is of infinite depth, how are you going to take a fathom reading? It is also shoreless, so you cannot really measure how far you have gone.

Q.: It is so peaceful not to have worry about all of that.

N.: It is so peaceful not to worry about the individual's concerns.

सिद्धस्य वित्तिः सत एव सिद्धिः
स्वप्नोपमानाः खलु सिद्धयोऽन्याः ।
स्वप्नः प्रबुद्धस्य कथं नु सत्यः
सति स्थितः किं पुनरेति मायाम् ॥ ३५ ॥

siddhasya vittiḥ sata eva siddhiḥ
svapnopamānāḥ khalu siddhayo'nyāḥ |
svapnaḥ prabuddhasya kathaṁ nu satyaḥ
sati sthitaḥ kiṁ punar-eti māyām || 35 ||

35

The Knowledge of the established Truth (Being) alone is accomplishment.
Comparable to (resembling) a dream, indeed, are other accomplishments.
The dream of one who is awakened, how can it now be true?
Does one who abides in Truth (Being) again approach illusion?

N.: The word "siddhi" can mean "accomplishment," or it can mean "miracle." Sri Natarajan has interpreted it as miracle, and has presented the verse as a commentary on real Knowledge versus that which seems to be miraculous. It is not uncommon for aspirants to assume that the power of Supreme Knowledge will endow somebody, as a body, with certain unusual, superhuman powers. Whether such powers exist or not, is really not a matter of discussion, for those who perform them say that they exist; but, in Reality, are such things existent? They are like dreams. If the belief is that, when one attains Realization, he possesses additional unique abilities, such as the power of knowing things from afar, power of healing, and such, he must ask why should Knowledge of the supreme, ever-existent Reality endow the illusory, embodied individual with special powers? What could Self-Knowledge, or Self-Realization, have to do with knowing what is in someone else's mind, as in the case of telepathy? One can see that Self-Knowledge can make one utterly disinterested in what is on anyone's mind, including one's own, but why would it make one interested in this power that would be much like keeping an open telephone connection with everyone else's mind? Or, why would the realization of bodiless Being result in the ability to exert influence over other bodies? Or, why would the realization of bodiless Being enable one's body to do unusual or miraculous acts? For those who are fascinated or impressed by such phenomena, the verse declares that all of this is a dream. One who knows Reality does not even approach such things. He looks at this as a dream after he has awakened. If, in a dream, you see a magician who can do all sorts of marvelous things, when you wake up, what do you think of his act? It is no more real than the rest of the dream. The magician may seem to have different powers, different abilities, or a different knowledge of things, but he still is just part of the dream. Realization is like waking up.

"The Knowledge of the established Truth, the Knowledge of Being, alone, is accomplishment." For this one should spiritually strive. It is proof of itself. Its bliss, which can be only inwardly perceived, is proof of itself. There are no other proofs of the Realization of pure Being, which is the highest accomplishment and the only true accomplishment. If one considers that there must be some other sign of Self-Realization, in this dream, or some advantage in this play of illusion, he is entirely mistaken. If one thinks that such spiritual Knowledge will give him some added advantage in the world, such as an ability to manage events in a better way, or some miraculous powers, to which the verse directly alludes, such as the ability to know something far away, to read someone else's mind, as if that would be that interesting, (laughter) the ability to heal the body, the ability to contradict the usual laws of nature, walking on places upon which one usually does not walk, and one thinks that this would be the sign of realizing the Truth or of having realized the Truth, or that this would be a sign that someone else has realized the Truth, it is entirely deluded. All that is dream stuff.

If we see some peculiar accomplishment in a dream, such as something that does not follow the waking state's usual laws of nature, or, if in a dream, a magician has the ability, in your dream, to make impossible things appear, and they seem real as far as the dream is concerned, how do you view all of this once you wake up? If someone in the dream has the advantage of being able to predict the future events of the dream, how do you view that when you wake up? Does any of that have any significance whatsoever? Is any of that even remotely related to waking up? Is it not all just dream stuff by dream characters who do not actually exist?

Q.: Where one's Knowledge of the Self deepens and steadies, it feels more and more like the appearance or disappearance of the dream subject and his dream adventures, their vanishing or not vanishing, and abidance in the Self is less and less interrupted.

N.: For the jnani, the appearance and disappearance of the body, the senses, and world are of no consequence. He knows that which exists at all times and sees no differences. Even the so-called differences of life and death do not perturb him. He treats them as a dream after one has awakened. The dream does not persist for him.

The term siddhi can mean "accomplishment," in which case, the verse is, "The Knowledge of the established Truth (Being), alone, is accomplishment. Comparable to (resembling) a dream are other accomplishments." Any other accomplishment in life is within the context of the dream of maya. The one thing to be accomplished is Realization of the Self, for this deals with Reality. Everything else is like dream accomplishments. If you accomplish something in a dream, after you wake up, what happens to that accomplishment? What happens to the entire dream life? It is gone, without a trace. The waking up would be the only real accomplishment. Waking up to the Self is the only real accomplishment. The rest seem to have value only in the context of a dream.

"The dream of one who has awakened, how can it now be true?" This is indicative of two points. First, viewing all of our accomplishments as a dream, there is no desire for such, but only the desire for the Truth, in which one comes to steadily abide. Secondly, how can the dream of one who has awakened now be true? Of last night's dream, whatever was dreamed, what remains now? There is not a trace of it. All the experiencer, the experiencing, and the objects of experience have gone. The outer things and the inner things, within the dream context, are completely gone. They do not continue. It is only from a residual standpoint of illusion and for the purposes of explanation for an aspirant that it is said that a sage sees everything as a dream, as if the dream were still going on but he sees it as insubstantial. Does the dream continue after you wake up? Not at all. In the same way, the world and accomplishments in the world do not exist at all when you know yourself. To say that you are in relation to them, to the extent that even to describe you as being detached from them, is ridiculous in the terms of the things of last night's dream. In one sense, you are supremely detached from the things of last night's dream, because the things of last night's dream do not exist for you. Just so is it for those who have realized the Truth. "Does one who abides in Truth, in Being, again approach illusion?" If you abide in Being, will you recreate the maya? One who abides in Being is Being. The Truth abides in and as the Truth, and that One will never approach illusion.

Another Q.: You asked, "Is any of that even remotely related to waking up? Is it not all just dream stuff by dream characters who do not actually exist?" It is just dreaming about waking up.

N.: It is not even dreaming about waking up. It is just dreaming and, in the dream, wrongly associated with a seemingly far away waking state. In a similar way, a person may assume that spirituality confers some special power over the phenomenal things or that possession of some special abilities, subtle, mental, or physical, will be proof of having awakened from this dream. How could that be proof? How could that even be a sign? The magician in your dream is not really an awakened one. He is just a magician dream character in a dream.

This text is directed toward the aspirant for Liberation. So, the meaning of the verse is that one should not aspire for or be impressed with those kinds of phenomena. What is necessary for complete peace and happiness is to be awake to the Reality of the Self. Nothing else can substitute for that.

Although many wondrous stories are retold of events that happened in the Maharshi's presence, and still continue to happen because of his Grace, what is it about him that is really extraordinary? It is the glorious Self-abidance in which neither individuals nor phenomena exist, in which there are no differences, in which there is nothing more to be done, nothing to be accomplished, nothing else to be known, but in which there is just the one, absolute Existence, which is utterly devoid of individuality and the world.

He says, "Does one who abides in Being, the Truth, again approach illusion?" Realizing yourself as the Self, the non-perceiver, the non-doer, the non-conceiver, would you return to a position of being a perceiver, a doer, or a conceiver? It would be stepping back into illusion. Know for certain the Knowledge of the absolute Truth. Your Being is what is real, is what is truly spiritual, is what is important, is the only thing that endures, and is the only thing that is truly spiritually precious.

The Knowledge is its own proof. It cannot be seen with the eyes. It cannot be conceived by the mind. It is always invisible to others, because, in it, there are no others. Your own continuous experience of the bliss of its Perfect Fullness is the proof, if proof be needed.

सोऽहंविचारो वपुरात्मभावे
साहाय्यकारी परमार्गणस्य ।
स्वात्मैक्यसिद्धौ स पुनर्निरर्थो
यथा नरत्वप्रमितिर्नरस्य ॥ ३६ ॥

so'haṁ-vicāro vapur-ātma-bhāve
sāhāyyakārī para-mārgaṇasya |
svātmaikya-siddhau sa punar-nirartho
yathā naratva-pramitir-narasya || 36 ||

36

The "He am I" inquiry, when in the "body is the Self" state (conception),
Is helpful for the search for (the path to) the Supreme.
In the true Self (one's own Self) Oneness Accomplishment, that again is purposeless (useless, meaningless),
Just as the correct notion (conception) of man-ness (manhood) of a man.

N.: If you are within the context of the conception, or state of, "I am the body," meditation on "He am I," or "That am I" can be helpful. For a man, the idea of "manhood," or of "being a man," is redundant. The fact is obvious. To think, "I am a man," does not make one more a man. It is redundant. In the same way, to think, "I am the Self," "I am Siva," and "I am Brahman," is redundant. "Siva," "Brahman," "He," and "That," are terms for the Self, and the Self is what you are. If you think that you are the body, the instruction and meditation upon "That I am" is very helpful. There is no doubt about it. Yet, when illusion is dismissed, that is, when the ignorant conception of being the body is dismissed, the positive assertions or affirmations that "I am the Self," are seen to be like a man repeating, "I am a man." It is not needed. Therefore, the primary approach is the negation of the false conception of an ego and the misidentification with the body. If this much is accomplished, the Truth of such statements, "So'ham," "He am I," are abundantly clear, without any repetition of the same and without any thinking about it. There is, instead, the deeper Knowledge of your own Existence as it is.

Just as the notion of the manhood of a man is simply redundant, so, the Maharshi says, the spiritual notion is "purposeless, meaningless, useless," and inapplicable to the spiritual Knowledge of the Self. The statements, or the thoughts, "I am He," "I am That," "I am the Self," and so forth and so on are redundant for one who has the direct, interior experience. The statements may be of help in instruction and for purposes of reflection and meditation while on the path to realizing the Self, but, once that Self is realized in the "Oneness accomplishment," in which there is no division between meditator and That upon which one meditates, in that undifferentiated state, what would be the significance of thinking, "I am the Self?"

The state of Self-Realization, therefore, is not a state of consistent thinking along even the loftiest of spiritual lines. It is certainly not a state of thinking to the contrary, that one is not the Self and not Siva. It is a different kind of knowledge. It is non-thought Knowledge.

If you are a human being, and you know that you are a human being, thinking that you are a human being is rather purposeless, is it not? Thinking that you are a human being does not make it any more so. If you stop thinking that you are a human being, you don't become any less of a human being. Elsewhere, the Maharshi has pointed out that if there is a doubt, so that you think that you are something else, such as a cow or a water buffalo, it may be useful to think that you are a human being, but, he adds, of course, no one would think, "I am a cow or water buffalo." It is absurd. If you think, "I do not exist," it may be helpful to remind yourself, "I am the Self. I do exist," but do you actually ever think, "I do not exist"? The entire inquiry and the fruit of inquiry, which is pure Knowledge, are thought-transcendent. The Knowledge is quite beyond all the thoughts to the contrary, and it is quite beyond all the affirmations in the mind that are expressions of it.

Q.: It seems that meditation starts with thought as an intention.

N.: Does it start with a thought or with an intention?

Q.: With an intention.

N.: Where is the source of the intention?

Q.: Intention must come from that depth, which is the Self.

N.: So, meditation starts in the depth of the Self, which is beyond thought.

Q.: Then, thought turns its wheels.

N.: In itself, that may not be harmful if the wheels are turning in the right direction. The actual meditation of inquiry occurs at a level that can not be described as thinking.

Q.: First there is the intention, and then something deeper takes over.

N.: When "something deeper takes over," that actually is the meditation, is it not?

Q.: Yes.

N.: Without that "something deeper," if you think, "So'ham, Sivo'ham, Aham-brahmasmi," but you do not have that depth of intention to meditate, what will it be? It will be hollow, will it not?

If the actual meditation depth does occur, thinking those thoughts are not harmful. They are somewhat redundant and are not doing anything more for the meditation.

Q.: The important part is the depth of meditation. The thoughts seem to help in some way.

N.: How do they help?

Q.: They help as aids to remember the teaching, which is deep.

N.: How do you remember it? The Maharshi asked this in the invocation.

Q.: It must be the experience. It always comes to the depth of experience.

N.: Remembrance is truly the deeper Knowledge and never the thoughts. Were the mahavakyas and other declarations of Truth, such as So' ham, originally uttered as thoughts or as a declarations of pristine experience? Were they not declarations of profound Realization beyond the domain of thought that was given expression so that the expressed would be realized by the one who hears it?

Q.: That is a perfect description of the Truth of the Maharshi's words and the explanations of the text.

N.: All of it is from and for the depth of real Knowledge, which is true experience. The mere repetition of the words is not of much significance. If we have the depth of Knowledge, the words are, at best, expressions. What really occurs now? Is it words? Is it thoughts? What is actually occurring for you?

Q.: It clearly is not words. Without experience, reading a spiritual book and an electrical engineering book are almost equivalent. They both rest in thought.

N.: So, spiritual literature is to be read in a different way. It is not merely the collection of ideas. The topic is always something that is nonobjective, that is, not a thing. When you read an electrical engineering book, you learn something about a topic, and hopefully it is applicable to what you are doing. When you read a profound spiritual work and come to an understanding of its meaning, you have become the author. So, if you read Sri Bhagavan's verses, and you really absorb the meaning, you are, by virtue of that meaning, absorbed. You become the Truth that has been indicated. The author, himself, stands as that Truth, so you have become the author. That does not usually happen with electrical engineering books. (laughter)

Q.: In the selection of the verses in this book, it did not matter if they were composed by the Maharshi or someone else. It is the depth that mattered most.

N.: In the text known as the *Anubandham*, the Supplement to the Forty Verses, many of the verses were derived from other works, such as *Yoga Vasistha*. Though they can be found in other works, they are still his words. When differences disappear, it is revealed that you, yourself, are the source of the Vedas. Of course, you cannot say that from the individual standpoint, but when individuality is no more and only Brahman remains, you, yourself, are the Origin. Is it possible for the Origin not to know what he, himself, has said? However, in this verse, the Maharshi elucidates the point that it is not necessary for the jnani to repeat it any more, since he is what he knows, and he cannot forget himself.

द्वैतं विचारे परमार्थबोधे
त्वद्वैतमित्येष न साधुवादः ।
गवेषणात्प्राग्दशमे विनष्टे
पश्चाच्च लब्धे दशमत्वमेकम् ॥ ३७ ॥

dvaitaṁ vicāre paramārtha-bodhe
tvadvaitam-ityeṣa na sādhu-vādaḥ ।
gaveṣaṇāt-prāg-daśame vinaṣṭe
paścāc-ca labdhe daśamatvam-ekam ।। 37 ।।

37

"Duality in inquiry, but in the Knowledge of the Supreme Truth,
Nonduality," thus. This is not good (holy) speech (doctrine, advice, proposition).
Prior to the search, when the tenth [man] was lost,
And after, when found, the tenth-ness is one (that one only, the same).

N.: The Self is not elsewhere. It is ever existent. In the Vedanta parable of the ten fellows who crossed a stream, the tenth man was never really lost. Likewise, the Self has never actually been lost. The Self has always existed, and you have always been the Self. The ideas that you are different from the Self and that the experience of the Self has been diminished or is at a distance or is in the future or is in the past are as erroneous as the idea that the tenth man is missing. The tenth man was never missing. The Self has never been missing. If you think it is missing, count again, but count yourself this time. That is, pay attention to who you are. You will find the Self to be your only self.

The Maharshi critiques the idea that there is dualism in practice and Nonduality at the end. It is "not good advice." It is "not a good proposition." It is "not holy doctrine." Nonduality is the Truth in the beginning, the middle, and the end. That which is regarded as the end is actually the starting place. The practice of the inquiry that attempts to realize the Self occurs entirely within this sphere, or the context, of the Self's Existence. You are involved in a search to find the satsang hall, and you are in the satsang hall. All of your moving about and investigating here, looking for the satsang hall, is in the satsang hall. Likewise, all of the practice, inquiry, and meditation are in the Self and by the Light of the Self. That one nondual Self is always present. It is ever existent. You can never be outside of it. It can never be other than what you are. Nonduality is the Truth, before the beginning, all through, and after the end. It is immutable.

In the story of the ten men who ford a stream and counted nine when on the other side, at no point was the tenth man lost.

The tenth-ness, his existence, was the same from beginning to end. It did not increase or decrease at all. Just so is it with the nondual nature of the Self. The Maharshi instructs that the idea that there is duality in inquiry and Nonduality at the end is not good and is not holy. What is holy is directly expressive of the Absolute. This dualistic conception does not lead to the highest good, so it is not good. It is not good advice to give or to take. It is not good doctrine to follow. It is not a good proposition to consider. It is not holy speech.

Nonduality is in the beginning, the middle, and the end. Just as the tenth man was there from the start, your Self, which is the nondual Truth, is present from the start. It is delusive to say, "There will be nondual realization at the end, but I must start with where I am." Where are you? That is the question to ask. Where are you? Who are you? There is no point in saying that we must delay the nonduality of the Truth and assume duality, or illusion, to be valid for the time being. If one would take that approach, when would it ever end? One would never catch up to the tenth man.

As in the story, one has to start with counting oneself. In inquiry, you start with yourself. The inquiry is into the nature of the inquirer. "Duality in inquiry": there is no duality in inquiry. In non-inquiry, there is plenty of duality. In inquiry, from the start, it is the Light of your own Consciousness shining inwardly to know its own nature. It is a matter of your own Being reposing in itself. From the start, it is your own Existence and the inherent Knowledge of existing that form the core of the inquiry.

Therefore, your inquiry does not take you from a real duality to a real Nonduality. Inquiry dismisses the delusion of duality and shows Nonduality to be the Truth. Since inquiry depends on nothing but your Existence, it is nondual from start to finish. The old adage is that the way of the world is sweet in the beginning but bitter in the end, while the spiritual way seems bitter in the beginning, because of its renunciation, but is sweet in the end. What the Maharshi has revealed is sweet in the beginning and sweet in the middle and sweet in the end. It is complete.

करोमि कर्मेति नरो विजानन्
बाध्यो भवेत्कर्मफलं च भोक्तुम् ।
विचारधूता हृदि कर्तृता चेत्
कर्मत्रयं नश्यति सैव मुक्तिः ॥ ३८ ॥

karomi karmeti naro vijānan
bādhyo bhavet-karma-phalaṁ ca bhoktum |
vicāra-dhūtā hṛdi kartṛtā cet
karma-trayaṁ naśyati saiva muktiḥ || 38 ||

38

"I do karma (action)," thus a man considering (regarding)
A bound one becomes and enjoys (experiences) the result (fruit) of karma.
If, by inquiry in the heart, doership is removed (cast off)
The triple karma perishes (is destroyed). That alone is Liberation.

N.: If there is the notion "I do," you experience the result. If, freeing yourself of the "I"-notion and the "I am the body" misconception, you realize that you never do anything ever, you have no karma. Not only do you have no karma now, but you have no karma in the future or in the past, because you never will do or did anything. It is not that one is a doer, or an experiencer, at one time, and one ceases to be such in Liberation. One can speak only figuratively in that manner. In Liberation, you find that you were never "you," or a "body." You were never an "experiencer." You have never been and never will be a "doer." For that which you are, pure Brahman, there is no karma.

The reference to three kinds of karma pertains to sancita, which is the whole collection of all karma, prarabdha, which is the karma to be played out in this life and which is regarded by some as their destiny, and agami, which is what is being done now with results stored for a later time. Thus, the karma is described as three-fold. In some teachings within Vedanta, for the purpose of instruction, it is said that the collection of karma dissolves, and the karma for the future that has not yet begun to bear results dissolves, but the prarabdha continues. This is an explanation, for the onlooker, of why the jnani's body still appears and still seems to go through experiences. From the position of Jnana, Knowledge, though, there is no body, and there is no conception of the body being oneself. Therefore, there is no set of experiences in life through which one passes. So, in truth, there is no prarabdha karma. The explanation of prarabdha is to conform to the aspirant's idea that the world is real and that the body has some connection with the Self. When those ideas are obliterated, by being known to be false, and are regarded as only ignorance, the Liberation from the triple karma becomes obvious.

I have not done anything. I am not doing anything, and I never will do anything. I have never experienced anything else. I see nothing other than the Self. I am not experiencing anything but the Self. I never will experience anything but the Self, because the only "I" that there is, is the Self, which is infinite and eternal and is never modified in its nature. Such Realization alone is Liberation, as declared by the Maharshi.

The word "enjoys" should be understood as "experiences." Not all karma is enjoyable, in the sense of being pleasant. One reaps the fruits good and bad. If there are the notions "I," and "I do," the law of karma is inexorable. As is done, so is the effect, and that continues apparently endlessly. By that, one becomes bound. In the initial verses of *Upadesa Saram,* the Maharshi instructs that it is an ocean of bondage to be within the context of doing karma, of "I do." If you do, you reap.

If you become a non-doer, that is, if you realize your bodiless Existence and know that your ego is not a performer of action, if you understand that you do nothing at any time and comprehend that you are not endowed with mind, speech, body, and such, but ever remain still and silent, and if such is your experience, this is "inquiry in the heart." In that, Sri Bhagavan declares, the performer of action, "the doership," "is cast off."

What is the result? The triple karma perishes. Karma is analyzed in a three-fold way. There is sancita karma, which is the collection of karma. There is prarabdha karma, which is the karma that plays out as this life. If we do not recognize it as karma, we call it fate. There is agami karma, which is done now in the present life and the results of which will be reaped later. Together, all of them are loosely called "karma."

Sri Ramana says, "The triple karma is destroyed." This is an unusual statement. In Advaita Vedanta works, it is often said that, for the mukta, the liberated one, the storehouse of karma is obliterated and there is no karma being produced in the present life. The mukta will not take birth again, for there is no future karma. Yet, to explain how his manifest life continues and how his body and mind seem to operate in the eyes of others, it is said that prarabdha karma continues until it is exhausted. The analogy presented is that of an arrow. Once it has been shot by being released from the bow, even though no more arrows are coming, that arrow continues to fly until it meets its target or hits the ground. When its motion is exhausted, its flight is over. That is said to explain the remaining lifetime of a jnani, one who has realized the Truth.

Yet, Sri Bhagavan says, "The triple karma perishes." That pertains to all the karma. There is no karma playing out in the present life, because from what viewpoint does the present life appear? For whom is the appearance? Sri Ramana said, "He knows nothing that is other than the Self." For the Self for which there is nothing other, there is no karma. He has no identity other than the Self. He has no lifetime to play out. He remains only as the space, and the arrow does not affect him. There is no target. The bow has been snapped. The space in which all that appeared is utterly unaffected. This, he teaches, "alone is Liberation." There remains no identification whatsoever with the body, with the mind, or as any kind of individual.

बद्धत्वभावे सति मोक्षचिन्ता
बन्धस्तु कस्येति विचारणेन ।

सिद्धे स्वयं स्वात्मनि नित्यमुक्ते
क्व बन्धचिन्ता क्व च मोक्षचिन्ता ॥ ३९ ॥

baddhatva-bhāve sati mokṣa-cintā
bandhas-tu kasyeti vicāraṇena ।
siddhe svayaṁ svātmani nitya-mukte
kva bandha-cintā kva ca mokṣa-cintā ।। 39 ।।

39

With the being in the conception of bondage, is the anxious thought of Liberation.
But bondage of whom? Thus, by the inquiry,
In the accomplishment of himself (of itself), in one's own (true) Self, one is ever-liberated.
(or: Is established of itself, in one's own Self, the ever-liberated.)
Where is the anxious thought of bondage, and where is the anxious thought of Liberation?

N.: When there is bondage, one thinks of liberation. It is a lifesaver for one who is dreaming that he is drowning in an ocean. The inquiry, "but bondage of whom?" is like waking up from that dream of drowning. Thus, by the inquiry, "in the accomplishment of himself," waking up to his own nature, one finds one's true Self, and that Self is ever liberated. You are never drowning. It was only a mistaken notion. You find that which is established of itself, in your own Self, and that is the ever-liberated. The ever-liberated nature is thought of as the state of liberation when one conceives of bondage. When the conception of bondage is gone, where can there be the thought, or conception, of liberation? Not being anxious over being bound, one is not anxious for Liberation. One is not anxious for Liberation, for it is ever-existent. One is not anxious about being bound, because one simply is not bound.

If you conceive of bondage, you conceive of liberation. The hardship of bondage causes the anxious urge for Liberation, but Ramana asks, "bondage of whom?" This should be the inquiry.

Who is it that is bound? If you inquire in such a manner, what do you accomplish? You accomplish of yourself, by yourself, in yourself, the Realization of your own true Self, which is, by nature, ever liberated and has never known any bondage. Since it has never known any bondage, it has no idea of such, and, likewise, it has no idea of Liberation.

Bondage and liberation are spoken of from the supposedly individualized perspective. If one is bound, one is told to seek Liberation. The only way to truly seek this Liberation is to inquire into the nature of the one who is bound. He proves to be nonexistent, as does his bondage. What happens to the separate, happy state called "Liberation"? It is found to be the innate, happy Being of your own true Self and not a state at all. Liberation, then, is not truly attained by anyone. Bondage is not actually lost by anyone. The bondage does not exist. It is not that one is bound and then becomes free. There is no bondage, and there is no bound individual. There is no one striving for liberation, there is no one liberated, and there is no liberated state. Being, which is ever free, is the highest Truth. It is the only Reality. So, Ramana says, thus "established in one's own Self, where is the anxious thought of bondage, and where is the anxious thought of Liberation?" The question is rhetorical. The answer is obvious in the Silence that is stateless and ever free.

रूपिण्यरूपिण्युभयात्मिका च
मुक्तिस्त्रिरूपेति विदो वदन्ति ।
इदं त्रयं या विविनक्त्यहन्धी -
स्तस्याः प्रणाशः परमार्थमुक्तिः ॥ ४० ॥

rūpiṇyarūpiṇyubhayātmikā ca
muktis-trirūpeti vido vadanti |
idaṁ trayaṁ yā vivinaktyahan-dhī-
s-tasyāḥ praṇāśaḥ paramārtha-muktiḥ || 40 ||

40

Having a form, having no form, and of the nature of both kinds,
Liberation is of three forms, thus, the knowers say.
The complete destruction of that "I"-notion (conception of individuality) that examines (ponders) this triad
Is the Supreme Truth of Liberation.

N.: By the destruction of the falsely assumed individuality, the supreme Truth of Liberation is known directly. If the Truth is not known by actual direct experience, conceptions of liberation are made within the mind. Reference is made to "with form," "without form," and "of both kinds." Jivanmukti and videhamukti, liberation in life and liberation after death, are sometimes described as with form and without form. Others consider liberation with form and without form as having a vision of God and of seeing God as formless. There is also the definition of liberation in the context of videhamukti, liberation at the time of death. Some consider liberation in the context of when the body drops away, thinking that the realized one remains "with form," "without form," or "with and without form." Those who favor "with form" say, "He remains in some subtle way." Others say, "No, he merges with the formless, like space." Still others say, "No, he merges with space, but some subtle essence remains in order to bestow compassion and to do good for other living beings who are still caught in samsara."

The Maharshi says that, with all these conceptions of liberation, the thing to do is eliminate the false notion of "I." If the "I" disappears, who is to be with the form, without the form, and with and without the form? If the "I" disappears, what is the difference between Liberation in life and Liberation after death? If the false individuality is gone, the only Truth that exists is Being, and that is the Truth of Liberation. Therefore, in the final verse composed by the Maharshi in this text, he has summed up the practice and the highest truth regarding Realization. The practice is to discern that individuality is merely a false assumption and is utterly unreal. That is its destruction. The complete destruction of the "I"-notion is the practice. He has simultaneously revealed the Truth regarding Realization, which is "I"-less. By the power of Self-Knowledge, eliminate the false assumption of individuality, and you will know everything that there needs to be known about Reality and about Liberation. It will be self-evident, Self-known, and doubtless, for it is the differenceless state.

Variety and difference are the characteristics of the assumption of individuality. Where there is the "I," there are "many" regarding "this," even if the "this" is the consideration of Liberation. Where there is no "I," there is no difference. From the position of the "I," one can imagine degrees of liberation, stages within liberation, and kinds of liberation. Where there is no "I," which alone is Liberation, such imaginings are cast far away.

Liberation while still apparently endowed with a body is referred to as jivanmukti. Liberation that is disembodied is referred to as videhamukti. Liberation conceived of as videhamukti with the retention of some subtle form not physically seen through the senses in order to grace and bless devotees is "with and without form." In this manner, Liberation can be considered in three different ways, but the Maharshi says that the complete destruction of the "I" that ponders this triad and that conceives of liberation while alive, liberation after death, and liberation after death but still retaining some form in order to benefit sentient beings, reveals the Truth about Liberation. All of these ideas are conceived from the perspective of the "I" and are not true. The "I" is not true, and it is the complete destruction, the obliteration, of that "I"-ness that alone is Liberation.

The individual does not become liberated; the individual does not become realized. Realization is Liberation from the individual; it is not liberation of the individual. Understand like this, and you will find this Liberation in yourself.

सद्दर्शनं द्राविडवाङ्निबद्धं
महर्षिणा श्रीरमणेन शुद्धम् ।
प्रबन्धमुत्कृष्टममर्त्यवाण्या -
मनूद्य वासिष्ठमुनिर्व्यतानीत् ॥ ४१ ॥

sad-darśanaṁ drāviḍa-vāṅ-nibaddhaṁ
maharṣiṇā śrī-ramaṇena śuddham |
prabandham-utkṛṣṭam-amartya-vāṇyā-
m-anūdya vāsiṣṭha-munir-vyatānīt || 41 ||

41

Saddarsanam composed in the Dravida language,
By Maharshi Sri Ramana pure,
The composition excellent (highest, best), in the immortals' language
Spoken afterward by Vasishta Muni was composed.

सत्तत्त्वसारं सरलं दधाना
मुमुक्षुलोकाय मुदं ददाना ।
अमानुषश्रीरमणीयवाणी -
मयूखभित्तिर्मुनिवाग्विभाति ॥ ४२ ॥

sat-tattva-sāraṁ saralaṁ dadhānā
mumukṣu-lokāya mudaṁ dadānā |
amānuṣa-śrī-ramaṇīya-vāṇī-
mayūkha-bhittir-muni-vāg-vibhāti || 42 ||

42

Giving honestly (straight-forwardly, sincerely) the Essence of the Truth of Being (Existence),
Giving joy to the world of seekers of Liberation,
The divine (not a man) Sri Ramana's (delightful, agreeable) voice,

The rays of Light, as a wall-like surface (as a fragment), the Muni's speech (words) shines.

N.: Dravida is Tamil. The language of the immortals is Sanskrit. Muni and Vasishta Muni, here, refer to Ganapati. Ganapati says that what he has written is like a reflecting wall that catches the original Light of the Maharshi's teachings. The word for "a wall-like, reflecting surface," can mean "like a fragment." So, a fragment of this Light is in Ganapati Muni's own words. Thereby, he gives all credit to the Sadguru, recognizing the Maharshi as the original Fullness and all the Light. Extolling the text, he says that it reveals the essence of the Truth regarding Being in a very straightforward and honest manner, making it the ideal text of the highest instruction for those who seek Liberation. The Maharshi's Truth is the clearest of the clear.

He humbly indicates that the words he has used to translate this into Sanskrit act like a fragment of the glorious Light of Sri Ramana, like a reflecting medium that shines with the Light from the original, which is Sri Ramana, His Voice and His Silence.

He calls the Maharshi's voice, "the divine." "Amanusa" literally means "not a man" and can mean "divine." He addresses the Maharshi as not being a man. The Sadguru should never be mistaken to be a person. Those who follow his teaching are awakened from their own personhood. You are not men and women. You are That. The teaching makes this abundantly clear. You are not a body. You are not a mind. You are not any form whatsoever. You are That, the eternal Absolute. From where could such Knowledge come, except from One who abides as That, and as That alone? So, he says that the Maharshi is not a man. This does not mean that he is of a nature different from us, but it would be absurd to think that he is a man. That which is called, "God," that which is realized as "Brahman," that which is known as the "Supreme Self," is He, in all its perfect fullness, and He causes us to realize the same.

The comments given here are to be considered as reflections of that Light.

Thus the Saddarsanam Svatmavicaram.

Om Namo Bhagavate Sri Ramanaya
Om Shanti Shanti Shanti Om
In the Temple of Being, the Space of Consciousness,
Om Sri Ramanarpanamastu

ॐ

Other SAT Publications available are:

SAT
SOCIETY OF ABIDANCE IN TRUTH
1834 OCEAN STREET, SANTA CRUZ, CALIFORNIA 95060
(831) 425-7287 ~ www.SATRamana.org ~ sat@cruzio.com